English

General Certificate English

Fourth edition

Alan Etherton

First edition published in 1983 by Thomas Nelson & Sons Ltd
Second edition 1987
Third edition 1994

This edition published in 2001 by:
Nelson Thornes Ltd
Delta Place
27 Bath Road
CHELTENHAM
Glos.
GL53 7TH
United Kingdom

07 08 / 10 9 8 7 6

A Catalogue record for this book is available from the British Library

ISBN 978-0-17-420340-7

Illustrations by Ellis Nadler, Peter Edwards, Trevor Huckwell and Garry Davies
Page make-up by Acorn Bookwork, Salisbury, Wiltshire

Printed and bound by Multivista Global Ltd

Contents

PART 4 Vocabulary Development

PART 5 Language Practice

PART 6 Oral English

The main aim of this book is to help students who are preparing for the GCE (Overseas) English Language examination. The contents are based on the syllabuses and past papers of the University of Cambridge and the University of London.

The success rate in this type of examination is lower than it could be. In addition to problems with the use of English, many students lack a sound understanding of the techniques required in writing acceptable compositions, in answering comprehension questions and in making a summary. Even when they have the intellect and command of language needed at this level, they lose marks unnecessarily by laying out their answers incorrectly and by being unaware of the standard expected by the examiners.

A major purpose of this book, therefore, is to give students enough guidance to enable them to reach the highest standard they are capable of, without being handicapped by ignorance of what they are expected to do or of how to do it.

The book is divided into six parts:

Part 1 – Summary

Students are shown quite clearly how to understand a passage, how to make notes and extract information, how to summarise different types of passages, and what the examiners expect as an answer.

Part 2 – Comprehension, Summary and Directed Writing

This part of the book shows students the techniques required when giving accurate answers to comprehension questions. Students are taken step by step through a wide variety of questions from past papers and are then required to answer questions on other past papers or on passages of a similar standard. The importance of understanding the question (as well as the passage) is stressed, and there is work on Directed Writing based on some of the comprehension passages. Students may at first find some of the work challenging but past results show that the examiners are looking for something more than a superficial understanding of the facts.

Part 3 – Communication in Writing: Composition

This part of the book deals with the basic techniques involved in writing *any* composition. It then deals with common types of composition in detail. It also includes guidance in writing friendly and business letters, reports and applications for a job. In other words, the material is not entirely examination-oriented.

Part 4 – Vocabulary Development

This part stresses vocabulary building, common types of questions in examinations, and the known problems of students at this level. There are separate units on phrasal verbs, problem words, idioms and common errors.

Part 5 – Language Practice

This part deals primarily with the common weaknesses of students at this level. Because of limitations of space, it is not practical to give a comprehensive review of each area, but the material has been chosen to test and strengthen those areas with which students are known to have particular problems.

The ultimate aim of language learning is to be able to receive or initiate communications in the language. However, advocates of a communicative approach will be aware there is little effective communication without an adequate language base. This book seeks not merely to help students pass the GCE examination but to establish a base from which they may later proceed in accordance with their careers and personal needs.

Part 6 – Oral English

This part provides practice in various aspects of oral English tests: pronunciation, reading aloud, picture description and discussion, and conversation.

This book was written without intending to exclude either gender; if there is a bias towards the use of 'he' this is for convenience rather than for any other reason.

Teachers are urged to be selective in using this book and not to feel obliged to work right through everything in it. They may also like to know that a teacher's handbook is available.

A.R.B.E.
2001

Acknowledgements

The author and publishers are grateful to the University of London, School Examinations Department, for permission to use questions from past University of London GCE English Language (International syllabus) examination papers. Thanks are also due for the use of past questions from the Cambridge (International) GCE examination, which are reproduced by permission of the University of Cambridge Local Examinations Syndicate. Every effort has been made to contact copyright holders of any of the extracts used and we apologise if any have been overlooked.

In addition, the author and publishers would like to thank Neal Simpson/ Empics for permission to reproduce the photograph of Denise Lewis on page 334 and HM Customs and Excise for permission to reproduce the photograph on page 335.

PART I

Summary

Making a summary is easy. Here are some examples from daily life. Perhaps you can find more examples in your own daily life.

■ Yesterday Peter saw an exciting film at a cinema or on television. Half an hour ago, a friend asked him about the film. Peter replied: 'It was very good – all about life on another planet.'

Peter has given a summary of the film.

■ A friend or cousin has just arrived from Canada. You are curious about the weather there, so you ask him or her: 'What was the weather like when you left?'

The friend may reply: 'Fine – sunny and warm.'

He or she has given a summary of the weather.

■ A friend has just bought a new typewriter. You are thinking of buying a typewriter yourself, so you ask your friend for his opinion. This friend could give you a detailed description of the typewriter but he knows that you don't need this, so he replies: 'It's not bad but it's rather noisy unless you put a pad under it.'

■ You saw a traffic accident. A police sergeant asked you what happened. Instead of giving all the details, you replied: 'The taxi swerved to avoid a cat. It ran into a van coming from town.'

Later on, the police sergeant may ask you to give all the details but at this point he just wants a rough idea of what happened.

■ At 7 a.m. this item appeared on the news in a radio programme:

'A case of suspected rabies has been found in the Fanling area. A man was bitten by a dog which has been taken to Government kennels for tests. The man has been given anti-rabies treatment at the Fanling Clinic and is reported to be in a good condition. Early tests on the dog show that it may have rabies. Further tests are being carried out. Meanwhile, the Department of Agriculture has sent teams of dog-catchers to the area. Twelve people known to have been in contact with the dog have been given treatment...'

The report may give many details. However, by 8 p.m. this news item is no longer very important. The radio may make a summary and say: 'A man was bitten today by a dog suspected of having rabies.'

Every day, we make many summaries of different things: of rumours, books, films, news items, amusing incidents, accidents, and so on. Don't be afraid of summary work. It is easy if you follow a few principles.

2 What the examiners say

In this unit, we will first look at the general method and then study the comments in past examiners' reports.

GENERAL METHOD

1 Get a blue pencil and a red one (or an ordinary pencil and a pen). This is useful because in an examination there may be **two** parts to the summary or directed writing question.

   Use the *red* pencil to underline important points for the first part of the question. Use the *blue* pencil to underline points for the second part of the question. This method prevents confusion and saves time.

2 Read the question before you read the passage. This may help you to find the theme of the whole passage or of part of it.

3 Read the passage quickly to find out its theme, that is, the main idea(s) and how the author develops it (or them). Look for the way he arranges his points. He may use one of these methods:

   - Time order – step by step
   - Advantages and disadvantages
   - Cause – event – result
   - Place order – what happens in different places
   - Order of importance

4 Read the question again very carefully. Find out exactly what you must do.

5 Read the passage again but more carefully than before. Make rough notes of the important and relevant points. Leave out details, examples, illustrations and irrelevant points. Your rough notes should be about half as long as your target. This means that if you have to write a summary 'in not more than 120 words', your rough notes should contain about 60 words.

   Remember that the examiners have already made a check-list of all the important points, so try not to omit any of them.

6 Look back at the question again to check that you are answering it correctly.

7 Use your rough notes to write your draft or (if you are good at this work) your final summary.

   Add words to make your final summary fluent.

8 Check for length. Add or omit words to get to the right length.

Later in this book, we will consider some of these points in detail. Let us first consider what the examiners say.

GENERAL COMMENTS

- 'It is evident that few candidates have any idea of what is required in the summary question, and marks are consistently low.'

- 'It is in the summary question that the majority of candidates show that they have not had adequate preparation for the examination.'
- 'This was by far the weakest part of the candidates' work.'

What mistakes did candidates make? We will consider them below.

1 Be confident. Don't be frightened.

If you know how to do this type of work, it is easy. The examiners said: 'Candidates need to learn to command their material, and not to let the material command them.'

2 Find the theme of the whole passage (or of the part you must deal with).

1 'The main purpose of the précis question is to find out whether, from a straightforward passage, candidates can unearth a central theme, and trace its development through a series of clearly defined stages ... For the examiners, the saddening thing was not so much that most candidates failed to find this theme, but that so few even looked for it.'
2 'Almost invariably candidates failed to discover the simple theme.'
3 'Most candidates failed because they did not try to grasp the passage as a whole.'

Exercise 1

Read each passage and then choose the sentence which best gives its theme.

1 My sister is very interested in dressmaking. Yesterday evening, she went to visit a friend. The two girls discussed the latest fashions for some time. When my sister left her friend's flat, she got in a lift. Then she had the surprise of her life. The lift stuck between the fifth and sixth floors. At the time there was another girl in the lift, and they were trapped for over an hour. Eventually they managed to attract the attention of a boy, who informed the janitor. A mechanic arrived and succeeded in repairing the lift sufficiently to move it down to the fifth floor. The girls got out and left the mechanic to complete the work.

    a) My sister often visits her friend to discuss dressmaking.
    b) Yesterday my sister went to a friend's flat to talk about current fashions in dressmaking.
    c) Yesterday my sister was trapped in a lift for an hour.
    d) When people are trapped in a lift, a mechanic comes to free them.

2 Ten or twenty thousand years ago, men lived on what they could catch rather than on what they could grow. Whether as fishermen or as hunters, they had to rely for survival on their ability to trap, kill and eat other animals. In the process of time, men learnt that seeds produce plants. (They already knew with some accuracy which plants were edible.) It is no surprise that our ancestors gradually learnt to grow their own food. This, coupled with skill in taming and domesticating animals, enabled them to store food – whether in bins or on the hoof. With more experience, farmers learnt to produce more food than they needed for their own families. They used this surplus as a form of money with which to buy tools, weapons and even ornaments. Thus trade started and

craftsmen (who were neither hunters nor farmers) managed to earn a living.

    a)   Our ancestors gradually learnt to grow their own food.
    b)   Early men were mainly hunters, who relied on what they could catch.
    c)   When men tamed animals, they could get their own food.
    d)   Early men were hunters, then farmers and eventually traders as well.

3   All countries feel the effects of any sharp decline in world trade. One might suppose that countries that are rich in natural resources – such as rubber, tin and oil – would remain unaffected, but this is not so. Any decline in world trade is accompanied by a fall in the demand for products. Manufacturers either reduce their output or close down altogether. The demand for raw materials falls sharply and this inevitably has an effect on primary producers. The prices of raw materials fall, often to a point at which it is unprofitable to produce them. Indeed, the producers of raw materials are sometimes more seriously affected by a recession than industrialised countries are.

    a)   Countries that produce raw materials are greatly affected by a world recession.
    b)   When developing countries stop producing raw materials, there is a fall in world trade.
    c)   Rubber, tin and oil are examples of natural resources.
    d)   Countries which have many raw materials are not affected by a fall in world trade.

3 Leave out details, examples and illustrations.

Details	The farmers grew rice, maize, wheat and barley.
Generalisation	The farmers grew cereals. (or *crops* or *food*)
Details	She could play the piano well and even had some idea of how to play the violin and guitar. She could read music and had written several of her own songs.
Generalisation	She was an excellent musician.
Details	The population was two million in 1965, over three million by 1970, and then rose rapidly to four million by 1976. Much to the surprise of the Government, it reached six million by the end of 2000.
Generalisation	The population increased rapidly between 1965 and 2000.

These are some of the comments of examiners in the past:

- ◼ 'Candidates made the basic mistake of retaining masses of detail and irrelevant statements. These were often taken unchanged from the passage, showing that candidates had not understood the main theme and had no idea of how to generalise.'
- ◼ 'Copying was the main fault; the candidates tacked together a random selection of phrases and sentences from the original, and the result was gibberish. There was seldom any attempt to discard or generalise details . . .'

1 It is quite clear to everybody that large numbers of taxis, lorries, vans, buses and private cars use King's Road every day, and one often sees motor-cycles and bicycles trying to squeeze through the dense traffic.

2 Lack of care, particularly on the part of the drivers of vehicles, is probably the major cause of traffic accidents, although pedestrians are sometimes to blame. This carelessness can take many forms. A driver may be chatting with a companion. He may be watching somebody in another vehicle. He may be thinking about some trouble at work or at home. He may be smoking and trying to find the ash-tray. Whatever the reason may be, there is no excuse for many of the accidents that occur.

3 When they leave school, girls have a wide choice of careers in most countries. They may become teachers, secretaries, nurses or shop assistants, for example. They may decide to become a doctor, a lawyer or even an engineer. Many women are highly successful in business, where then tend to be conscientious, creative and very hard-working. The modern girl cannot complain that she is forced to stay at home and look after her parents, or later, her children.

4 Nature has provided each living thing with its own means of defence. Sometimes this is obvious to anybody. Cats can climb trees to escape from dogs. A lizard can 'freeze' in the grass when chased by an inquisitive dog. It can shed part of its tail if necessary, thereby distracting an enemy. Birds can fly away. Frogs can jump into water and hide in the mud at the bottom of a pool. Each creature has its own way of staying alive.

4 Don't copy from the passage.

Use your own words as far as possible.

This is what the examiners say

■ 'Once again it must be emphasised that candidates are required to use their own words as far as possible. This does not mean that no words from the passage are to be used. It always happens that certain words cannot readily be replaced, and the use of such words is not penalised, but when the candidate offers merely a string of short passages, all exactly copied from the original, or even, as often happens, whole sentences without alteration, such work cannot be given much credit.'

■ 'Copying from the passage was the main fault.'

1 (Ex. 1, no. 1)
   a) My sister is very interested in dressmaking and yesterday she was stuck between the fifth and sixth floors with a friend.

b) Yesterday my sister was caught in a lift for more than an hour.
c) When my sister left her friend's flat, she got in a lift but she was trapped, and later a mechanic arrived and succeeded in repairing the lift.

2 (Ex. 1, no. 2)
a) Whether as fishermen or as hunters, they had to rely on their ability to kill animals until they learnt to produce more food than they needed for their families.
b) Farmers managed to produce more food than they needed and so trade started and craftsmen managed to earn a living.
c) At first men were hunters but later they became farmers and produced a surplus of food which was used for trade.

3 (Ex. 1, no. 3)
a) A recession affects all countries.
b) All countries feel the effects of any sharp decline in world trade.
c) A recession is accompanied by a fall in the demand for natural resources.

4 (Ex. 2, no. 2)
a) Lack of care is probably the main cause of accidents on roads, although pedestrians are at times responsible for the accidents.
b) Most traffic accidents are caused by carelessness.
c) There is no excuse for many of the traffic accidents that occur.

5 (Ex. 2, no. 3)
a) When they leave school, many women are highly successful and are not forced to stay at home.
b) Many careers are open to girls now.
c) Many girls do not have a wide choice of careers in some countries.

5 Use your notes to write a fluent summary with no errors of spelling, punctuation or grammar.

■ Do not omit 'a' and 'the'. Your summary must be in complete sentences and not in note form.
■ Use linking words to connect the idea in one sentence with the idea in the next sentence.

Exercise 4

Make correct sentences from each set of notes. Only one sentence is needed in each case. Use your own punctuation.

1 carelessness – cause – accidents
2 girls – many careers
3 King's Road – many vehicles
4 recession – all countr. affect
5 petrol – price – risen – recent yrs
6 AIDS – research – no cure yet
7 airport crowded – tourists – new one needed
8 mechanisation – workers afraid – lose jobs

9 found abandoned cubs – forest – took to camp
10 China and India – over 1 billion people each – still increasing

6 Don't do these things:

- Don't add information to a passage. Don't comment on information given in a passage. Give a summary of the main points – whether you agree with them or not.
- Don't write on alternate lines. Some examiners complain that this is a waste of paper and makes the work more difficult to read.
- Don't draw vertical columns and put one word in each column. This is an artificial way of writing. The examiners have asked schools not to do this.
- Don't forget to cross out (very clearly) any rough work or draft summaries. An examiner gets annoyed if he marks a summary and then turns over the page to find the final summary on the other side.

7 Use the correct number of words.

- Follow the limit given in your question. You will lose marks if you exceed it. If your summary is too short, you will probably leave out important points.
- Do not use 90 per cent of your words on 50 per cent of your facts. This will force you to omit important points in the second part of the passage. If you keep your rough notes very short, you will not have this problem.

8 Remember that, as in composition work, you will lose marks for all errors of spelling, punctuation and grammar.

Some students are very careful when they write a composition but think th they can use any kind of English in a summary. This is wrong.

3 Summary – practice passage 1

In an examination you may have to make a summary of any of these:

- a prose passage (or more than one passage)
- dialogue or an interview
- evidence in a court or to a committee
- a diary
- a letter or a series of letters

You may have to do one or two of these things:

a) Make a summary of the whole of a passage or of part of it.
b) Make a summary of one point or topic in a passage or in more than one passage. This topic may be mentioned throughout the passage(s) or occur in one part only.

c)   Give a numbered list (in single words, short phrases or sentences) of kinds, factors, causes, characteristics, evidence, and so on in the passage.

d)   The summary question may be called 'Directed Writing'. You may be asked
(i)   to bring together and summarise what the author says about a topic.
(ii) to gather information about one topic from two or more passages.
(iii) to write about a theme related to the passage(s). This may not involve making a summary.

Practice passage 1

Read this passage and then answer the questions about it.

While the intelligence of ants is limited – for example, they have no proper language, cannot be said to reason (to think things out), and do not, except in one case, use tools – their mental powers should not be underrated. Experiments have shown that they can learn the correct route in simple
5 mazes which have six blind alleys, and individual ants vary in their ability to do this and in the speed (or number of runs through the maze) with which they learn their lesson. Just as in the maze, so it is in the world of work; some individuals learn to do jobs better and more quickly than other ants in the nest.

10   These quicker learners are the primitive leaders of the community, the 'excitement centres'. They are called 'excitement centres' because, although they determine what activities are carried out and when, they do not do so by sitting down and thinking about it and then giving directions to the other ants, but they excite the ants into doing the different jobs by
15 starting to do them themselves. The excitement centre ants are in effect the first individuals in each colony to respond to the stimulus of jobs needing to be done. The settling down to work of the twenty or thirty excitement centre ants soon arouses in the other ants feelings of their own hunger and need to go out foraging, or of their own instincts to repair a broken part
20 of the nest or to build new chambers to provide accommodation for a rapidly expanding brood.

Thanks to this leadership, the seemingly complex round of jobs of the ant community is fairly economically and successfully achieved. Food-getting is the most important task. It is no light one to get in food enough for from
25 40,000 to half-a-million individuals each day. A colony of 40,000 carnivorous ants will eat a quart of insect food (equivalent to over 20,000 insects) every day during the active summer months. Yet there are always several times more ants in the nest than there are out foraging. Inside the nest, the queens must be carefully tended and guarded, and the eggs they
30 lay carried off to the appropriate chamber. The brood require constant attention, for the larvae (grubs) must be fed and unceasingly licked, so that their skins are kept moist, and the cocoons must be watched so that ants ready to hatch out can be helped to emerge. Few ants can escape from their cocoons or pupal skins unaided. The nest structure also requires continual
35 care and must be kept scrupulously clean, properly drained and proof against enemy invasion. Then there are the aphid cows (greenflies, blackflies and whiteflies), both inside and outside the nest, to be milked, or other guests to be tended or kept from prowling too near the queens or brood. For in each ants' nest there are many such insect guests, especially of the beetle kind.
40 Some 5,000 species of insects and spiders are found only in the nests of ants, living there permanently as either welcome or tolerated lodgers.

9

1 In your opinion, which of these best sums up the theme of the whole passage?
   a) Ants
   b) The intelligence, leadership and life in a colony of ants
   c) Scientific experiments with ants
   d) Life inside an ants' nest

2 Which of these best sums up the first paragraph?
   a) Some ants are more intelligent than others.
   b) The intelligence of ants is not particularly great.
   c) Ants may be more intelligent than we think.
   d) Ants have their own way of communicating.

3 Which of these best sums up the ideas in the second paragraph?
   a) The more intelligent ants are the natural leaders.
   b) The role of excitement centre ants in a colony
   c) How ants get their food
   d) How disputes are settled in a colony of ants

4 What is the theme of the last paragraph?
   a) The importance of the queen ants
   b) How ants defend their young against their enemies
   c) How ants get their food
   d) Essential duties inside a colony of ants

5 If you have to make a summary of about 120 words of this passage, how many words will you try to get in your rough notes?

   a) 110   b) 180   c) 50   d) 98

This is what the examiners said about candidates when they made a summary of practice passage 1:

■ 'Lack of proper preparation and practice was even more evident in the précis, and it is extremely difficult to understand why the majority find beyond their powers the simple object of the exercise. Anyone who has learnt to read properly should be able to read and understand the argument of a straightforward passage, and reproduce it faithfully in a shortened form. But almost invariably candidates failed to discover the simple theme, a very plain picture of how an ant colony conducts its existence. Masses of detail and irrelevant figures were retained and commonly these were lifted in exactly the original terms: details such as 'a quart of insect food', 'their skins are kept moist', 'greenflies, blackflies and whiteflies', 'the beetle kind', 'spiders', were retained because apparently candidates had not learnt that they must find general terms such as "parasites".'

■ 'The passage had a clear intention, and progressed logically from an introductory paragraph on the particular type of intelligence possessed by ants, followed by a paragraph on the methods of work observable in an ant community with special reference to the leaders and their instinctive urge to work, concluding with an analysis of the essential activities engaged in by an ant community. Surely no simpler or more naturally developed theme could be demanded, but candidates failed to discover the key ideas, and so presented a mere jumble of little bits unrelated and ill-coordinated. They need to learn to command their material, and not to let the material command them.'

■ 'Many candidates forgot that the passage was about "ants" and faced with the sentence "Just as in the maze, so it is in the world of work; some individuals learn to do job better and more quickly than other ants in the nest", they wrote on human beings, failing to appreciate that "individuals" was a term that could be used for ants. Garbling was common. Ignoring the passage "Experiments have proved that they can learn the correct route in simple mazes that have six blind alleys", they wrote that "ants nests are built in six blind alleys", and there were countless examples of inaccurate facts and extraneous matter being introduced.'

1 What is extraneous matter?
2 Can we introduce extraneous matter when making a summary?
3 Why did the examiners object to the use of *a quart of insects* and *their skins are kept moist* in the summary?
4 Where did candidates get their *little bits of unrelated material* from? Do you think they were right or wrong to include this type of material?
5 Are these the main tasks mentioned in the last paragraph?
   a) Get food.
   b) Look after the queen, the eggs and the larvae.
   c) Keep the nest in good condition.
   d) Deal with the aphid cows and any guests.

4 Making notes – practice passage 2

FINDING THE THEME

In the previous units, examiners stressed the importance of finding the theme of a passage before you start to make a summary. There are two main ways of finding the theme:

1 In many cases, it is given in the question. You are told which facts to summarise. For an example of this, please see practice passage 2 below.
2 If no theme is given in the instructions,

   a) Read the passage once and see if you can find the theme. It may be shown by the paragraphing. A new paragraph may start a new topic or aspect of a topic.
   b) Read the passage again and search for the theme and its development. Summary passages are usually expository and follow one of a number of patterns, e.g.
   Historical development from the past to the present
   Advantages and disadvantages

Different causes for something
Different attitudes to something

3 Once you have found your theme, you know which facts in the passage are important and which are not.

Read the following passage carefully and then, in not more than 150 words of continuous writing, summarise the ways deserts are created by man or nature.

Read the whole of this unit before you make your summary.

In the past 50 years the Sahara has engulfed 251,000 square miles of arable land. More than one-fifth of India is being overrun by the Thar Desert. Hundreds of square miles of northern Chile have been swallowed by the Atacama since 1960. The situation in Iran, the Middle East, southern
5 Africa, Argentina and parts of Siberia, China and the USA is almost as grim. Deserts, arid and semi-arid areas, now cover 43 per cent of the earth's land surface.

What happened to transform these once-thriving lands into deserts? We assume climatic changes were responsible, but this is not necessarily so,
10 say meteorologists. The 3.5 million square miles of desert that have appeared since civilisation began were mostly man-made.

When man first turned to agriculture, he cleared the land of trees and vegetation, usually by burning. After a few seasons, the nutrients in the soil depleted, he moved to the next virgin tract. This slash-and-burn method
15 is still common in Africa, Latin America and Asia. The degraded fields became grazing lands for cattle and sheep. As the number of animals increased, edible grasses and herbs were devoured before they could reseed. Such unpalatable woody plants and shrubs as thorn-bush, cactus and mesquite took over. Finally, in the Middle East and Africa, the land was
20 opened to omnivorous goats that stripped all vegetation. At the same time, man had been cutting down forests for timber. Rain washed earth from hills, causing floods and gouging deep gullies in the bare lowlands.

When droughts came, as they do in most generations, winds removed the anchorless topsoil that had taken thousands of years to develop. Eventually
25 the denuded hills were stripped down to 'desert pavement', a tightly wedged mosaic of rock and stones in which nothing can grow.

The desertification of Mesopotamia, where agriculture was practised some 6,000 years ago, was due to a different set of circumstances. With insufficient rainfall to support cultivation, man irrigated his crops. But not
30 for thousands of years did he recognise the importance of proper drainage. Without it, irrigation led to salinisation. As the waters that were let into the fields each spring evaporated, they left behind salts, alkalis and other minerals. As the salinity increased, harvests became progressively poorer. Timber felling in the mountains to the north compounded the problem.
35 Rains rushing down the denuded slopes carried silt, which raised the river beds and clogged the irrigation canals, causing water to overflow the dykes.

The building of great dams has intensified the problem. For 50 centuries, the Nile flooded Egypt every spring, washing away salt and depositing a thin film of fertilising silt. Since the construction of the Aswan dam, water has
40 had to be pumped to the fields. There is no way to wash away the salt deposits and the rich silt is trapped behind the dam. For the first time in the

nation's history artificial fertilisers must be used. Agronomists predict that soon Egypt may produce fewer crops than before the dam was built.

Perhaps the most significant cause of the proliferation of deserts is the
45 proliferation of man himself. In many arid regions, human and animal populations double every 25 years. When a cultivated field or a pasture is exhausted, people can no longer move on to a new one because the land is already occupied. Fourteen inches of rain a year are necessary to raise a crop, but land-hungry farmers are ploughing up ranges receiving as little as
50 an average of six inches annually. In the next drought, the soil on these lands will dry up and blow away. Other farmers are ploughing slopes so steep that erosion sets in from the moment cultivation begins.

Can desertification be stopped? If there is still enough soil for plants to take root, the desert can be halted, and even turned back. Ecologists'
55 recommendations are quite simple:

1 Make an inventory of which arid lands are best for grazing, which for agriculture, and which should remain untouched.
2 Limit livestock to what each range can sustain. Goats and sheep should be confined to certain areas.
60 3 Rotate crops and specify the number of years arable land must remain fallow. Keep production stable even in rainy years.
4 Reafforest the hills; plant stabilising trees and shrubs on dunes and plains.
5 Promote solar energy, propane and other fuels.
65 6 Clear brush and inedible plants from ranges.
7 Redesign irrigation works to provide crops with only as much water as they need. Line canals to prevent leakage and install adequate drainage systems.

Please do not make a summary of this passage yet.

FINDING THE THEME

Very roughly, these are the main points in the passage:

good land is turning into desert (ll. 1–11)

Causes	primitive farming, then grazing, then goats	(ll. 12–20)
	cutting trees on hills (+ rain)	(ll. 21–23)
	drought (+ wind)	(ll. 23–26)
	lack of drainage	(ll. 30–37)
	dams (lack of silt and cleansing)	(ll. 38–45)
	population increase – farming of marginal land	(ll. 46–54)
Remedies	check suitability of land	(1)
	restrict livestock	(2)
	rotate crops; let fields rest	(3)
	reafforestation	(4)
	solar and other fuels	(5)
	clear useless vegetation	(6)
	improve irrigation and drainage	(7)

The theme is in the question

The question tells us to look for 'the ways deserts are created by man or nature'. This means that:

1 We can almost ignore lines 1–11.
2 We can completely ignore line 55 to the end.
3 All we have to do is make notes on the 'ways deserts are created by man or nature'.

Then we can make these rough notes:

By man ...
primitive method of farming takes goodness out of soil
grazing and goats cause further deterioration – no plants left
cut timber on hills – causes erosion and flooding
lack of irrigation – increases salinity, reduces crops
dams – no silt, no cleaning away of salt deposits
increasing population – over-intensive cultivation, causing erosion on hills

By nature ...
rain – erosion and floods
droughts and winds – remove topsoil
? salinity caused by deposits of salts
? increase in population of human beings

These notes add up to about 71 words with the two doubtful points in them or 59 words without them. I propose to leave them out, so I have to write out an answer of 'not more than 150 words' using about 60 words to start with.

Now it is time for you to write your summary. You can use the above notes or you can make up your own notes. Try *not* to copy from the passage. You can start in this way: 'Primitive methods of farming helped to create deserts by...'

---

5 Extracting information – practice passage 3

Note: *Get your coloured pencils ready or use a pen and a pencil.*

Read the following passage carefully, and then:

a) Using a separate line for each, make a numbered list of not more than **ten** kinds of stamps the passage mentions as being collected. Most of these should be expressed in a single word.

b) In not more than 80 words of continuous writing, summarise the reasons given in the passage for issuing and collecting stamps.

Philately, or stamp-collecting, has never been more popular than it is today. Indeed, there has been a colossal rise in recent years in the number of collectors of all ages, the amount spent, and the number of stamps issued.

Basically, a postage stamp is a receipt for the money paid for services
provided by the post office in collecting, sorting and transporting mail. The
first adhesive postage stamp to be issued was the famous 'Penny Black',
which appeared on 6th May 1840, followed two days later by the 'Twopenny
Blue'. Both showed the head of Queen Victoria.

Most of the very early stamps showed only the head of the monarch, or
ruler, or the value of the stamp, or a simple motif. However, it was not long
before pictorial stamps appeared, illustrating features of life in the country of
issue. Stamps were also seen as a means of publicising anniversaries and
other great occasions, and the resulting commemorative issues quickly
gained popularity. Commemoratives and pictorials appealed to those who
wanted to learn more about the world; indeed, many a schoolboy has found
geography and history much more exciting in a stamp album than in a dry
textbook!

Commemoratives are usually short-term issues simply because there are
other anniversaries to celebrate, and a centenary, for example, is not a
centenary the year after. Most countries, however, continue to make long-
term issues with a wide range of values, which are used on the bulk of mail
over a period of several years. These are called definitive issues, or simply
definitives. Special stamps were also issued for mail carried by air, and 'air-
mails' became popular with collectors.

As more and more stamps were issued, so more and more people of all
ages swelled the ranks of collectors. Postal administrations paid increasing
attention to the apparently insatiable appetite of collectors. Strange shapes –
the triangulars and diamonds – and extra large stamps, or 'giants', tempted
the young. Thematics – stamps on particular themes such as birds or aircraft
or Scouts or Christmas – were issued in colourful profusion, appealing to the
varied interests of potential collectors. International events or interests
inspired international issues, and sometimes groups of countries took part in
an 'omnibus' issue. Miniature sheets appeared combining one complete set
of stamps in a single conveniently sized sheet. Collectors were wooed with
specially produced envelopes bearing new sets of stamps and postmarked on
the day of issue; these are known as first-day covers.

Of course, the more stamps issued, the greater the likelihood of printing
errors; reprints of stamps would differ from the originals in small ways. Thus
varieties were found, and more advanced collectors began to specialise in
these.

After the Second World War newly independent nations saw philately as
a useful source of revenue, and smaller and smaller islands broke away from
their parent bodies to form postal administrations and issue stamps of their
own. There are even states and islands whose main source of income is the
sale of stamps.

Having been attracted to the hobby by the more recent issues, many
collectors have sought obsolete issues. Others have taken up stamp-
collecting as an investment, or a hedge against inflation, or a means of
providing for retirement. There are even collectors who never see the
stamps they purchase. They commission agents to buy for them, the stamps
are then locked away in some vault, not to see the light of day again until
the right time for them to be sold at a very much higher price than was paid
for them.

Usually the stamps collected for investment are very old or 'classic' issues.

These are relatively scarce and therefore quite expensive, and, as more and more people become serious collectors trying to obtain classic issues from a decreasing number available on the open market, so increasing scarcity forces values up rapidly.

However, the vast majority of collectors are mainly interested in building up collections of certain countries or groups of countries or themes for the satisfaction and pleasure it gives. Philately is a world-wide hobby and must play some part in increasing understanding and goodwill between the ordinary people of the countries of the world.

Do not answer questions 1 and 2 yet.

1 With an ordinary pencil or a red one, underline all the different kinds of stamps mentioned in the passage. Do that now.

When a student started to make a list of the different kinds of stamps, he produced this list. To save space, it is given as three columns but on the answer paper each word would have to be on a separate line.

postage stamp	air-mails	omnibus
adhesive stamp	triangulars	miniature sheet
pictorials	diamonds	varieties
commemoratives	giants	classics
definitives	thematics	

Which four of these would you omit to obtain ten kinds? Have you any different kinds in your list?

In setting out the answer, is it necessary to number these kinds of stamps? Give a reason for your answer.

2 Now use a blue pencil or a pen to underline (or make rough notes about) the reasons given in the passage for issuing and collecting stamps. Put your reasons in two rough lists. Do that now.

A student made these two lists. Compare your own lists with them and discuss any differences in class.

Issuing
receipt for dealing with mail
show life in country
commemorate important or international events
air-mail
get revenue from stamp-collectors

Collecting
pleasure and interest
learn about world
interested in varieties, thematics, sheets, first-day covers
as investment

These notes come to about 35 words and can form the basis of an answer. Now write your summary as in b). You can use the above notes or your own (if you think they are better).

Read the following passage and answer the question that follows.

Despite the billions of pounds spent over the past 35 years on efforts to eradicate malaria world-wide, financial cut-backs mean the killer disease flourishes, as does the insect responsible for spreading it.

With an estimated two million people a year dying from malaria (mainly
5 in Africa) out of an annual 400 million clinical attacks of the disease, it is the world's second biggest killer (after the combined diarrhoeal diseases which afflict Third World children). Malaria is rife in parts of Mexico, Turkey and the Middle East as well as Papua New Guinea, the Solomon Islands and other parts of the Pacific. The Far East has patches of malaria
10 which are very resistant to drugs.

In Britain, which has around 2,000 imported cases of malaria annually, resulting in an average of six deaths, more than half the cases involve the malignant *Plasmodium falciparum*, the most serious and potentially fatal form of the disease which can be caught in most malarial countries. The majority
15 of British malaria victims – many of whom had been taking anti-malaria precautions – caught the disease in Africa. About 2 per cent of British travellers to Ghana come back with a malignant form of the disease.

Of the 3,500 species of mosquito, only the female *Anopheles* mosquito carries the four malaria parasites. This is one of the 50 species found in
20 Britain, although our climate is not warm enough for the parasite to complete the 10-day lifecycle inside the insect needed to pass on the disease. The only recorded cases of people catching malaria in Britain in recent years were the result of mosquitoes arriving at Gatwick on planes from malarial countries.

25 Other mosquitoes found in tropical climates are responsible for the spread of yellow fever, the virus infection dengue, encephalitis (inflammation of the brain), and elephantiasis – gross thickening of the skin, due to chronic obstruction of the lymphatic vessels.

The transmission of diseases is carried out exclusively by the female
30 mosquito, which bites and sucks the blood of mammals in order to breed. (The male mosquito prefers a diet of fruit juices.) After the female has fed, it finds some water in which to lay its eggs, which hatch within days. Mosquitoes are particularly fond of breeding in old car tyres in which water has collected; a recent shipment of tyres from Africa to the southern states
35 of America resulted in the introduction into the United States of the *Aedes* mosquito, which carries yellow fever and dengue.

Mosquitoes feed mainly at dawn and dusk and tend to search for food at ground level, which is why they frequently bite their victims' ankles, feet and legs. Some live indoors, while others hunt for food under trees. Nobody
40 knows why some people are more susceptible to mosquito bites than others.

The official line to help prevent mosquito bites is basic: cover up as much skin as possible and wear long trousers tucked into socks; take whatever anti-malarial tablets are recommended for your particular destination, and continue them for 28 days after arriving home. Sleep under a mosquito net
45 impregnated with insecticide.

If you catch malaria – which causes flu-like symptoms and can take up to a month to manifest itself – get treatment immediately. It is particularly dangerous for pregnant women, as all forms of malaria can cause abortions.

Note: *When you answer this type of question, pay particular attention to the layout of your answer. In this case, you have to write a leaflet for travellers. You may need to use a heading and sub-headings. You may wish to list important points.*

You have been asked to write a leaflet of advice on malaria for overseas travellers from Britain. Write **two** paragraphs, totalling not more than 170 words in all, on the following aspects:

a) How the mosquito breeds and transmits malaria.
b) The likelihood of a British traveller contracting malaria and what to do if it happens.

Your leaflet should be written accurately, with attention to grammar, spelling and punctuation. Use only information taken from the passage.

7 Practice passage 5

Read the following passage carefully, and then:

a) On a separate line for each, make a numbered list of not more than **ten** very important points over which the writer advises candidates to exercise care. Most of these points can be expressed in a single word; you will receive no marks for any point that takes more than six words.
b) In a paragraph of continuous writing of not more than 100 words, summarise what is said in the passage about the reader of the essay written in the language examination.

The essay in the language examination is an exercise in communication. As in all forms of written communication, there are two parties to the transaction, the writer and the reader. These two are separated by time and space, they are likely to belong to different age-groups and different
5 backgrounds, and the chances of their ever meeting face to face may be very small indeed. But, through the medium of the written word, they do meet, each in solitude, one giving, the other receiving.

The original essay is different from answers to most other examination questions: in most other cases the pattern is predictable, and is merely an
10 extension of the classroom situation; the candidate is the learner whose knowledge is being tested and the examiner is the teacher, the expert, testing what the student has learnt. But the teacher-learner roles are reversed in the essay; it is the examiner who is the learner, the candidate the teacher. The pattern is not predictable, for there are no right and wrong
15 answers. If the examiner and the candidate are separated by national boundaries, there is so much that the former can learn about a different way of life, so much that can be added to his store of knowledge, and it is most likely that the examiner is someone who wants to learn.

The candidate is thus in a position of considerable power: what is written
20 must be read, even if it is completely irrelevant. How he uses that power is of considerable importance.

If he is going to communicate, he must have something to communicate, and his first consideration will be what he is going to write, his material. He will not choose a topic about which he knows nothing, but one within his
25 experience or his imagination. If the writing is to have real value, the material must be worth passing on, and it will be selected with great care, so that the most effective use may be made of the amount of writing that the candidate is expected to produce.

When the material has been selected, the next step is to arrange it in a
30 sensible way. A jumble of ideas in random order will leave the reader bewildered. The pattern of description should be clear, or the resulting picture will be like an unmade jigsaw puzzle; the narrative should be in orderly progression, or the point of the story will be lost; the argument will fail if it is merely a series of loosely connected dogmatic assertions. The wise
35 candidate, therefore, makes a plan, a very brief outline of what he is going to communicate. This may or may not be committed to paper, but the successful essay carries within itself plenty of evidence that the writer has planned what he has written. The plan may be modified, of course, during the actual writing, but the writer will aim to produce material that is
40 adequate, interesting, coherent, orderly, and neatly rounded off, so that the reader feels a satisfaction, a sense that he has received something worth receiving and that his time has been well spent.

It is not only the material, of course, that is important. Good material that has been sensibly planned can be ruined for the reader by the manner
45 of presentation. For one thing, the reader is entitled to politeness, and politeness demands that the handwriting shall be as readable as the writer can make it. The language that is used, too, should be a suitable vehicle for carrying the material that has been selected. This presupposes a reasonable competence in handling the language. The examiner will not demand the
50 same standard from the candidate that he himself has reached, but he will expect intended meaning to be apparent without his having to make constant guesses. Incoherence and ambiguity spoil the effectiveness of the material, as do constant errors of grammar, poor punctuation, and hopelessly incorrect idiom.
55 Finally, having made his communication and completed his writing, the wise candidate will have left himself sufficient time to read through and check his work. Even the best writers make slips, and it is obviously in the candidate's own interests to ensure that what he has written is as free from error as he can make it.

Do not answer a) and b) on page 18 yet.

A student made this rough list of points when he was preparing to answer a). Which of the points should be changed or deleted? Which points should be added?

1 choose the right topic
2 arrange ideas properly
3 make a good plan
4 unity of ideas
5 courtesy
6 good handwriting
7 suitable and correct language
8 should be coherent
9 comparatively free from error

10   adequate punctuation
11   correct use of idioms
12   checked for accuracy

Write your answer to (b) but notice that you are concerned only with information about the reader (that is, the examiner) and not with the candidate.

8   Making a summary of letters – 1

In an examination you may be asked to make a summary of the whole or parts of two or more letters. Normally, there is no need to give the address of the people concerned but it is necessary to use reported speech and to make the identity of each writer clear. Read the letters on page 21 and 22 and then make a summary of the correspondence in not more than 150 words.

Theme

The theme of the letters is very clear. Mrs Lawson paid for some goods but did not receive them – or a reply to her letters. The suppliers explained that their records had been lost in a fire and promised to supply the goods immediately.

Notes

Lawson – pd £30 on 2 March for dishes (from Lapsup Company)
wrote twice and received no reply
4 May – threatened to take legal action

Lapsup – replied on 7 May
apologised
explained records destroyed in fire
had tried to trace customers
promised to send goods on 7 May

These notes amount to about 45 words, which is a little on the short side if my answer must be between 135 and 150 words, so I must be prepared to do a little padding when I write the draft summary.

Draft

On 2nd March 2001, Mrs Anne Lawson sent a cheque for thirty pounds to Lapsup Company Ltd, and ordered a set of Sando dishes. When the goods did not arrive, she wrote twice in April and tried (but failed) to contact the firm by telephone. Finally, on 4th May, she threatened to take legal action unless she received the goods or a refund of her money by 15th May.

24 Market Street,
Anytown,
AN5 6ZX

4th May 2001

The Manager,
Lapsup Co. Ltd,
498 High Street,
Dawmouth DX4 9UG

Dear Sir,

In response to your advertisement in 'Country Fair', I sent you a cheque for £30 on 2nd March, and ordered a set of your Sando dishes. The advertisement said that there might be a delay of 14–21 days before the goods were supplied.

However, nothing had arrived by the middle of April, so I wrote to you on 18th April, asking you to supply the goods or return my cheque. I received no reply. I wrote again on 26th April and still received no reply. When I tried to telephone your office in April, the operator said that your line was out of order.

I have consulted my solicitors and now propose to take legal action against you unless the goods are supplied or my money is refunded by 15th May

I regret having to take this action but your failure to reply to my letters leaves me with no alternative, particularly since my bank informs me that my cheque was presented for payment in the middle of March.

Yours faithfully,

Anne Lawson (Mrs)

LAPSUP COMPANY LIMITED

279 City Road, Dawmouth, DX4 7SL
Tel: 02124-563867

7th May 2001

Our Ref: M/3149/TD

Mrs Anne Lawson
24 Market Street,
Anytown,
AN5 6ZX

Dear Mrs Lawson,

Thank you very much for your letter of 4th May. I am extremely sorry that there has been such a delay in supplying the Sando dishes, and that you did not receive a reply to your letters.

You are correct in saying that your cheque for thirty pounds was paid into our bank in March. Unfortunately, on 24th March, our office at 498 High Street was completely destroyed by fire. As a result, all our records were destroyed and we were unable to trace you.

We advertised in 'Country Fair' in early April, asking customers to contact us but perhaps you did not see this advertisement. It is true that in April our old phone was out of order but I am surprised that the operator did not give you our new phone number at our City Road office.

Please accept my sincere apologies for the delay. Your dishes are being despatched today. I am sure that they will reach you safely and that you will be delighted with them. Please write or phone me if you have any further queries. We are anxious to keep in touch with our customers and to provide as good a service as possible.

Yours sincerely,

J. Goodenough

John Goodenough
Manager

22

*(Before I finish the draft, I will count the number of words to see whether I must finish quickly or must use up more words. I do **not** count the words until I am near the end of the draft summary. I notice that I have used 110 words up to 'advertisement'. I can use another 40.)*

On 7th May, the manager of Lapsup Company wrote and apologised to Mrs Lawson. He explained that the firm's records had been destroyed in a fire during March, so that he had been unable to trace Mrs Lawson, despite an advertisement.

The manager repeated his apology and explained that the goods were being sent that day. He asked Mrs Lawson to contact him if she had any further queries. (= 138 words)

Final summary

I can use the draft summary as my final summary or, if I like, add another 10 words. I have not omitted anything important, so I do not intend to add any more words.

9   Making a summary of letters – 2

Read these two letters and then make a summary of them in not more than 120 words.

On 14th July, this letter appeared in a newspaper:

Examinations

As a mother of two teenage children, I write to suggest that the Form 5 examination should be abolished. The pressure from this examination starts in Form 4 and even in Form 3 in some schools. Students have to spend valuable time studying books, writing notes and memorising facts when they could be playing sports or watching interesting programmes on television.

I very much doubt whether the examination results are reliable. I have known some excellent students do poorly in their final examination – through nerves or bad luck with questions – whereas other quite weak students have managed to get excellent results.

Similarly, I doubt whether much of what young people are studying is of much value to them. Who wants to bother with History or Geography in this modern world? The children would be far better off learning how to grow crops, repair machines or write business letters. In mathematics, a lot of the material is of no value later in life. Neither my husband nor I have ever had to use the geometry or algebra we studied at school.

It is about time our educationalists woke up and faced reality. For a start, they could abolish the Form 5 examination and revise the syllabuses thoroughly.

Mary Downton

On 19th July, this letter appeared in the same newspaper:

Examinations

May I, as a teenager, reply to Mrs Downton's suggestion that the Form 5 examination be abolished and that syllabuses be revised extensively.

Up to a point, I agree that our syllabuses should be revised. I do not agree that history, geography and mathematics are a waste of time but it might be possible to include subjects or topics which help to prepare students more obviously for current problems. For example, classes on career guidance, marriage and commerce would be useful but I would definitely not get rid of the above three subjects at the same time. Certainly we could improve the contents of the syllabuses but I think it would be a great pity if we stopped studying the history and geography of our own country and of others.

Mrs Downton suggested that the Form 5 examination should be abolished. I definitely do not agree with this. Many students (including some good ones) would not work hard without the stimulus of a public examination. Business companies want some proof that applicants have reached a good standard of education. Watching television may be enjoyable but it is not a good training for adult life.

If examinations are to some extent unreliable, by all means improve them but don't make the mistake of throwing the baby out with the bath water.

John Stocker

Notes

Do not always expect a summary question to deal with the whole of both letters. Other possible questions are:

a) Make a summary of what both writers have to say about syllabuses and school subjects.
b) Summarise the views of both writers on examinations.
c) In 60 to 80 words, summarise the points on which both writers appear to agree.

Practice passage 6

Read the following two passages describing successful ascents of Mount Everest, the world's highest mountain.

After an hour or so we came to a vertical rock step in the ridge. This appeared quite a problem. However, the step was bounded on its right by a vertical snow cliff and I was able to work my way up this forty-foot crack and finally get over the top. I was rather surprised and pleased that I was
5 capable of such effort at this height. I brought Tenzing up and noticed that he was proving a little sluggish, but an excellent and safe companion for all that. I really felt now that we were going to get to the top and that nothing would stop us. I kept frequent watch on our oxygen consumption and was encouraged to find it at a steady rate.
10   I continued on, cutting steadily and surmounting bump after bump and cornice after cornice, looking eagerly for the summit. It seemed impossible to pick it out and time was running out. Finally I cut around the back of an extra large hump and then, on a tight rope from Tenzing, I climbed up a gentle snow ridge to its top. Immediately it was obvious that we had reached
15 our objective. It was 11.30 a.m. and we were on top of Everest!
    To the north an impressive corniced ridge ran down to the East Rongbuk glacier. We could see nothing of the old North route but were looking down on the North Col and Changtse. The West ridge dropped away in broad sweeps and we had a great view of the Khumbu and Pumori far below us.
20 Makalu, Kangchenjunga and Lhotse were dominant to the east looking considerably less impressive than I had ever seen them. Tenzing and I shook hands and then Tenzing threw his arms around my shoulders. It was a great moment! I took off my oxygen and for ten minutes I photographed Tenzing holding flags, the various ridges of Everest and the general view. I left a
25 crucifix on top for John Hunt, and Tenzing made a little hole in the snow and put in it some food offerings – lollies, biscuits and chocolate. We ate a mint cake and then put our oxygen back on. I was a little worried by the time factor so after fifteen minutes on top we turned back at 11.45.
    The steps along the ridge made progress relatively easy and the only
30 problem was the rock step which demanded another jamming session. At 12.45 we were back on the South Summit both now rather fatigued. Wasting no time (our oxygen was getting low) we set off down the great slope in considerable trepidation about its safeness. This was quite a mental strain and as I was coming down first I repacked every step with great care.
35 Tenzing was a tower of strength and his very fine ability to keep a tight rope was most encouraging. After what seemed a lifetime the angle eased off and we were soon leading down onto the narrow snow ridge and finally to the dump of oxygen bottles. We loaded these on and then, rather tired, wended our way down our tracks and collapsed into our camp at 2 p.m.

Breathing becomes such a strenuous business that we scarcely have strength left to go on. Every ten or fifteen steps we collapse into the snow to rest, then crawl on again. My mind seems almost to have ceased to function. I

simply go on climbing automatically. The fact that we are on Everest, the
highest mountain in the world, is forgotten – nor does it register that we are
climbing without oxygen apparatus.

The only thing that lures me on is that little point ahead, where all the
lines come together, the apex, the ultimate. The exertion now must be
terrible, and yet I am insensible to it. It is as if the cortex of my brain were
numb, as if only deeper inside my head is there something making the
decisions for me. I don't want to go on. I crawl, I cough, but I am drawn on
towards this farthest point as if it were some magnetic pole, perhaps because
to be there offers the only solution. My mind is disconnected, dead, but my
soul is alive and receptive, grown huge and palpable. It wants to reach the
very top so that it can swing back into equilibrium.

The last few metres up to the summit no longer seem so hard. On
reaching the top, I sit down and let my legs dangle into space. I don't have
to climb any more. I pull my camera from my rucksack and, in my down
mittens, fumble a long time with the batteries before I have it working
properly. Then I film Peter. Now, after the hours of torment, which indeed I
didn't recognise as torment, now, when the monotonous motion of plodding
upwards is at an end, and I have nothing more to do than breathe, a great
peace floods my whole being. I breathe like someone who has run the race
of his life and knows that he may now rest for ever. I keep looking all
around, because the first time I didn't see anything of the panorama I had
expected from Everest, neither indeed did I notice how the wind was
continually chasing snow across the summit. In my state of spiritual
abstraction, I no longer belong to myself and to my eyesight. I am nothing
more than a single, narrow, gasping lung, floating over the mists and the
summits.

Only after I have drawn a couple of deep breaths do I again sense my
legs, my arms, my head. I am in a state of bright, clear consciousness, even
if not fully aware of where I am. In the instant that Peter joins me and flings
his arms around me, we both burst into tears. We lie in the snow, shaking
with emotion. The camera is cast aside. Our tears express everything we feel
after such a concentrated effort of will; they are our release.

We lie next to each other, there on the summit, lost to oblivion. And so
we remain for some while, up to our necks in drifted snow, mouths open,
recovering. When I do stand up, Peter stares at me as if he wants to impress
my face on his memory, as if indeed he doesn't recognise my face at all.

Standing now in diffused light, with the wind at my back, I experience
suddenly a feeling of completeness – not a feeling of having achieved
something or of being stronger than everyone who was ever here before, not
a feeling of having arrived at the ultimate point, not a feeling of supremacy.
Just a breath of happiness deep inside my mind and my breast. The summit
seemed suddenly to me to be a refuge, and I had not expected to find any
refuge up here. Looking at the steep, sharp ridges below us, I have the
impression that to have come later would have been too late. Everything we
now say to one another, we only say out of embarrassment. I don't think
any more. As I pull the tape recorder, trance-like, from my rucksack, and
switch it on wanting to record a few appropriate phrases, tears again well
into my eyes. 'Now we are on the summit of Everest,' I begin. 'It is so cold
that we cannot take photographs...' I cannot go on. I am immediately
shaken with sobs. I can neither talk nor think, feeling only how this

55 momentous experience changes everything. To reach only a few metres
below the summit would have required the same effort, the same anxiety
and burden of sorrow, but a feeling like this, an eruption of feeling, is only
possible on the summit itself.

Everything that is, everything I am, is now coloured by the fact that I
60 have reached this special place. The summit – for the time being at least –
is the simple intuitive answer to the enigma of life.

The questions that follow are based on the two passages. Using only the
information you have obtained from reading these passages, answer questions
1–5, each in a short paragraph. You may make notes to help you but put a line
across all your notes when you have answered all the questions.

Questions

These questions carry equal marks.

1 In passage one, what particular problems do the climbers experience on
their ascent and descent and how do they overcome them?
2 What equipment do the climbers take with them to the summit in
passage one?
3 In passage two, what evidence is there that fatigue and lack of oxygen
have numbed the writer's reactions?
4 Describe the changes in the writer's spiritual state during this experience.
5 In what ways do the two writers differ in their behaviour in the final stage
of the climb?

11 Practice passage 7

*Notice that this past examination question contains two summaries followed by
directed writing.*

'I was cycling to school with my lunch box and tennis racquet balancing on
my handlebars, and my school bag over my shoulder, which kept slipping
down – and I was late.

I was thinking about what I wanted for my birthday – I was going to be
5 fourteen on Saturday.

As it was, I woke up in hospital with a fractured head and a headache
that lasted for a week.

I can't remember what happened but someone in a car behind said I was
going down this straight bit of road and my bag got caught in the front
10 spokes and I took a header over the handlebars.'

Cycling is the most efficient form of transport known to man as far as
distance travelled per unit of energy expended – but it is not the safest.

In the UK roughly 300 people are killed and 30,000 injured each year
riding bicycles, along with 1,000 motorcyclists killed and 60,000 injured.

15 *The facts – recent surveys*

To understand how and why bicycle accidents occur, someone has looked at

645 serious non-fatal bicycle accidents and 46 fatal ones involving children living in Queensland, Australia over a 10-year period.

In 70% of the fatal cases the children had head injuries and 87% of the fatalities were due to a collision between a cyclist and a motor vehicle or train.

Boys aged between 12 and 14 had most of the accidents (86% of the cases). These occurred most frequently on a straight road, between 3 and 5 pm, in daylight, and in clear weather conditions.

Another recent study of cycling accidents, carried out in England, showed that amongst the injured children, only 30% had taken the cycling proficiency test and that half of the accidents were caused by poor riding techniques.

A separate study of head injuries resulting from accidents indicated that 58% were due to inability to control the bike and 38% were due to collisions.

Of the cyclists who died 70% did so from head injuries. This is not surprising given that landing on your head on a road or a car is rather like an egg dropping onto a concrete floor.

You've only got one head and it does contain your most valuable organ – the brain.

So what were the conclusions of these studies?

The findings

(1) Under the age of 12, children's brain development is not sufficiently advanced to coordinate cycling skills to a degree where they can manage open roads. Children younger than 12 find it difficult to judge the speed of traffic.

(2) Much thought should go towards the design of bicycles – it should be possible to design a bike that is both safe and showy.

45 (3) There should be more cycleways separating cyclists from motor traffic.

(4) Children should only be allowed to ride to school if they have passed a cycling proficiency test.

(5) Children who cycle should wear crash helmets.

Questions

1 a)   Look at the report of cycle accident surveys ('The facts – recent surveys'). Summarise what they say about the causes and the results of accidents.

Write a paragraph of no more than 90 of your own words. Use ideas from this section of the article only.

b)   Summarise the ways in which bicycle accidents can be reduced, firstly by cyclists and their parents, and secondly by manufacturers and town planners.

Use ideas from the first and third sections of the article only.

2   Imagine you are a road safety officer and that there have been several bicycle accidents in your area. You have been asked to visit a local school to talk to students aged up to 13.

Write what you would say. Use an idea or two from the article to start your talk and to catch the audience's attention. Write about 200–250 words.

I2   Practice passage 8

*Read this extract and then answer the questions a) and b) about it. Question c) is given for your information but you are **not** asked to answer it here.*

When Tristan da Cunha suddenly blew up in 1961, the entire community was rescued and taken to live in England. The volcano had appeared very near to the main settlement, and it erupted as people were in the middle of their escape. As you read it, try to imagine that you are one of the islanders.

Smoke was billowing from the new volcano – a raw, fiery wound that had opened at the top of the huge swelling which, like a giant-sized boil, now towered high above the spring-green plateau. Out of the gaping hole at the top red-hot cinders were rocketing into the sky with a low menacing roar.
5 This, clearly, was only a foretaste of what was to come. What could already be seen was awesome enough, but they had no time to stand and stare. There wasn't a moment to lose.

The men moved silently, like automatons, towards the village, some to save what they could from the houses – a Bible, a new pair of homemade
10 moccasins, a baby's dress, anything that came to hand – while another group, led by Joseph Glass, ran down to Little Beach. There, about 200

metres from the spitting volcano, they hauled four long-boats down from a grassy ledge and launched them into the surf, swiftly manning the oars to row round to Boat Harbour Bay. The rest returned on foot, carrying
15 everything possible and sighing for a donkey or an oxen cart. But the cattle had already been turned loose and driven from the settlement the night before as it would clearly be impossible to evacuate any of the livestock.

Having to leave the animals behind was one of the hardest blows for all, for apart from the small amount of money deposited in the Tristan Bank,
20 the livestock represented the entire total of the islanders' worldly wealth.

But all thoughts of personal possessions were swept aside by a new crisis when it was realised that the long-boats would be unable to land in Boat Harbour Bay. There was only one narrow approach between the rocks, and the wind, which had veered to westerly since dawn, had whipped up a
25 choppy sea. The oarsmen were game enough, but even if they landed their craft without accident, ferrying out the women and children in the teeth of that treacherous wind and through that narrow gap of turbulent water was likely to be more dangerous than running the gauntlet of the volcano and returning to Little Beach.
30 So, signalled to go back, the tossing long-boats pulled away and disappeared round Hottentot Point, leaving the rest of the islanders to climb wearily up to the top of the cliff again and set out once more with their belongings towards the settlement. By now the sun was high in the sky and the morning was bright and clear – much too beautiful a morning for
35 tragedy. Nor were any in that tired procession prepared for the astonishing assault on eyes and ears as they reached the village and realised, for the first time, the full horror of what a volcano could do.

By now the smoke had turned black. The air was fogged with flying ash, and from the incandescent mouth of the erupting cone thundered glowing
40 rocks and flames of fire. And spilling down its sides like thick black treacle were two broad, bubbling, hissing streams of lava that crept towards their only escape route – the sea.

From *The Glass Island* by Nancy Hosegood

a) If you had been on the island and had been watching the volcano, what exactly would you have seen and heard? Use your own words, and be careful to note the differences between what you saw at first (lines 1 to 17) and what you saw on your return when the sun had risen (lines 30–42). Write about 100 words.

b) All the way through the extract, the writer hints at the different feelings the villagers had. Using evidence from the passage, write about four of those feelings and suggest a reason for each.

c) Imagine that you are Joseph Glass. Tell your story of what happened next. Be careful to make your story fit the facts that you have read in the extract. Go on thinking about how the islanders would feel as the escape went on. Make their feelings realistic.

Please see Part 2 of this book for further practice in Summary and Directed Writing.

There is no need for you to answer question c). It is given here to show you what was included in this past examination paper.

30

PART 2

Comprehension, Summary and Directed Writing

13 Figurative language

> We can use many words with a literal meaning or a (quite different) figurative meaning. Make sure that you can understand whether a word is used literally or figuratively. Make sure that you know the meaning of a word when it is used metaphorically.
>
> In this unit try to understand the meaning of four words: literal, figurative, simile, metaphor(ical). Examples will make the meanings clear.

Literal

When a word is used with its normal meaning, we say that it is used in a literal sense (or with a literal meaning).

Struck   a)   The thief **struck** me on the arm with a piece of wood.
            b)   A plank fell from a building and **struck** a pedestrian.
Sharp   c)   Be careful! That knife is very **sharp**.
Sweet   d)   This tea is too **sweet**. You put too much sugar in it.
Sailed   e)   Two yachts **sailed** gracefully into the harbour.

Figurative

When a word is used with a special, non-literal meaning, we say that it is used in a figurative sense (or with a figurative meaning).

Struck   f)   Suddenly a clever idea **struck** her. (= came into her mind)
Sharp   g)   He has a very **sharp** tongue. (= critical, perhaps bitter)
Sweet   h)   Mary is a **sweet** girl. (= good-natured, cheerful, friendly)
Sailed   i)   My brother **sailed** through his driving test. (= went without difficulty)
            j)   At the reception, the bride's mother **sailed** into the room, wearing a beautiful blue dress. (= entered in an impressive way)

Exercise 1

In each pair of sentences, say whether the words in bold type are used literally or figuratively. If they are used figuratively, explain what they mean.

1   a)   Venus Williams **breezed** by her opponent to enter the final of the tennis tournament.
   b)   When we went out, a gentle **breeze** was blowing.

2   a)   **Brush** your hair, John. It looks untidy.
   b)   **Brush** up your English before you go to London, Jane.

3   a)   John has had a **swollen** head ever since he won first prize in the competition for amateur photographers. Now he thinks he knows everything about photography.
   b)   Mary had a **swollen** jaw, so I think she had toothache.

4   a)   Soldiers **combed** the jungle to try to find the terrorists' camp.
   b)   My brother **combed** his hair before he went out.

32

5 a) Yesterday I took the last paper in my examination. Now that the final **hurdle** is behind me, I can relax.
  b) An American has just broken the world record for the 110 metres **hurdle** race.

6 a) In some parts of the world, pollution is killing **fish** in coastal waters.
  b) Don't worry about John. He's not the only **fish** in the sea. You'll soon find another boyfriend.

7 a) The manager is a bit of a rough **diamond** but he certainly gets things done.
  b) The weight of a **diamond** is expressed in carats.

8 a) Several fishing-boats **sank** during the storm last week.
  b) Luther's heart **sank** when he saw his mother take out the forged letters which he had written.

9 a) Mrs Brimlow **flew** into a temper when Mr Armroyd accused her son of theft.
  b) I saw a cat stalking a bird in my garden. So I clapped my hands and the bird **flew** away.

10 a) If you borrow money from a loan **shark**, you will get into trouble.
  b) We saw a triangular fin above the water, so we knew that there was a **shark** not far from the shore.

In speech and written work, many people use words figuratively. So be prepared to understand and explain figurative meanings in an examination.

A simile

We use a simile (plural: similes) when we compare two people or things in respect of one or more qualities. We often use 'as' or 'like' to start the simile.

a) Peter was as white *as a sheet*.
b) The manager makes us work *like slaves*.
c) The shop assistant followed the tourists around the shop *like a fox stalking a group of rabbits*.
d) This meat is as tough *as a piece of old leather*.

Exercise 2

Complete these sentences in any suitable way by using similes.

1 A drunken person often walks like _____.
2 He is a slow worker. In fact, he's as slow as _____.
3 My friend can run like _____.
4 He eats his food like _____.
5 She never loses her temper. She is as cool as _____.
6 When the man was accused of theft, he broke down and began to cry like _____,
7 Don't trust him! He's as cunning as _____.
8 When the two motorists wanted to park their cars in the same place, they began to quarrel like _____.

A metaphor

A metaphor is a figure of speech. When a person uses a metaphor, we say that he is writing figuratively (and not literally). A metaphor takes the comparison of a simile a step further by saying that a person or a thing is or does something that is not literally true. For example, an idea cannot physically hit a person but we can say 'an idea suddenly struck me'. A man cannot use a boat to sail through a driving test but we can say 'he sailed through his test easily', meaning that the test was very simple for him and he had no difficulties.

In the following examples, the words in bold type are used metaphorically:

a) That is a **glaring** error. (= a very obvious one)
b) We were short of money, so we **dropped** the idea of moving to a new house. (= abandoned)
c) He gave a **sweeping** glance round the room. (= rapid and covering everything in sight)
d) I **ploughed** my way through the mathematics problems. (= worked slowly and steadily, and perhaps reluctantly)
e) Mistakes **crept** into his work. (= came almost unnoticed)
f) The Government is going to **axe** expenditure. (= cut, reduce)

Why do people use figurative language?

Similes and metaphors make a statement more concrete and vivid. They make a statement easier to understand and often more interesting or striking. For example, compare these sentences:

1 He is a very cunning boy.
2 He is as cunning as a fox.

In sentence (2), many people can imagine a fox and they may know many stories about how cunning foxes are. These memories help the reader to realise how cunning the boy is. Now compare these sentences:

3 An idea suddenly came into her mind.
4 An idea suddenly struck her.

By using 'struck' in (4), the writer makes the statement more vivid and effective. We can almost imagine an idea (coming like a flash of lightning) hitting somebody's head and entering the person's mind.

You must be able to recognise similes and metaphors, and to explain why they are used. If a word is used metaphorically, do not give its literal meaning when you have to explain it.

Check that you are familiar with the different kinds of vocabulary questions and know how to answer them.

1 Give a single word or short phrase with the same meaning as each of the following as they are used in the passage.

Look at the instructions to see whether the answer should be a single word, a short expression or a complete sentence. In most cases, a sentence is not needed.

Examples

a) Few prisoners managed to **get out of** Alcatraz prison.
   (escape from)
b) In some countries, the standard of English is gradually **deteriorating**.
   (slowly becoming worse *or* falling in standard as time passes)
c) These are the main points to follow when you are driving. *Above all,* concentrate on what you are doing. Watch other road-users carefully and try to *anticipate* what they may do.

   (most important of all; say (or guess) in advance)

In an examination do not waste time copying the words from the passage or question. Write the number of the question and then write your answer in this way:

1 a) escape from
   b) falling in standard as time passes
   c) most important of all; guess in advance

Exercise 1

Give a word or short phrase with the same meaning as the words in bold type in the sentences below.

1 Have you seen Jo **lately**?
2 I had **hardly** finished lunch when the telephone rang.
3 If a car costs US $80,000, we can **hardly** call it cheap,
4 When I first met Anna, I was **struck** by her obvious intelligence.
5 Mrs Smith gave her husband an **icy** stare, and so he kept quiet.
6 This law is too lax. The Government should **put teeth** in it.
7 Be very careful when you deal with him. His politeness is only a **cloak**. Beneath it, he has a cold, **calculating** mind.
8 She is a **strong** supporter of a **conservation** group and is very concerned about the environment.
9 It seems likely that those men are planning some **illicit** activity.
10 There was nothing we could do **but** wait patiently for the next bus.
11 Mr Jones **invariably** comes home very late at night.
12 I can't help you. My English is very **rusty**, so you'd better look the word up in a dictionary.

Look at the sentences in Exercise 1 again. Say whether these words are used literally or figuratively.

1	(4)	struck	6	(7)	cloak	
2	(5)	icy	7	(8)	strong	
3	(6)	Government	8	(8)	environment	
4	(6)	teeth	9	(11)	late	
5	(7)	politeness	10	(12)	rusty	

2 Explain in your own words the meaning of...

Look at the instructions to see whether or not you must use a complete sentence. It is safer to use a complete sentence unless the instructions say that only single words or phrases are needed.

If you quote words from the question or passage, put them in quotation marks.

a) Convinced that he was being pursued by a gang of thugs and murderers, Wilson fled blindly through the night. He ran straight into a tree and fell to the ground unconscious. When **his wits gradually came back to him**, he found two boys kneeling beside him.

either This means that he slowly became conscious again and aware of what was happening.

or The expression 'his wits gradually came back to him' means that he slowly became conscious again and aware of what was happening around him.

(The first answer is shorter and simpler, so it is better here.)

b) After years of wrangling with his neighbours, Mr Jones finally decided to **bury the hatchet** and concentrate on improving his farm.

either This means that he decided to make peace with his neighbours.

or Here, 'to bury the hatchet' means 'to make peace'.
or Here, 'to bury the hatchet' means that he decided to make peace.

(The first answer is the best because it has no problems with punctuation marks.)

Explain in your own words what the words or expressions in bold type mean as they are used in the following sentences. Answer in complete sentences.

1 Mary **blamed** Ben for the accident.
2 When we went to the factory, the production manager explained to us, **step by step**, how palm oil was transformed into neat bars of soap.
3 We carried the unconscious swimmer from the water and tried to **revive** him.

4   We applied artificial respiration. A few minutes later, the man **came round** and opened his eyes.

5   The men bought large quantities of watches and stored them near the border. Then, when their informants assured them that **the coast was clear**, they carried the watches across the border by means of a path through the mountains.

6   The Government needs to increase its income. **Nevertheless**, it has decided not to increase income tax **for the time being**.

7   Uncle is nearly an hour late. He may have been delayed by the traffic. **On the other hand**, he may have decided not to come this evening because of the heavy rain.

8   The Government has decided to make interest-free loans available to small businessmen. This is being done as one way of **boosting** the local economy and of **creating** more jobs.

9   In the winter months, influenza is a **common** illness in many countries.

10 When another employer offered her more money, Mary was **tempted** to change her job but she finally decided to stay with her existing employer.

3 Quote the words that ...

You may be asked to copy from the passage a word or expression which shows or proves something.

Example

In question 9 above, which single word shows the time of the year when influenza is common?

(Answer: *winter*)

Exercise 4

These questions are based on the sentences in Exercise 3 above.

1   In question 1, which word tells us that Mary believed that Ben had caused the accident?

2   In question 2, which word suggests that the writer admired the soap?

3   In question 3, which word tells us that the swimmer was not aware of what was happening?

4   In question 4, which word tells us that more than one person helped the man?

5   In question 5, which expression shows the route taken by the men?

6   In question 6, which expression shows us that the decision is only a temporary one?

7   In question 7, which single word shows us that the writer is not certain of the reason for the lateness of his uncle?

8   Which two words in question 8 show us that there are other methods of helping the economy?

9   In question 10, which word tells us that Mary considered leaving her present employer?

10 In question 10, which word first tells the reader that Mary had a job at this time?

4 Multiple-choice questions

At a market, inspectors visit hawkers to check their weights and scales. They want to ensure that the equipment is true and that buyers are not cheated.

Write down the word from the following list which is closest in meaning to *true* as used in line 2 of the example.

accurate   credible   honest   sincere   valid

(Answer: *accurate*)

Exercise 5

In each case, choose the word that is closest in meaning to the given word in the passage.

1 During the year, the company ran into **unforeseen** difficulties which had a bad effect on its trading position. As a result, the profit for the year is less than forecast.

   Here, *unforeseen* is similar in meaning to

   unfortunate   impossible   unanticipated   disastrous   technical

2 In the passage in question 1, *ran into* is similar in meaning to

   was ruined by   managed to avoid   hurried to meet   experienced   prepared for

3 Mr Brown offered Mrs Green US $125 000 for her house, not really expecting that she would agree to sell. Contrary to his expectations, Mrs Green accepted the offer without hesitation and asked for a 10 per cent deposit.

   Here, *Contrary to* is most similar in meaning to

   despite   following   according   beside   against

4 In question 3, *deposit* is used with the meaning of

   fee   receipt   commission   down payment   purchase price

5 Make sure that children receive adequate food, especially in their **crucial** early years, since malnutrition may affect both mental and physical development.

   Here, *crucial* is most similar in meaning to

   valid   vital   first   initial   sensitive

6 In question 5, the word *malnutrition* is used. In this word, the prefix *mal-* has the meaning of

   before   after   delayed   excessive   bad

7 In question 5, *adequate* is most similar in meaning to

   good   tasty   sufficient   healthy   abundant

8 The editor of a leading newspaper has been accused of contempt of court by a judge because the paper published information about the accused

man which might prejudice the jury and prevent a fair trial from being held.

Here, *contempt of* is used with the meaning of

failure to appear in   wrongly reporting the   lack of respect for trying to attack   wrong criticism of

9   In question 8, *prejudice* is used with the meaning of

anger   please   influence   prevent   attack

10   'I appreciate what you did to help my grandmother,' Mary said to John. We can tell from this that Mary was _____ to John.

helpful   thankful   useful   careful   grateful

5 Replacing a word in a passage

If you have to replace (or explain) a word in a passage, make sure that you use the right part of speech or the right form of a verb.

Example

The man *claimed that he had not* stolen the money.

Give a short expression which we can use in the passage without greatly changing its meaning.

right	denied that he had
wrong	deny he took
wrong	to deny he had

Exercise 6

Give a word or short expression which we can use in these sentences to replace the words in bold type without greatly changing the meaning of each passage.

1   The chief clerk has promised to **look into** the matter for us.
2   According to the radio, the Government has **put up** the fees for using car parks.
3   There has been a drop in the number of traffic accidents in the **previous** two years.
4   The plate was **shattered** when it fell off the table.
5   My brother is **suffering from** a bad cold now.
6   Have you ever **been** to London by air?
7   The prices of houses have risen considerably in recent years. **Consequently** many young couples are now unable to buy their own home.
8   This road has been closed **for the time being** but will probably be reopened some time next month.

15 Obstacles to understanding

Check that you understand the expressions and sentence patterns in this unit. A passage consists of many different sentences. If you fail to understand a key expression, you may fail to understand an important part of the passage.

1 Passive and active verbs

When a verb is **active**, the action often moves from left to right:

a)   A spectator attacked a player at a football match.

However, when a verb is **passive**, the action moves from right to left:

b)   A spectator was attacked by a player at a football match.

Test

We will call the spectator Peter. We will call the player John. Then:
In a) who was hurt?
In b) who hurt somebody?
In a) who assaulted another person?
In b) who may have been injured?

Conclusion

When you are reading, do not confuse 'he was arresting' and 'he was arrested'.

2 So . . . that

You already know this pattern:

a)   He was so angry that he could hardly speak.
b)   She was so delighted that she started to cry.

However, a writer can start a sentence with 'So' in this way:

c)   So angry was he that he could hardly speak.
d)   So delighted was she that she started to cry.

3 Had hardly . . . when

We can use this pattern with the meaning 'one thing had only just happened when something else happened.'

a)   He had hardly sat down when the telephone rang.
b)   We had hardly started to play when it began to pour with rain.

Remember that 'hardly' means 'only just' here.

4 Anything but = not; nothing but = only

a)   He is anything but intelligent.   (= not intelligent)
b)   We were anything but pleased.   (= We were not pleased at all.)

40

c) It was nothing but borrowing.   (= It was only borrowing.)
d) He is nothing but a fool.   (= He is a fool.)

5 Dashes = brackets

Some writers use dashes in place of brackets. Both of these sentences are correct:

a) My wife and I – we live next door – have just come here to settle some matters.
b) My wife and I (we live next door) have just come here to settle some matters.

6 What about . . .?

This is a short form of 'What shall we do about . . .?'

a) *Mary*   What about Peter?
   Anne   We'd better invite him, too.

The expression can also be a suggestion or an invitation:

b) *John*   What about going for a swim?
   Tom   That's a good idea.

7 Sometimes it is helpful to simplify a long sentence

When a sentence is very long, it is sometimes helpful to look for the key words and find out what the main idea is. When you have done this, you can consider the details.

a) Despite the mud and surge of flood water, **Peter managed to** struggle slowly towards the slippery bank of the river and at last, with one major effort which almost completely exhausted him, to **drag himself** up **to safety.**
b) Consequently **people** who are habitually engaged **in** some form of **agriculture, can** generally **keep whatever they have gained** or earned through their hard work **unless,** indeed, **they are conquered** or plundered by some stronger and more violent people from outside.

8 Three at a time

Many sentences make three statements at one time. This pattern can take various forms:

a) She was tired, disappointed and rather angry.
b) The ship's activities, now that they are exposed, embarrass South Africa (from where she operates), Britain (who insures her), and Norway (who provided her harpoons and whaling equipment).
c) Someone had quarrelled over its possession, someone else had joined in, and suddenly, without anyone knowing exactly why, the volcano of passion had erupted and a lava of blood had flowed.

9 Inversion of subject and verb

After words with a negative sense and after certain adverbial expressions, the subject may come after the verb (or after part of the verb).

a) Only on one estate, where the spraying programme was maintained, **did the insects continue** to cause damage.
b) Never **had Mary seen** such a remarkable sight.

Notice that this type of sentence is not a question.

10 Words with different meanings

Note: *In your own written work, avoid starting a sentence with 'As', 'For' or 'Since', so that the meaning of each sentence is immediately clear to your reader.*

Words such as 'as', 'for' and 'since' can have different meanings. In each sentence, check which particular meaning each word has.

a) As I was waiting for a bus, I could not cross the road to talk to Mary.
   (= Because)
b) As I was waiting for a bus, I happened to see a traffic accident.
   (= When, While)

11 to be + an infinitive

Planned future action is sometimes shown by a suitable form of the verb 'to be' + an infinitive. This method can be used to give orders.

a) She is to be at the manager's office by 3 p.m. tomorrow.
b) According to this programme, the Minister is to be met at the airport by local businessmen.

12 Starting with an adverbial expression

When we want to emphasise an adverbial expression (or for another reason), we can start a sentence with it. Then the main subject may not come until much later in the sentence.

a) Inside the cage-like structures, small private battles were being fought.

or

b) Inside the cage-like structures and, indeed, as far as one could see within the walls of the castle, small private battles were being fought.

Participle expressions often occur at the start of a sentence. The reader may then have to wait until he finds the main subject of the sentence.

c) Horrified at what he had done and worried about the consequences, the man rushed away, hotly pursued by a crowd of angry villagers.
d) Not realising that the last bus had already gone, we waited nearly an hour for a bus to arrive. Then we gave up and decided to walk home.

16 Practice passage 1

Read the passage and then answer the questions about it. Use your own words as far as possible.

Note: *In this past GCE examination question, all seven paragraphs were given before the questions. In this book, each paragraph is followed by the questions above it so that you will not have to turn back pages all the time.*

In this story the author describes a journey deep into the Amazon jungle where, to the surprise of the explorers, they came across creatures which they believed no longer existed.

1   We passed very slowly through the woods, partly because Lord John acted as a scout before he would let us advance, and partly because at every second step either one or the other of the two professors would stop, with a cry of wonder, before some flower or insect which presented him with a new type.
5   We may have travelled four or five kilometres, keeping to the right of the line of a stream, when we came upon a considerable opening in the trees. A strip of brushwood led to a tangle of rocks – in fact the whole plateau was strewn with boulders. We were walking slowly towards these rocks, among bushes which reached our waists, when we became aware of a low babbling
10   and whistling sound, which filled the air with a constant clamour and appeared to come from some spot immediately before us. Lord John held up his hand as a signal for us to stop, and he made his way swiftly, stooping and running, to the line of rocks. We saw him peep over them and give a gesture of amazement. Then he stood still as if forgetting us, so utterly
15   hypnotised was he by what he saw. Finally he waved to us to come on, holding up his hand as a signal for caution. His whole manner made me feel that something wonderful but dangerous lay before us.

Question 1

1   a)   (i)   State two reasons which prevented the team from moving faster than they were doing.
         (ii)   How many explorers were on this expedition?
         (iii)   'A strip of brushwood' (lines 6–7). What does this tell you about the shape of the brushwood?

     b)   (i)   From this paragraph, write out the phrase containing three consecutive words that means the same as 'there were large rocks scattered about.'
         (ii)   Lord John made his way, 'stooping and running' to the rocks. Explain why he moved like this.
         (iii)   'Finally he waved to us to come on' (line 15). Explain in your own words the reason why Lord John did not beckon them on immediately.

2   Creeping to his side, we looked over the rocks. The place into which we gazed was a pit, and may, in the early days, have been one of the smaller
20   volcanic blowholes of the plateau. It was bowl-shaped, and at the bottom, some hundreds of metres from where we lay, were pools of green-scummed stagnant water fringed with reeds. It was a weird sight in itself but its occupants made it look like a scene from hell. The pit was the habitat and nesting ground of pterodactyls. There were hundreds of them congregated
25   within our view. All the bottom area around the water's edge was alive with

young ones. Their hideous mothers brooded upon leathery yellowish eggs which were still to hatch. The birds looked more like reptiles than birds. The babbling and whistling that we had registered before had come from this mass of obscene reptilian life. Now it was combined with a horrible
30 odour which made us feel sick. But above, perched sentinel-like, each upon its own stone, tall, grey and withered, sat the males. They were absolutely motionless save for the vigilant movement of their eyes or an occasional snap of their rat-trap beaks as dragonflies went past them. Their huge membranous wings were closed by folding their forearms, so that they sat
35 like gigantic old women wrapped in crinkly grey shawls, their ferocious heads protruding above them. Large and small, not less than a thousand of these filthy creatures lay in the hollow below us. Like penguins, they lived in colonies.

Question 1
(continued)

c) (i) The explorers were gazing into a pit (line 19). What, according to the author, could have accounted for the existence of this pit and others like it?
(ii) What do we learn from the passage about the size of the pit?

Question 2

2 a) (i) List any two similarities between pterodactyls and ordinary birds.
(ii) The male pterodactyls were keeping watch. From the evidence in the paragraph, explain in your own words two ways in which they did this.

3 Our professors would gladly have stayed there all day, so taken up were they
40 by this rare chance to study the life of a prehistoric age. They pointed out the bones of fish and birds pecked clean and lying about among the rocks as proving the nature of the diet of these creatures. I heard them congratulating each other on having cleared up the point why the fossilised remains of this flying dragon are, even today, found in such great numbers
45 in certain coastal areas.

Question 2
(continued)

b) What particular discovery about the pterodactyls' diet 'cleared up the point' (line 43) about their fossilised remains?

4 Finally, however, Professor Challenger, intent on proving some point which his colleague Summerlee had contested, thrust his head over the rock and nearly brought destruction upon us all. In an instant, the nearest male gave a shrill whistling cry, and flapped its five-metre span of leathery wings as it
50 soared into the air. The females and young ones huddled together beside the water, while the whole circle of sentinels rose one after the other and sailed off into the sky. It was a wonderful sight to see at least a hundred creatures of such enormous size and ugly appearance swooping like swallows with such swift, shearing wing strokes above us; but we soon realised that it
55 was not a sight over which we could afford to linger or daydream. At first the great brutes flew round in a large ring as if to make sure what the extent of the danger might be, in just the same way as a great white shark would circle its would-be victims before mauling them. Then the flight grew lower and more threatening, like modern jets zeroing in on a target. The circle
60 narrowed, until the birds were buzzing round and round us, the rustling flap

of their wings filling the air with a sound that made me think of an aerodrome back home on the day of an air show. 'Make for the woods and keep together!' cried Lord John. We needed no further encouragement.

5 The moment we attempted to retreat, the circle closed in upon us, until the
65 tips of the wings of those nearest to us nearly touched our faces. We beat them with the stocks of our guns but there was nothing solid or vulnerable to strike. Then suddenly, out of the whizzing slate-coloured circle, a long serpentine neck shot out, and a fierce beak made a thrust at us. Another and another followed. Summerlee gave a cry and put his hand to his face,
70 from which blood was streaming. I felt a prod at the back of my neck, and turned dizzy with shock. Challenger fell and, as I stooped to pick him up, I was struck again from behind and I dropped on top of him. At the same instant I heard the thunderous crash of Lord John's elephant gun, and, looking up, saw one of the creatures with a broken wing struggling upon the
75 ground, spitting and gurgling defiantly at us with wide open beak and bloodshot eyes. At such close quarters the creature looked like some horrible winged devil whose picture I had seen in an old book in the University Memorial Library. Its hideous comrades had flown higher at the sudden sound, and were circling above our heads, ready for another aerial
80 attack.

6 'Now,' cried Lord John, 'run for our lives!' We staggered through the bushes, and just before we reached the trees the birds broke their circle as if on cue and bore down on us. The boldest of them nose-dived and knocked Summerlee down, but we wrenched him up and made a stumbling rush for
85 the tree trunks. Once there we were safe, for those huge wings had no room to sweep beneath the branches.

7 As we limped campwards, sadly mauled and discomfited, we saw them for a long time flying above our heads, soaring round and round, no bigger than wood pigeons, with their eyes no doubt following our progress. At last,
90 however, as we reached the thicker woods they gave up the chase and we saw them no more. Our zeal for scientific exploration disappeared with the flying birds.

Adapted from *The Lost World* by Sir Arthur Conan Doyle

Question 2
(continued)

c) Why did the pterodactyls now look 'no bigger than wood pigeons' (lines 88–89)

d) Choose five of the following words or phrases. For each of them give one word or short phrase (of not more than seven words), that has the same meaning as it has in the passage.

constant (line 10)	save for (line 32)
stagnant (line 22)	taken up (line 39)
fringed (line 22)	retreat (line 64)
hideous (line 26)	zeal (line 91)

Question 3

Imagine that you were the male pterodactyl who spotted Professor Challenger first and then alerted the rest of the pterodactyls. Write a description of the battle between yourself and the explorers. You must write only about what you and the other pterodactyls did, both in attacking the explorers and defending yourselves. Use only material from line 46 to line 86.

Your account, which should be in continuous writing, must not be longer than 160 words, including the ten words given below.

Begin your account as follows:

Something moved at the edge of the pit, and I . . .

---

17 Practice passage 2A

Read the passage and then answer the questions about it. This passage is the first part of a past examination question.

Use your own words as far as possible. Questions marked with an asterisk (*) should be answered very briefly and in these answers complete sentences are not necessary. Other questions should be answered in complete and correct sentences.

Note: *Marks are awarded for correct facts and deducted for incorrect English.*

A My parents were hardly seated in the Brimlows' kitchen, and my father was still wondering how to open the unpleasant business, when the sound of a key in the front door was heard. Luther was not alone. He came into the kitchen pale and trembling, and with him was a tall, well-dressed man who
5 looked in a thoroughly black humour. Luther licked his lips and explained that this was Mr Armroyd, the stockbroker who employed him. Mr Armroyd began without preliminary: 'I'm saving the police a job by bringing your son along myself, Mr Brimlow.'

Luther immediately began to babble: 'I can explain everything, Mother.
10 It's all a mistake. It wasn't theft. It was nothing but borrowing.'

It was at once to his mother that he appealed. Poor old Brimlow from the first was hardly in the picture. Mrs Brimlow did not lose her self-possession. Her narrow cunning face sharpened, and she said: 'I think you and your husband ought to leave us, Mrs Pentecost.'

15 My father answered her sharply: 'I'm not so sure about that, Mrs Brimlow.' And turning to Mr Armroyd, he added: 'My wife and I – we live next door – have just come in here to settle some matters that concern this young man. They may be related to what you have to say, and if we have your permission we shall stay.'

20 Mrs Brimlow, sniffing danger like a vixen, cried: 'I won't have it! This is my house, and who stays in it is my business – not Mr Armroyd's or anyone else's.

Mr Armroyd said in a sharp reminding voice: 'Mrs Brimlow, I told you that I had brought your son along rather than permit the police to do it. If
25 you are unreasonable, I shall have to change my mind. Then it won't be a question of your next-door neighbour knowing what has happened, but of everybody knowing it.'

Questions

Answer these questions. The comments below were *not* given in the examination paper. They are given here to help you.

a)* Each on a separate line, list the people who were in the kitchen with Luther, and opposite each write his or her relationship to or connection with Luther.

Comments Use a separate line for each person.
Remember to show the person's relationship to or connection with Luther.
Do not bother about the author (a son or daughter of the Pentecosts).

b)* Explain the word *hardly* in
(i) *hardly seated* (line 1)
(ii) *hardly in the picture* (line 12)

Comment Do not explain *seated* or *in the picture*.
Set your answer out in this way.

b) (i) _____ Give one or two words to explain *hardly* in each case.
(ii) _____

c) Luther calls his theft borrowing. What is the real difference between these actions?

Comment Use a complete sentence this time. Think about permission and the intention to return something.

d)* In what two ways does the author compare Mrs Brimlow to a fox?

Comment Just copy out the words from the passage. A sentence is *not* needed.
In line 20, a *vixen* is a female fox.

e) What danger did Mrs Brimlow *sniff* (line 20)?

Comment This is very difficult question. Read lines 20–21 and line 2. Then explain what the danger was. Use your own words as far as possible.

f)* Quote the single word which explains *what has happened* in line 26.

Comment Read lines 9–10 again. Your answer must be one word only.

g)* Quote three words or phrases which show that Luther was afraid.

Comment Look at lines 4, 5 and 9. Put each word or phrase on a separate line.

h) In what way could Mr Armroyd be said to be less severe than one might have expected?

Comment Look at lines 7–8 and 23–27. Then give your answer in one or two sentences.

Now check all your answers. Correct any errors of English.

This unit contains the second two parts of the examination question in Unit 17. Learn how to lay out your answers correctly. Learn how to answer comprehension questions.

Every year some good candidates fail this examination because they do not know the standard or layout of the answers expected by the examiners.

1 Answer all parts of each question.
    When you have answered a question, look back at the question again. Check that you have answered all the parts.
2 Do not use a complete sentence when you are asked to give only a word or phrase.
3 Use complete sentences when asked to do so.
4 Do not copy most of the question when you give your answer.

Example

Why was Luther nervous when he came home?

Wrong type of answer

When Luther came home he was nervous because his employer had accused him of theft.

Right type of answer

His employer had accused him of theft and was going to tell his parents about this.

5 When you write in sentences, try to form each sentence in your mind before you start to write it. Then you will make fewer mistakes.
6 Keep your answers short. Long answers often contain more mistakes.

Passage 2B

Read passage B and then answer the questions about it.

B Mrs Brimlow was one of those fools who will not see reason. 'You can say what you like,' she shouted. 'I don't believe a word of it. Our Luther's a
30 good boy, and a hard-working boy, and a clever boy. What about your own letters? Haven't you written to say how good he was, more than once?'
    Mr Armroyd's eyebrows shot up, and Luther said suddenly: 'Oh, leave it alone, Mother. You'll do no good.' But already Mrs Brimlow was rummaging in a dresser drawer, and she brought out three letters headed with the name
35 of Mr Armroyd's firm. Luther made a snatch for them, but Armroyd intervened quickly and took the letters. He gave a sweeping glance through all three, folded them carefully, and put them into his pocket. 'These interest me enormously,' he said. 'It seems to me, Mrs Brimlow, that your son will go far – in one direction or another. Picking from the petty cash is
40 common enough with boys of his sort and at his age, but such a neat bit of forgery is unusual.'
    He looked with renewed interest at Luther, who was white and quaking.

'Are you such a poor stick,' he asked, 'that you must bolster yourself up like this even to your own parents?'

45 There could be no doubt now, even in Mrs Brimlow's mind. She put her arms round her son and shrieked at Mr Armroyd, 'You leave him alone! You slave-driver. You stingy old devil! Is it any wonder the poor boy steals when you pay him a wage I'd be ashamed to give to a washerwoman?'

Questions

i) (i)* What feeling is implied in the statement *Mr Armroyd's eyebrows shot up* (line 32)?

(ii) Why did Mr Armroyd feel like this?

Comment Write one word only for (i). Start your answer to (ii) with the words *He was very surprised because* _____.

j) What was wrong with the letters?

Comment Use *They* _____ or *Mr Armroyd had not* _____.

k) What further information are we given in this section about the crime of which Luther was suspected in passage A?

Comment The crime was theft. Start in this way, *In line 39, it is suggested that he had* _____. Do not put *picking* in your answer.

l)* Explain (i) *go far* (line 39)

(ii) *bolster yourself up* (line 43)

Comment Keep your answers short, if possible.

m) In what way was Mr Armroyd's reaction to the letters different from what might have been expected?

Comment You can start: *Instead of becoming angry, he* _____.

Passage 2C

Now read passage C and then answer the questions about it.

C Mr Armroyd intervened sharply, 'Mrs Brimlow, I came here to tell you that
50 for a long time your son has been stealing considerable sums of money. I have learned from you that he is also a forger. Now listen to me, if you can stop your tongue clacking for a moment. I'm surprised that one or two things haven't struck you. Your son dresses expensively for his situation. He travels first class on the railway. I've seen him at lunchtime in rather
55 expensive restaurants entertaining a young lady. This young man has got to be cleared out of Manchester. He's flying a bit too high, even though I recently increased his salary to a rate higher than is usually paid. But I imagine he hasn't told you that. However, I did it, and I'll tell you why.' He slapped the pocket containing the forged letters. 'If I had written these
60 letters they would have said just about what your son said of himself. He has shown exceptional insight into my business. If you like, I'll gratify Mrs Brimlow's vanity and say frankly that he's a prodigy. He could have gone a long way with clean hands. But in my office, he's not going any way at all with dirty hands. Nor in Manchester, so far as I can prevent it.'

Questions

n)* Explain (i) *struck* (line 53)

(ii) *flying a bit too high* (line 56)

(iii) *clean hands* (line 63)

Comments (i) Use the right tense or verb form.

(ii) Your first word can end in *-ing*.

(iii) You can use one word or two. Think of a word which starts with *hon*.

o)* Quote the single word or phrase of not more than *four* words which most clearly shows that

(i) Luther was guilty of more than one theft.

(ii) Mr Armroyd's loss had not been light.

(iii) Luther's tastes were not in keeping with the sort of job he held.

(iv) Mr Armroyd found what Mrs Brimlow said distasteful.

(v) Luther was highly intelligent at work.

Comments (i) See line 50 and find a plural noun.

(ii) There are two possible answers in line 50.

(iii) Possible answers are in line 53 to line 55, but do not use more than four words.

(iv) See line 49 or line 52.

(v) See line 61 or lines 62 and 63.

p) In what way had Mr Armroyd shown a very considerate attitude to his employee?

Comment The best answer is probably in lines 56 and 57, but you must express this in your own words. An alternative answer involves mentioning the police.

Vocabulary

Imagine that you have to explain the meaning of the words in bold type below. Which of the possible answers is/are correct? 1, 2, 3 or 4 of them may be correct or they may all be wrong.

1 My father was still wondering how to **open** the unpleasant business. (line 2)

A Open means start to talk about.

B 'Open' means 'start to talk about'.

C investigate

D first mention

2 a tall, well-dressed man who looked **in a thoroughly black humour.** (line 5)

A in a very angry mood

B in an angry mood

C with a dirty face

D with a completely dirty face

3 Luther **licked his lips.** (line 5)

This suggests to the reader that Luther was _____.

A hungry

B thirsty

C nervous

D frightened

4 Mr Armroyd began without **preliminary.** (line 7)

A nervousness

B introduction

C nervous

D introduce

5   *Luther immediately began to **babble**.* (line 9)
    A   accuse
    B   complain
    C   dribble
    D   cry like a baby

6   ***Poor** old Brimlow – was hardly in the picture.* (lines 11–12)
    The writer uses 'poor' to show us that...
    A   Brimlow was not a rich man
    B   Mrs Brimlow's husband had no money
    C   he felt sorry for Mr Brimlow
    D   he sympathised with Brimlow

7   *Mrs Brimlow did not lose **her self-possession**.* (line 12)
    A   the things she owned
    B   control of herself
    C   everything she possessed
    D   the furniture which belonged to her house

8   *Mrs Brimlow – cried: 'I won't **have** it!'* (line 20)
    A   own
    B   possess
    C   allow
    D   permit

9   *Mrs Brimlow was **rummaging** in a dresser drawer.* (lines 33–34)
    A   hiding
    B   concealing
    C   searching
    D   sitting

10 *He gave a **sweeping** glance through all three letters.* (lines 36–37)
    A   quick and going from top to bottom rapidly
    B   cautious and avoiding anything unpleasant
    C   angry and expecting to see bad things
    D   interested and noticing all details

11 *Picking from the **petty** cash is common enough ...* (lines 39–40)
    A   loose
    B   small
    C   business
    D   commercial

12 *... such a **neat** bit of forgery is unusual.* (lines 40–41)
    By using 'neat' here, Mr Armroyd showed that...
    A   he respected careful people
    B   he admired Luther's handwriting
    C   he somewhat admired Luther's skill
    D   he realised that the crime was very serious

13 *He looked with renewed interest at Luther, who was white and **quaking**.* (line 42)
    A   tremble
    B   trembling
    C   shiver
    D   shivering

14 *You* **stingy** *old devil!* (line 47)
   A   rude
   B   spiteful
   C   talkative
   D   proud

15 *He has shown exceptional* **insight into** *my business.* (lines 60–61)
   A   experience of
   B   understanding of
   C   profit from
   D   dishonest in

16 *I'll* **gratify** *Mrs Brimlow's vanity.* (lines 61–62)
   A   satisfy
   B   please
   C   challenge
   D   ignore

17 *. . . and say* **frankly** *that he's a prodigy.* (line 62)
   A   openly
   B   with regret
   C   jealously
   D   honestly

18 *He could have* **gone a long way** *with clean hands.* (lines 62–63)
   A   travelled
   B   travelled a considerable distance
   C   become very successful
   D   success

19   Practice passage 3

This passage gives you further practice in answering questions at the standard of the GCE examination.

Note: *In its original form, the three sections of the passage were given before the questions. As a matter of convenience, in this book the questions are given after each section.*

Brilliant detective work by just one man has proved that a single grubby little ship, flying a flag of convenience, is slaughtering great numbers of undersized whales in forbidden waters. Working by stealth, the ship earns an estimated £1.5 million to £2 million profit a year for its owners. She is
5 killing hundreds of whales every year, decimating the stocks of humpback, fin, sperm, killer and blue whales off the North African and Portuguese coasts.

Now the whale-chaser *Sierra* has been caught in the act of transferring a cargo of newly caught whalemeat to Japanese freighters for shipment to
10 Japan. The ship's activities, now that they are exposed, embarrass South Africa (from where she operates), Britain (who insures her), and Norway (who provided her harpoons and whaling equipment). Most of all, they acutely embarrass the world's largest commercial whaling nation, Japan.

Stories about an undercover whaling ship going 'cowboy-hunting' had
15 been circulating for some time. 'Greenpeace', the anti-whaling and conservation group, even named her last year. But nothing was sure until a whale enthusiast decided last summer to find out the truth for himself. Paul Brown based his search on logic and thoroughness.

Questions

Answer the following questions in your own words as far as possible. Questions marked with an asterisk (*) should be answered very briefly and in these answers complete sentences are not necessary. Other questions should be answered in complete and correct sentences.

a)   Give three reasons why the activities of the *Sierra* were illegal.
b)* Give a single word or short phrase which has the same meaning as each of the following as used in the passage:
    (i)   undercover (line 14)
    (ii) conservation (line 16)

His first thought was: who are the professionals at tracing ships? Lloyd's, of
20 course. He approached them as any commercial client would, and paid the necessary fees of several hundred pounds to become a recipient of their information. He first asked them if the *Sierra*, registered in Cyprus, was on their computer. She wasn't, so he asked if they would put her on. This meant that all Lloyd's agents would be told to report if the *Sierra* came into
25 port, when, where, and what she was doing.

That was in August, 1978. By October, Paul Brown began to get a list of the *Sierra*'s movements. But he needed more than that. Therefore he asked the Lloyd's computer to run a program of refrigerated cargo freighters to see if one of them kept coinciding with the *Sierra*. None of them did.
30 Paul Brown thought again, and asked Lloyd's a different question: did the *Sierra*'s movements into port ever match with any Japanese refrigerated cargo carriers of more than 10,000 tons? He began to get a print-out of 40–50 ships.

He still had to tie it down further. He reasoned that he would have to
35 catch the *Sierra* when she was transferring her whalemeat, if she had any, and that therefore a cargo ship would be expected to be hanging around in a port for a few days, waiting for her. So he asked Lloyd's to tell him if any of the 40 or 50 ships in the North Atlantic was sitting idle in port for more than five days, on the assumption she had a rendezvous with the *Sierra*.
40 This brought Brown a bite. Lloyd's told him that a Japanese freighter, the *Yamato Reefer*, had been lying idle in Las Palmas, in the Canary Islands, for over a week. Wasting no time, Brown caught the first flight to Las Palmas, arriving the same evening.

Questions

c)   Give in your own words the reason why Paul Brown paid a large sum of money to Lloyd's.

d) Why did Paul Brown ask for the *Sierra* to be put on the computer? Do not quote from the passage.
e) Brown asked Lloyd's two questions about refrigerated cargo freighters. In your own words say
   (i) how the questions differed;
   (ii) why he asked the second question;
   (iii) why he was anxious to discover if a ship might have a rendezvous with the *Sierra*.
f) Why should the *Sierra* wish to transfer its cargo?
g) Why did Paul Brown ask if there was a refrigerated cargo ship which was doing nothing for more than five days?
h) Explain in your own words the meaning of each of the following:
   (i) *He still had to tie it down further.* (line 34)
   (ii) *This brought Brown a bite.* (line 40)

He took a room in a hotel, with a good view of the bay. He began to study
45 the dock gates, to see which was lightly guarded. Dressing in old clothes, growing a beard and wearing a big hat, he went down to the docks every day, passing himself off as a fisherman. After a few days' fishing, no one gave him a second glance.
Thirteen days after he arrived, the *Yamato Reefer* moved from the bay into
50 the harbour. Brown saw it was time for action. He rushed down to the dock, and as he was sitting in his usual place the *Sierra* came right past him, just 40 feet away.
From the dockside fishing place, Paul Brown began to take a remarkable series of photographs. On the day after the *Sierra* came in, he chartered a
55 pilot boat, and took more pictures from the boat's cabin roof. What the pictures showed was the *Yamato Reefer* lowering her cranes and winches to transfer loads of cargo, each containing about 170 wrapped packs, from the decks of the *Sierra*.
But a crew member became suspicious of the pilot boat's repeated passes,
60 the harbour police were called, and loading stopped. The next day they continued – in the outer harbour, a container dock that undesirables could not get into. Paul Brown persisted. First, he found a truck driver who agreed to take him in for 100 dollars. From the truck's cab Brown took a stream of photographs of the unloading, the captain, the gunner, the crew, and, most
65 significant of all, four Japanese meat inspectors. He also found a fork-lift truck driver who agreed, for another 100 dollars, to hold up the lettering on one of the unloaded packs so that it could be photographed. It was marked in Japanese and also in English FRESH QUICK FROZEN WHALE MEAT.
Paul Brown had not yet finished. Another bribe got him a copy of the
70 *Sierra*'s manifest* from the harbour authorities. She was carrying 210 tons of frozen whale fillets.

manifest: a list of ship's cargo

Questions

i) Why did Paul Brown pretend to be a fisherman?
j) What did Paul Brown's photographs prove?
k)* What is the meaning of **undesirables** (line 61)?
l) What did Paul Brown achieve by the bribes he gave?
m) What evidence is there that the crew of the *Sierra* did not want anyone to know what they were doing?

Discuss in class (a) which of the following answers is the best, and (b) why the others are wrong or less suitable. The answers refer to some of the above questions.

i) 1 Paul Brown pretended to be a fisherman to take a remarkable series of photographs.
2 Paul Brown pretended to be a fisherman so that, when the *Sierra* entered the dock, he could get into the dock (which was guarded) and take photographs of the ship.
3 He wanted to enter a guarded dock and take photographs of the *Sierra*.
4 To take photographs of the *Sierra* and prove that it was taking part in illegal whaling.

j) 1 Paul Brown's photographs proved that the *Sierra* was a Japanese ship.
2 They proved that Paul Brown could get past the guards easily.
3 Paul Brown's photographs proved that a Japanese ship had been breaking the law by catching whales.
4 They proved that the *Sierra* had caught whales and transferred their meat to a Japanese ship.

k) 1 *Undesirables* mean 'people who break the law'.
2 Bad men.
3 People who were not welcome (because they were too inquisitive).
4 Robbers.

20 Types of comprehension questions

This unit gives examples of different types of comprehension questions. It gives you practice in answering them.

In previous units, most questions have started with 'What', 'Why', 'Explain' or 'Quote', or they have been vocabulary questions. In the past, the following types of questions have also been used.

I Give two/three reasons/results/factors. . .

Examples

Give three reasons why Mr Armroyd had suspected that there was something wrong with Luther's way of living.

What is your answer? Can you answer without referring back to the passage?

Give three problems which Paul Brown faced in his attempt to track down the *Sierra* and obtain evidence against it.

What is your answer?

55

2 Questions about the effects of words in the passage

Example 1

During supper, George's face was stony but by the time the meal was through he observed that his wife's was stonier.

> Q. What do the words 'stony' and 'stonier' tell us about how George and his wife looked?

What is your answer?

Example 2

Stories about an undercover whaling ship going 'cowboy-hunting' had been circulating for some time. 'Greenpeace', the anti-whaling and conservation group, had even named her last year.

> Q. Why does the author use 'even' here?

Can you explain the author's purpose in using this word?

3 Questions which force you to search for particular words in the passage

Example 1

Feeling somewhat ashamed of what he had done, Luther stared at the floor and carefully avoided looking at his mother or at Mr Armroyd. Mrs Brimlow was shrewd enough to guess which way the wind was blowing. She began to adopt a more conciliatory tone.

> Q. Quote the single word in the passage which best shows that each of these statements is true:
> (i) Luther did not feel proud of himself at that time.
> (ii) When Mrs Brimlow began to speak again, she was much more reasonable in her attitude.

What are the words?

Example 2

Paul Brown showed initiative and persistence in his attempt to track down the *Sierra* and demonstrate to the public what was going on. Not content with merely tracing the ship, he contrived to get photographic evidence which would attract publicity and could not be denied.

> Q. Quote the single word in the passage which best suggests that Paul Brown was not the sort of man who gives up easily.

What is the answer?

4 Questions asking about how a person (place or thing) changes during a passage

Example 1

What change, if any, occurred in Mr Armroyd's attitude in the passage (about Luther)?

| **Example 2** | How did Paul Brown's attitude to his task probably change during the period of time covered in the passage? |

What are your answers? These are challenging questions. Don't give up. Work out the answers.

5 True/false questions

| **Example** | Do the following sentences accurately describe the character of Paul Brown as shown in the passage about the *Sierra*? Answer **Yes** or **No** for each sentence. |

- a)   He probably supported the aims of the 'Greenpeace' group.
- b)   He was a resourceful man.
- c)   He was envious of the success of the *Sierra*.
- d)   He was unconcerned about the fate of whales.

Are these sentences right or wrong?

6 Questions which test your understanding of a situation and of its likely consequences

These may be questions about what somebody might have said or about what might have happened after an incident.

| **Example 1** | Write down **two** statements which the captain of the *Sierra* might have said to his crew after Brown was first seen taking photographs of the ship. |

Make up two possible statements.

| **Example 2** | When Armroyd returned home, his wife asked him if he had had a good day at work. Write down **two** statements in reply to this question. In the first statement let Armroyd say where he had been. In the second statement let him say what he thought of his visit to the Brimlows' home. |

Make up two statements which Armroyd might have made to his wife.

7 Questions which involve some knowledge of grammatical terms

In a few questions, you may need to know what a verb, adjective, phrase or clause is. These questions are not common but they have occurred in the past. These are typical examples. Do not try to find the answers because you do not know which passage they refer to.

- a)   Write down **three** verbs from the second paragraph which give the impression that inanimate (or lifeless) objects were actively on the young men's side.
- b)   Quote an adjectival phrase of five words from the third paragraph.

Please see Units 63 and 64, which deal with the grammatical knowledge you are expected to have.

8 Questions which deal with punctuation marks, the use of italics and other technical points

These questions are not common but they occur sometimes.

Example 1	In line 15, why is 'dead' in inverted commas?
Example 2	In line 74, why is FRESH in capital letters?
Example 3	In line 8, why is *poaching* in italics?
Example 4	How would the final sentence of the second paragraph be changed in meaning if we left out the comma after 'men'?

9. Questions about the author of a passage

These questions may deal with an author's aim, his attitude to his topic or to his tone.

Example 1	What seems to be the main aim of the author in writing this passage about locusts?
Example 2	As far as we can tell, what is the author's attitude to Paul Brown?
Example 3	The tone of this passage is (ironical, sarcastic, objective, humorous, cynical). Which of the five words is most appropriate here?

10 Questions about the main point of a passage or paragraph

These are not very common at GCE level because they are usually too easy. In any case, they are better tested in the summary question.

11 Questions asking what a pronoun or other word refers to

Example	At first Brown was uncertain whether information from Lloyd's about the movement of the *Sierra* was reliable, but he soon discovered that it was indeed, and this made his task less difficult.

Q. What does *it* refer to in line 2?

What is the answer?

12 Inferences and implications

Example 1

A university course for a first degree normally lasts three years.

> Q. What does the writer imply by using 'normally'?
> A. He implies that some courses may be longer or shorter than three years.

> Q. What may we infer from the writer's use of 'normally' in this sentence?
> A. (We may infer that) sometimes a university course lasts for less or more than three years.

Notice that the writer **implies** *but the reader* **infers**.

Example 2

The number of deaths and serious injuries as a result of traffic accidents has increased steadily in the past twenty years. Unfortunately, there is no sign that this increase will be checked or that the number of accidents will begin to fall.

> Q. What may we infer about the writer's attitude to road safety from his use of 'unfortunately'?
> A. (We may infer that) he thinks that more action is needed to reduce the number of accidents.

> Q. What does the writer imply by using 'unfortunately' in this passage?
> A. (He implies that) something should be done to reduce the number of accidents.

Example 3

Although living standards continue to rise throughout the world, there are large areas where unfortunate peasants are forced to struggle hard merely to find food for their families. In too many cases, failure to obtain food has led to malnutrition and death.

> Q. 1 What may we infer about the writer's attitude by his use of 'unfortunate' in line 2?
> Q. 2 What does the writer imply by using 'too many' in line 3?

21 Practice passage 4

Read the following passage carefully, and then answer questions a) to j) which follow it.

If people are to spend their lives cultivating the land, year in and year out, in the same place, certain things are necessary. The land must be reasonably fertile, not too cold or too hot, not too unprotected from the wind, not too heavily overshadowed with forest trees, not too swampy so that the grain is
5 drowned, but, above all, not too dry. Water is the first necessity for growing

food. There must be some sort of tools to do the field-work, spades and hoes and mattocks and ploughs, and oxen or horses to draw any but the smallest kind of plough. It will often be more economical and more convenient if everybody does not make his own tools, but one man does the blacksmith
10 work for the whole community, not growing any food himself but being kept by those who do, in return for making their tools. There must be granaries and barns built to store the food for the winter, and some sort of guard or defence to keep the settlement from being attacked by wild beasts or possibly by neighbouring peoples who are short of food themselves. There
15 must be arrangements to see that the ploughing and sowing and reaping are done at the proper times; there must be people who know the weather and calendar and can tell when the god of the harvest likes the harvest to begin and how to prevent the god of the river from getting angry and drowning the crops; and if the community trades part of its spare food for iron or
20 stone or salt or anything else, there must be roads or tracks along which goods can travel; there must be a market at which they can be sold or exchanged, and probably some people in charge of the market to see that the weights and measures are true, that there is no cheating, and no quarrelling between those who come to market. On the other hand a real
25 agricultural community does not need large towns, or main drains, or stock exchanges, or a post office, or the other things which our industrial society needs. It does not even need schools, because you do not learn to grow food out of books, but mainly by actually growing it.

One thing further about agricultural life: it changes very little year by
30 year. The land produces much the same sort of crop, and the same things have to be done to make the crop grow. Plough-time, seed-time, harvest, and winter follow one another year in and year out, and everybody's work is much the same as it was last year and as it will be next year, so that agricultural societies are generally conservative, and slow to change their
35 ways or their minds.

Consequently people engaged in agriculture can generally keep whatever they have gained or earned unless, indeed, they are conquered or plundered by some stronger and more violent people from outside.

Questions

a) Give briefly the meaning of the following words and phrases:
   (i) *year in and year out* (line 1)
   (ii) *above all* (line 5)
   (iii) *but* (line 7)
   (iv) *kept by* (lines 10–11)

b) What action does the word *do* (line 11) refer to?

c) How could the god of the river drown the crops? (lines 18–19)

d) Write down the word from the following list which is closest in meaning to *true* as used in line 23:
   accurate
   collect
   honest
   sincere
   valid

e) (i) List ten things which the writer says are necessary for agricultural communities, including those who trade. Write them on separate lines, using not more than six words for each.

(ii) Now make a second list to show the purpose of the items in the first list, using not more than six words for each. Use the same numbers as in your first list.

f) From the evidence in the passage, write down the most suitable word from the following list to complete the sentence:
One learns to grow food by _____.
cultivation
planning
practice
study
theory

g) In lines 25 to 28 the author gives a list of things which are not needed by a real agricultural community.
(i) Which of these does the author say is particularly surprising?
(ii) How does he indicate that it is surprising?

h) List four pieces of evidence which the writer uses to show that agricultural societies are conservative. Write each piece of evidence on a separate line, using not more than six words for each.

i) What, according to the writer, might threaten the safety of agricultural societies?

j) In the second paragraph the author describes the characteristics of agricultural life. In a paragraph of about 100 words describe how you think town life differs from the picture of agricultural life which is given in the passage.

Note: This passage and the questions are part of a specimen paper issued by a GCE examining board. The marking scheme was:

a)	4 marks
b)–d)	1 mark each
e)	10 marks
f)	1 mark
g)	2 marks
h)	8 marks
i)	2 marks
j)	10 marks

In an examination, read through the whole passage and then glance at the marking scheme (if it is given) before you start to answer the questions. In this way, you can make sure that you answer the questions which have the most marks.

---

22 Aids to better comprehension

In this unit we will consider quite simple ways in which you can improve your ability to understand a passage and to answer questions about it. The unit includes comments and advice from examiners' reports.

1 Read regularly, e.g. at least five pages a day.

You cannot understand a passage if you do not understand the words and sentence patterns in it. If you read regularly for at least three months, your English will improve very considerably. You may not notice the improvement (because it is gradual) but you will make fewer mistakes and improve your vocabulary at the same time.

This is the best and most practical way of improving your standard of English. The more you use a language, the more efficient you will become in understanding it and in expressing yourself in it.

2 Beware of the opening sentence of a passage.

In some cases, it does not tell you what the whole passage is about. We do not always find a topic sentence at the start of a paragraph.

3 Don't worry if you don't know the meaning of some words.

a) You may be able to guess their meaning from the context.
b) There may be no questions about them.
c) The meaning of a sentence may not be greatly changed if a difficult word is misunderstood or is omitted completely.
d) Don't waste time stopping to think about a single difficult word. Read right through the passage to find out what it is about. Later on, you can see whether a difficult word is important or not.

4 Sometimes it is helpful to make notes about a passage or to make a quick drawing.

In passage 2A (page 47), we had to make a list of people in the Brimlows' kitchen. We could make a rough list and then check that we have not omitted somebody. In another case, it might be useful to make a quick drawing to show where different people were when something happened.

5 Take some coloured pencils to the examination room.

If you have to answer questions about the actions or characteristics of people, you can use different colours to underline words about people or events in the passage.

6 Read the whole of each question before you answer part of it.

Sometimes instructions about how to answer a question are given after the last part. You could make a mistake if you answered the first two parts without noticing any instructions at the end.

7 Mentally simplify or re-express difficult sentences in a passage until you can find out what they mean.

Example

He did not think it completely out of the question that their house would remain undamaged when the floods came; indeed, he decided that this was something he should not rule out.

= (roughly) He thought the floods might not damage the house.

8 If you have to answer in complete sentences, try to form each complete sentence in your mind before you start to write.

Then you can avoid using tenses or words which are difficult.

9 Don't waste time by copying out the question on your answer paper.

10 Obey any instructions.

Some students lose marks because they ignore instructions to use a single word, a short phrase or a complete sentence.

11 Don't give alternative answers unless you are asked to do so.

Sometimes students give alternative answers (often with different meanings) in the hope that one of the answers will be correct. The examiner marks the first answer only. He ignores any other answers.

12 When you have to give the meaning of an expression, explain all key words.

For example, you may have to explain the meaning of 'an invariable routine'. You can say 'a fixed method (= routine) which never changes (= invariable)'. (But do not include the brackets and words in them in the above example.)

a) It is not necessary to explain the words in the order given in the expression. We can explain 'routine' first and 'invariable' afterwards.
b) Explain *all* important words.

13 Use the right part of speech.

Check that it fits the context, i.e. the sentence in the passage. For example, the passage may include 'The man showed great audacity in carrying out his plan'. Then we can use 'boldness' for 'audacity' but we cannot use 'bold' or 'boldly'.

14 Use short answers but give all the necessary information.

The examiners write: 'Good candidates answer each comprehension question in one or two short, clear sentences. It is only the weak candidates who write long, muddled answers, containing many different guesses, and these lose marks for unnecessary length and for the grammatical mistakes they contain.'

15 Use your own words if possible.

In some cases, you may be allowed to quote words from the passage. In other cases, it is wise to express ideas in your own words.

16 Try to improve your knowledge of the meaning of common idioms.

For example, what does 'dead' mean in these sentences?

a) Yes, you're dead right about the cause of the fire.
b) Through the fog, we saw a fishing vessel dead ahead of us.

It means 'exactly'. It has another meaning in these sentences:

c) This road is a dead end. (= It leads nowhere.)
d) He has a dead-end job. (= It has no future for him.)

17 Understand the difference between the literal and figurative meanings of a word.

Please see Unit 13. Here are further examples:

Similes

a) The disease spread through the villages *like fire sweeping through dry undergrowth.*
b) Mrs Brimlow defended Luther *like a lioness protecting a cub.*

Words used

a) literally and b) figuratively (metaphorically here)

sea

a) There are many fish in the sea.
b) She was surrounded by a sea of troubles.
   The landslide created a sea of mud.

exploded

a) When the bomb exploded, it made a great hole at the side of the road.
b) When Magellan's men sailed round the world, they exploded the myth that the world was flat.

volcano

a) When the volcano erupted, a great cloud of poisonous gases swept down on the village below.
b) Someone had quarrelled over possession of an axe in the prison, someone else had joined in, and suddenly, without anyone knowing exactly why, the volcano of passion had erupted and a lava of blood flowed everywhere.

Practice passage 5

Read the following passage, which is an extract from a newsletter from a branch of the RSPCA (Royal Society for the Prevention of Cruelty to Animals). Then answer the questions which follow it.

This Society is concerned about the growing number of people who have come to us, in the past year, with sick and dying animals which they say they have recently purchased from pet-shops. Almost invariably their concern is not for the welfare of the animal, which is our major concern, but
5 to seek our help in enabling them to recover their purchase money. Our procedure has been to issue a veterinary certificate, based on the animal's condition at the time of examination, and to tell these people to write to the Director of the Agriculture and Fisheries Department (who are the pet-shop licensing authority) and to the Consumer Council. When we
10 approached the Consumer Council on this matter we found that they had, quite independently, become greatly concerned about the condition of pets being sold by the pet-shops.

On 20th November, a meeting was held at the Consumer Council office between representatives of this Society, the Consumer Council, the
15 Agriculture and Fisheries Department and two major pet-shop owners. As a result of this meeting, the pet-shop owners agreed, in future, to issue a certificate with each animal sold stating that at the time the animal was sold it was in good health and that if the animal became ill or died within a certain period – the period has not yet been agreed – from the date of the
20 sale, the pet-shop would refund the entire purchase price to the purchaser.

We have not yet received confirmation that pet-shops are in fact now issuing these certificates but we are hoping that they will do so in the very near future.

It is the view of this Society that if members of the public refrain from
25 buying animals from pet-shops who refuse to issue a 'Good Health Certificate' in respect of animals they intend to purchase, the pet-shops will have to comply with the request from ourselves and the Consumer Council. If they fail to do this, it will not be very long before they go out of business. The long-term effect will be that pet-shops will have to show more concern
30 for the animals in order to sell them.

We appeal to you, our members, to help us in our fight for better conditions for animals sold in shops. If you pass a pet-shop, please make a point of looking at the animals on display. If you see that any of them are sick, overcrowded, in cages too small to give them freedom of movement,
35 neglected or mistreated, please report the facts as early as you can to this Society and the Agriculture and Fisheries Department. Please follow up all verbal complaints with written statements.

Questions

a) Briefly give the meaning of the following words and expressions as they are used in the passage:
   (i) quite independently (line 11)
   (ii) refund the entire (price) (line 20)

(iii) confirmation (line 21)
(iv) neglected (line 35)

b) In line 1 of the passage, there is a reference to a growing number of people. What do these people want to get from the RSPCA?
c) Why is the Agriculture and Fisheries Department mentioned?
d) Which of the following words is most similar in meaning to *growing* in line 1?

troublesome   initial   surprising   expected   increasing

e) In five separate sentences, list **five** things which the Society has done as a result of complaints from the people mentioned in line 1.
f) In five short sentences, list **five** things which visitors to pet-shops might complain about to the Society.
g) 'The pet-shops will have to comply with the request...' (lines 26–27) What was this request?
h) What action did the owners of pet-shops take concerning this request?
i) What might cause some pet-shops to go out of business (line 28)
j) Read lines 13 to 15 again. In 80 to 100 words, summarise the problems which faced the owners of pet-shops at the meeting on 20th November, and what they agreed to do as a result.

24 Practice passage 6

Read this passage carefully and then answer the questions about it.

Beware of the man who says he is never frightened! If I were choosing a party to climb a difficult mountain, or in war-time for a patrol behind the enemy's lines, the last person I should include would be one who claims he is incapable of being afraid.
5   Personally I love doing dangerous things, but as I am very easily frightened, and dislike being frightened, I have always gone out of my way to do adventurous things in order to drive out fear and develop confidence in my ability to overcome my lack of courage. I am sure you can develop and increase your stock of courage by experiencing fear and learning to
10 overcome it.
Never shall I forget how petrified I was when confronted with the microphone for the first time. As the studio light went from red to green and I knew that thousands of people were listening to me (at any rate at the beginning of my talk!) I could feel my heart pounding so loudly in my throat
15 that it seemed quite impossible there would be room for any voice to come through! And yet it did! I had won that battle.
Similarly in the Liberator bomber over Malaya, when once again I was waiting for the red light to go green, how terrified I was; but the parachute really opened, and no one shot at me as I came down, and I really enjoyed

20 it (at any rate in retrospect), and once more fear had been routed.

    But, in the two examples I have given you, the real terror had been in
    anticipation. More often the testing time comes upon you without giving
    you freedom of choice or time for anticipation. And there is just nothing
    you can do about it.

25 I remember once when John Rymill, the Australian explorer, and I were
    sledging down the coast of East Greenland in winter; the Arctic sea was
    frozen over to a depth of several feet. The rocky coast-line came down so
    steeply to the sea that it was impossible to sledge along the land, and to pass
    a headland we had to drive our dog sledges far out on the sea-ice where the

30 going was good. At dusk a storm suddenly came up and we had no
    alternative but to camp where we were. Above the noise of the storm we
    became aware of a rending noise, accompanied by a quivering beneath us,
    and we realised that the sea-ice was breaking up. Soon a crack appeared ·
    right across the floor of the tent and we could hear the seawater gurgling

35 between the edges of the two floes. At last the wind died down, and at
    dawn we discovered that we were still attached to land, though the open
    sea was now only a short distance from our tent. The worst of that
    experience was that we just could not do anything about it. We just had to
    wait and wait, getting more and more frightened. All we could do was to try

40 to divert our thoughts to something else.

    Defying fear on a mountain or at sea may be bad enough, but you do at
    least know the limits of what you are up against, though the weather can
    add an incalculable hazard. In warfare you have not only the human
    element of your enemy to contend with, but such demoralising things as

45 bursting shells, dive-bombing, tanks, and all the nerve-racking noise of
    modern battle. However, in an air-raid I feel curiously detached, and find I
    can almost enjoy it as a spectator; and in the normal course of infantry
    warfare one is sustained by one's training and regimental tradition and
    upheld by the presence of one's companions.

Questions

a) In your own words say what the author thinks of a man who says he is
    never afraid. Use one sentence only.

b) Quote an expression of six words from the passage which explains why
    the author often did dangerous things.

c) What was the author doing with a microphone (in line 12)?

d) In line 16, the author wrote 'I had won that battle'. Who was the enemy?

e) Which words does the author use to link the fourth paragraph with the
    preceding one? Write **only** the linking words.

f) 'The real terror had been in anticipation.' (lines 21–22) Explain in your
    own words what the author means.

g) Why did the author go across sea-ice?

h) According to the author, what purpose did his training (line 48) serve?

i) Briefly explain the meaning of the following as they are used in the
    passage:
    (i) stock (line 9)
    (ii) in retrospect (line 20)
    (iii) hazard (line 43)
    (iv) the human element (lines 43–44)
    (v) curiously (line 46)

j) Make a list of **six** examples from the passage of situations in which fear

was or may be experienced. Write each example on a separate line.
Complete sentences are not required.

k)   In this passage, the author mentions types of fear in military or
adventurous situations. In about 100 words, describe at least **three**
situations in which you are sometimes afraid.

25 Practice passage 7

Read this passage carefully and then answer the questions about it.

In some parts of the world malnutrition is due rather to unbalanced diets
and badly prepared food than to actual shortages. Because the value of
proteins is not understood by some peoples their diet is often grossly
unbalanced. As a result, they suffer from deficiency diseases. This reduces
5 their ability to work efficiently. The whole thing is a vicious circle: because
the people are underfed or ill-fed, they have no reserves of physical strength;
so they are more easily weakened by disease and lack energy; thus they
cannot work efficiently and agricultural productivity suffers; inadequate
production completes the circle, for the people must then go hungry.
10   Breaking the circle is no easy task but it must be done, for it is in those
parts of the world, e.g. in Africa, South-West Asia, Monsoon Asia and Latin
America, where people are underfed, that increased food production is
failing to keep up with the annual increase in population. Unless something
can be done to change these conditions, famine and disaster are likely to be
15 the ultimate result.
      Although millions of people in different parts of the world are crying out
for food, we frequently read of huge surpluses elsewhere, perhaps of grain in
North America or of fish in England. The question appears: why cannot
these surpluses be used to feed the hungry? They could, but often there are
20 certain difficulties in the way. Although a particular country might be
generous and give some of its surplus away – as the United States has often
done – a country, like an individual, must earn its keep, and it does this by
selling goods. Poor countries often cannot afford to buy food, even if they
are in desperate need of it.
25   In addition, world surpluses are usually of cereals, e.g. wheat and maize,
but it is not grain that is needed, but rather foodstuffs such as milk, meat
and fish, which are rich in protein. The problem is also further aggravated
by the fact that grains such as wheat and maize are not those to which the
underfed are accustomed, and food habits are not easy to change, even
30 when people are hungry.
      Let us conclude this brief account of the problem of population and food
supplies by saying that the question of feeding coming generations
satisfactorily is not an impossible one, even though it may present many
difficulties. If, for example, all the world's farmers were able to raise their

35 standards to those reached in parts of Holland or Denmark, the present
world area used for agricultural purposes could support many times its
present population. Progress is now being made on many fronts and great
efforts are being made by many peoples but a quickening in the rate of
progress and even greater efforts are urgently needed.

Questions

a) What does the author mean when he says that some people have a diet
   which is *grossly unbalanced* (lines 3–4)?
b) What causes people to have an unbalanced diet, according to the passage?
c) In line 5, in what way is it apt to call the circle *vicious*?
d) Briefly describe six stages in the vicious circle. Put each stage on a
   separate line and do not use more than three words to describe each
   stage. Complete sentences are not needed.
e) In a single sentence of your own, explain why, according to the author,
   there may be *famine* (line 14).
f) In three separate sentences, give three reasons why surpluses of food
   cannot always be sent where they are most needed.
g) Why is Denmark mentioned in this passage?
h) What evidence is there in the passage to support the writer's use of
   urgently in the last line? Give **two** possible reasons, each in a complete
   sentence.
i) Give words or expressions which we can use in the passage to replace the
   following words without greatly changing the meaning of the passage.
   (i) due to (line 1)   (ii) grossly (line 3)   (iii) ultimate (line 15)
   (iv) aggravated (line 27)   (v) coming generations (line 32)

j) In line 16, the expression *crying out* is used. Which of the following
   expressions is nearest in meaning to it?

   expressing sorrow about   begging earnestly   dying through lack of
   shedding tears   suffering badly

k) In 60 to 100 words, summarise what the author says in the passage about
   the causes and effects of malnutrition in some parts of the world. Do not
   add information about other points.

26 Practice passage 8

Read this passage carefully and then answer the questions about it.

On 29th August 1973 the midget submarine *Pisces III* (the name is Latin for
'fish' and is pronounced 'pie-sees') was lying on the bottom of the Atlantic
Ocean, about 100 miles from Ireland. The two men in it were just finishing
a six-hour work shift, for the submarine's job was to help in laying trans-
5 Atlantic telephone cables. On the surface above them was the mother ship,
Voyager, a specialised cable-laying ship.
   Their work done, the men were looking forward to breakfast and some
sleep. They requested permission to rise, and this was granted, so the *Pisces*

III slowly surfaced. But just as it was nearly back on board the *Voyager*,
10 something went wrong. A cable slipped and the small submarine fell back
into the water. As it did so, part of the submarine – not, fortunately, the
main working area where the two men were – flooded, and *Pisces III* went
into an uncontrollable dive towards the sea-bed, finally coming to rest nose-
down at a depth of 500 metres.
15   The men were uninjured and had enough air for three days. They could
still communicate with *Voyager* by radio. The captain of the *Voyager*
immediately reported the accident to his head office, and an international
rescue attempt began. A submarine had never before been recovered from
such a depth. There were few submersible vessels in the world which could
20 operate at that depth, and these could work only with the help of
specialised surface ships. Meanwhile, the men's life-support system would
run out after three days. The experts were privately very pessimistic.
    Simultaneously, several things were arranged. *Pisces II*, a sister-ship to the
unlucky submarine, would be flown out from England to Cork, in Ireland,
25 which was the nearest place to the accident having both an airport and port
facilities. *Pisces V*, another sister-ship just built, would be flown over from
Canada. Royal Navy ships would go to where the *Voyager* was, so that they
could stay in contact with the men on the sea-bed while *Voyager* sailed to
Cork to collect the two submarines. In addition, an American submarine
30 known as CURV (for Controlled Underwater Reconnaissance Vessel) would
also be flown to Cork, and a Canadian cable-laying ship would arrive there
to collect it and its team of operators.
    At first all went well, but because of the distances involved it was late on
Thursday before *Voyager* returned with its cargo to the scene of the
35 accident. The two submariners were cold and hungry but were otherwise
well after a day and a half below the water. Soon they were relieved to hear
on the radio that *Pisces II* had been sent down to look for them. After
several hours of searching, it failed to pin-point their location. Then it
developed a small leak, which forced it to return to the mother-ship for
40 repairs.
    Next it was the turn of *Pisces V*, with its Canadian crew. It too made the
long descent, and began to search through the thick black water. Eventually
it found *Pisces III*, and moved in to attempt to attach a line. But here too
there were problems. *Pisces III* had come to rest on the bottom of the sea at
45 a sharp angle, so it proved impossible to attach the normal hook and line.
All that *Pisces V* could do was attach a thin line, not strong enough to lift
the trapped vessel. *Pisces II* was being repaired and CURV was not yet
ready, so *Pisces V* stayed down until, after 19 hours in the sea, its batteries
were exhausted and it had to be taken to the surface. *Pisces III* had then
50 been under the water for 51 hours, with only 24 hours remaining before the
life-support system would fail.
    At 4 a.m. on Saturday, 1st September, *Pisces II*, its leak repaired, and
armed with a specially-made locking mechanism, dived again. This time, in
little over an hour, success came. The mechanism worked, and a strong line
55 was attached to *Pisces III*. But would this be enough? If the line should slip
off when the attempt to lift the submarine was made, the rescuers might
lose contact with *Pisces III* again. It was therefore decided to put CURV into
operation. There was just enough time to give it one chance to fix a second
line.

60   Here the technique was different, for CURV was unmanned. Its operators stayed on a ship above water, directing it by remote control, seeing its movements only through the eyes of its television cameras. But again luck was with them, and at 10.35 a.m. CURV succeeded in attaching a second strong line to *Pisces III*.

65   With only a few hours of oxygen remaining, the two men were finally on their way up. The lift was rough, and they were knocked around, but the lines held firm, and when the vessel was within 50 feet of the surface frogmen were able to reach it and fasten several more lines, just in case. Eventually, at 1.17 p.m. on Saturday afternoon, *Pisces III* surfaced again, and

70 the men were immediately helped out and on to the *Voyager*, exhausted and starving, but otherwise in good condition. Thanks to an efficient international rescue effort, the deepest ever submarine recovery had been safely completed.

Questions

a)   What were *Pisces III* and *Voyager* trying to do when the accident happened?

b)   What was the most important part of the life-support system in *Pisces III*?

c)   Give **three** reasons why the men trapped in *Pisces III* were in danger. Put each reason in a separate sentence.

d)   In line 22 we are told that the experts were privately very pessimistic. Why?

e)   Briefly explain why *Pisces II* made two voyages to the sea-bed.

f)   What was the major difference in the way *Pisces II* and CURV operated?

g)   Why were frogmen not used in this rescue?

h)   Briefly explain the meaning of these words as they are used in the passage:
  (i)   midget (line 1)
  (ii)   communicate (line 16)
  (iii)   relieved (line 36)
  (iv)   attach (line 45)
  (v)   little (54)

i)   In 80 to 120 words, summarise the way in which the *Pisces III* was rescued.

---

27   Practice passages 9 and 10

Read the following extract from Cry Freedom; *then answer all the questions.*

Passage 9

This is part of a story about a five-year-old coloured boy growing up in South Africa in the 1920s. The children in the story lived in special sections (locations) in the towns, set apart from whites, and were expected to address whites as superiors ('baas'). 'The Veld' refers to open land.

Wednesday was crackling day. On that day the children of the location made the long trek to Elsberg siding for the squares of pig's rind that passed for our daily meat.

I finished my breakfast and washed up. Aunt Liza was at her washtub in the yard. A misty, sickly sun was just showing. And on the open veld the frost lay thick and white on the grass.

'Ready?' Aunt Liza called.

I went out to her. She shook the soapsuds off her swollen hands and wiped them on her apron. She lifted the apron and put her hand through the slits of the many thin cotton dresses she wore. The dress nearest the skin was the one with the pocket. From this she pulled a sixpenny piece. She tied it in a knot in the corner of a bit of coloured cloth.

'Take care of that ... Take the smaller piece of bread in the bin but don't eat it till you start back. You can have a small piece of crackling with it. Only a small piece, understand?'

My friend Andries came trotting out of the yard. His mother's voice followed; desperate and plaintive:

'I'll skin you if you lose the money!'

I glimpsed the dark, skinny woman at her washtub as we trotted across the veld. Behind, and in front of us, other children trotted in twos and threes.

There was a sharp bite to the morning air I sucked in; it stung my nose so that tears came to my eyes; it went down my throat like an icy draught; my nose ran. I tried breathing through my mouth but this was worse. The cold went through my shirt and shorts; my skin went pimply and chilled; my fingers went numb and began to ache; my feet felt like frozen lumps that did not belong to me, yet jarred and hurt each time I put them down. I began to feel sick and desperate.

We went faster. We passed two children, sobbing and moaning as they ran. We were all in the same desperate situation. We were creatures haunted and hounded by the cold. It was a cruel enemy who gave no quarter. And our means of fighting it were pitifully inadequate. In all the mornings and evenings of the winter months, young and old, big and small, were helpless victims of the bitter cold.

For us, the children, the cold, especially the morning cold, assumed an awful and malevolent personality. We talked of 'It'. 'It' was a half-human monster with evil thoughts, evil intentions, bent on destroying us. 'It' was happiest when we were most miserable.

Andries had told me how 'It' had, last winter, caught and killed a boy.

Hunger was an enemy too, but one with whom we could come to terms, who had many virtues and values. Hunger gave our crackling a feast-like quality. We could, when it was not with us, think and talk kindly about it. Its memory could even give moments of laughter. But the cold of winter was with us all the time. 'It' never really eased up. There were only more bearable degrees of 'It' at high noon and on mild days. 'It' was the real enemy. And on this Wednesday morning, as we ran across the veld, winter was more bitterly, bitingly, freezingly, real than ever.

Eventually we reached the pigfarm, and turned to the distant shed where the queue had already formed.

The line moved slowly. The young white man who served us did it in leisurely fashion, with long pauses for a smoke. Occasionally he turned his back.

At last, after what seemed hours, my turn came. Andries was behind me. I took the sixpenny piece from the square of cloth and offered it to the man.

'Well?' he asked.

55   'Sixpence crackling, please.'

Andries nudged me in the back. The man's stare suddenly became cold and hard. Andries whispered in my ear.

'Well?' the man repeated coldly.

'Please baas,' I said.

60   'What d'you want?'

'Sixpence crackling, please.'

'What?'

Andries dug me in the ribs.

'Sixpence crackling, please baas.'

65   'What?'

'Sixpence crackling, please baas.'

'You new here?'

'Yes, baas.' I looked at his feet while he stared at me. At last he took the sixpenny piece from me. I held my bag open while he filled it with crackling

70   from a huge pile on a canvas sheet on the ground. Turning away, I stole a fleeting glance at his face. His eyes met mine, and there was amused, challenging mockery in them. I waited for Andries at the back of the queue, out of reach of the white man's mocking eyes.

Adapted from *Cry Freedom* by Peter Abrahams

Questions

Please note that questions 1–6 were not included in the Cambridge paper. We are not permitted to reproduce the multiple-choice questions, so original questions (asking about the same point) have been given.

1   What evidence is there in the passage that the families at this place did not each much meat?
2   What did Aunt Liza tell the writer to do about bread before he set off on his journey?
3   Explain why the writer felt both *sick* and *desperate* (in line 27).
4   What do you understand by *malevolent* in line 35?
5   The writer refers to hunger and the cold as enemies. Which one was the greater enemy and why?
6   Why do you suppose that the writer waited for Andries at the back of the queue instead of near the front of it?
7   When the author mentioned Aunt Liza's hands he says they were 'swollen' (line 8). Why do you think he included this detail?
8   In lines 35–36 the author describes cold as a 'half-human monster'.
   a)   Why does he do this?
   b)   In what ways is the cold like a monster? Be careful to use your own words.

9   Look at the conversation between the man and the boy (lines 54–68). Explain why the man spoke like that to the boy and did not serve him immediately.
10   The author is telling the story of something he remembers when he was a little boy. What reasons may he have had for telling it, and why did he include the events you have been reading about?

This question consists of two parts and is taken from a University of London GCE examination paper. In the original paper, the questions were given separately from the two passages. In this book, the questions follow the passages as a matter of convenience for readers. Spend 40 minutes on the questions in section A. Spend about an hour on the question in section B.

Section A

Answer *all* parts of this question, (a)–(k). **Take care to answer starred (*) questions in your own words.**

One: The War of the Worlds

On an October evening in 1938, an American radio network broadcast a dramatic programme which told of the invasion of the earth by creatures from the planet Mars. The realism and the newslike technique of the production and the acting ability of Orson Welles caused a national panic.

5　The story begins with the discovery of an astronomical phenomenon falling to earth. It continues as follows:

Then came the night of the first falling star. It was seen early in the morning, rushing eastward, a line of flame high in the atmosphere. Hundreds must have seen it, the strangest of all things that ever came to
10　earth from outer space. Some of those who saw its flight say it travelled with a hissing sound.

Early the next morning it was found, soon after dawn, by someone who was convinced he had seen a meteorite. An enormous hole had been made by the impact of the projectile, and sand and gravel had been flung violently
15　in every direction. The heather was on fire eastward and a thin blue smoke masked the sunrise.

The Thing itself lay almost buried in sand, but what was visible was a huge cylinder, about 30 yards in diameter, rather rounded like a meteorite. The early morning was wonderfully still and the sun was already warm. The
20　lone observer did not remember hearing any birds that morning; there was certainly no breeze stirring and the only sounds were of faint movements from within the cylinder, which he assumed came from the unequal cooling of its surface, still hot from its flight through the air.

From *The War of the Worlds* by H.G. Wells

Questions

a)　What three features of the radio productions caused such a panic? [3 marks]

b)　The object from Mars is referred to several times. Give five different names or descriptions from the passage. [5 marks]

c)*　**In your own words**, describe the scene when the object was first found. [4 marks]

d)　What made the observer decide it was not a meteorite? [2 marks]

e)*　Give another word or phrase (maximum 5 words) for the following, as used in the passage:
masked (line 16)
lone (line 20) [2 marks]

Two: Marvels and Mysteries

In July 1978 a middle-aged couple in Manchester saw a brilliant red cog-wheel float across the sky. They thought they had seen a UFO (Unidentified Flying Object). Not knowing anything about the subject, they wrote to an astronomer whose programmes they had watched on television.

5 Perhaps they did not express themselves fully and he did not question them in depth. In any event, he advised them that what they had seen was probably a meteor, albeit a spectacular one. The couple thought no more of the matter until, six months later, they happened to watch a programme in which a well-known UFO investigator appeared.

10 They contacted her and related their story. Whatever it was they had seen, it was now clear that it was not a meteor. The object had been too large, and had been seen in daylight for several minutes. (Meteorites usually remain visible for only a few seconds.) What they had experienced, according to the UFO investigator, was an impressive close encounter of the

15 first kind: and it was only by chance that their valuable eyewitness report was not lost forever.

This case illustrates the importance of what can happen after someone has sighted a true UFO. But, as this case also shows, it is not always easy to find out who is the right person to contact. So if you have seen something

20 strange in the sky, what should you do?

If you believe that what you have seen might be a true UFO, first of all it is important to try to find corroborative witnesses. It is not, however, advisable to knock on people's front doors – some may not take too kindly to your intrusion. This does not mean that you should not try to call the

25 attention of those close by. Their presence may add weight to your sighting, or they may be able to provide some other explanation of the phenomenon you have seen. It could, after all, simply be an identified flying object (or IFO).

Another important step is to make notes about the environment and the

30 area in which the sighting is made. Factors such as the barking of dogs or the sudden silence of birds may be significant. Of course, if you have a camera within reach, use it. It is surprising how many people who are perfectly equipped to take photographs are so overwhelmed by what they have seen that they fail to do so. If it is dark, and there is a controlled

35 shutter speed on your camera, set it for a reasonably long exposure – probably about one second. This offers a much better chance of recording what may be a relatively dim phenomenon, even if it appears to the eye to be reasonably bright.

If you are in a car, switch on the ignition and, if you have one, the radio.

40 There are enough stories to support the belief that some UFO phenomena can cause interference with electrical systems; UFO encounters rarely last for long, and there is unlikely to be the opportunity to telephone anyone while the object is still in view. Time is better spent taking in as much detail as possible. The importance of being able to recall in detail what you have

45 seen is paramount.

After the UFO has disappeared, do not discuss details of what you have seen with anyone else who might be around. Simply exchange telephone numbers and addresses, just as you would if you were involved in a road accident. Agree with other witnesses on who is to report the sighting and to whom. Finally, advise all the witnesses that, at the first possible opportunity, they should draw the object you have all seen, and write out a statement describing the sighting. Each witness should do this independently, and not talk about it to anyone else until they have done so. It is surprising how easy it is to be unwittingly influenced by what others say.

To whom should you report your UFO sighting? There are several possibilities, and you should think carefully before acting. The most obvious choice is the police. They will probably regard it as their duty to check your story; but in most countries, with the exception of France and the USA, where certain procedures exist, there will be little they can actually do.

As far as newspapers, radio and television are concerned, try to resist the temptation to approach them. The media will probably be interested only if they think they can use your story, and that may depend on whether it is quiet or busy in the newsroom, rather than the credibility or intrinsic interest of your sighting.

The most sensible step to take if you have seen what you believe to be a UFO is to contact a UFO investigator as soon as possible. They are trained to help you and to record accurately the necessary information for scientific appraisal. There are many kinds of UFO investigators and groups. Some are motivated by an almost religious belief in UFOs and will be biased. Others border on the eccentric, attracting cranks and frauds. Most, however, are serious-minded and will be concerned with establishing the authenticity of your sighting. Each report is treated confidentially and almost all UFO groups use a standard report form. You will probably be asked to fill in one of these forms. You might also be asked if it is possible for a UFO investigator to come and see you at a time and place of your choosing.

Naturally, if you happened to come face to face with what you may think is a UFO, it is not always easy to remember exactly what to do. The oddness of the occasion may well lead you to panic. Yet it is always worth trying to remain calm and to remember the procedures outlined in this article. The more well-authenticated, well-documented cases there are, the more will eventually be discovered about these elusive intruders.

From *Marvels and Mysteries, UFOs*

Questions

f) Give two reasons given as proof that the object seen in 1978 was not a meteor. [2 marks]

g) Why should you look for witnesses after sighting a UFO? [2 marks]

h) Why should you not discuss the event in detail with witnesses? [2 marks]

i) Why are you advised not to contact the media? [2 marks]

j)* Give another word or phrase (maximum 5 words) for the following, as used in the passage:
corroborative (line 22)
overwhelmed (line 30)
eccentric (line 70)
elusive (line 81) [4 marks]

Refer to both passages.

k) Give two features that occur in both passages. One feature should be a possible explanation for UFOs, the other a natural event. [2 marks]

Section B [35 marks]

You are advised to spend about 1 hour on this section.

Use ideas from Passage Two only.
You have been asked to take part in a radio programme about strange phenomena from the skies.
   Write the text of your talk, which should:

- give **clear instructions to follow** if suspected UFOs are seen
- give **some advice about what actions to avoid** after a sighting.

Use your own words as far as possible, and try to make the talk both interesting and informative. Marks will be given for both style and content.

28 Practice passage 11

This passage is in two parts and is taken from a University of London GCE examination paper. For the convenience of readers, the questions are given directly after the passage to which they refer.

Section A (about 40minutes)

1   RMS Titanic Incorporated was granted salvage-in-possession rights to the wreck of the great liner by a United States court in 1994. Those rights can only be maintained so long as the company keeps a presence at the site and continues to undertake salvage work. Should the company abandon the site, it would be a free-for-all.

5   When the wreck of the ship was discovered in 1985, there were very few scientific research bodies capable of reaching her; the passage of a dozen years has meant that the floor of the Atlantic is no longer so far away. The outrage and recriminations – like the public interest in the collapsing wreck – can surely only increase.

10   It was announced last year that RMS Titanic Incorporated would be mounting an exhibition at Greenwich of items recovered from the site of the most famous shipwreck in the world. The company has recovered hundreds of items scattered two and a half miles under the sea. One hundred and twenty of these items – crockery, suitcases, hairbrushes, letters,

15   clothing, all the detritus of 1,500 lost lives – were displayed for more than a year at Greenwich Museum in an exhibition, *The Wreck of the Titanic*, that was seen by more than 720,000 people.
      This venture is the company's latest scheme to raise money for further salvage efforts. Each dive costs more than $100,000. The company receives

20   no public funding. It has undertaken never to sell any of the personal objects recovered, but to keep them together as a single exhibit. It has sold hunks of *Titanic*'s coal at $25 a time. Bass Ale joined in by sponsoring a

hunt for the 12,000 bottles of ale that went down with the ship. The
company, now filming the current salvage efforts for a documentary, is also
25 providing an Internet site with live footage from the salvage vessel,
interviews with crews and scientists and information about the ship and
salvage operations. The site also provides a forum for an on-line argument
about the fate of the wreck.

The Titanic Historical Society of Massachusetts condemns the salvage
30 efforts outright, deploring the crass commercialism of the venture. Eva Hart,
one of the last survivors of the disaster, spoke out against the salvage: 'The
ship is its own memorial. Leave it there.' Many view the wreck as a tomb.
The arguments swirl around the *Titanic*'s hull – now, snapped in two,
disintegrating slowly on the ocean floor – like so much wreckage. Many
35 claim that valuable lessons about ships' construction and new historical
information are to be gleaned by exploring the wreck; in any case, the
public fascination remains undiminished. Maybe we care about the *Titanic*
because somehow, among its passengers – men, women and children from
all social classes, from more than 20 nations – we can always imagine
40 ourselves, and we wonder what we would have done on a dark night, on a
cold sea, when the last lifeboat was about to be lowered away.

Questions

a) What connection has RMS Titanic Incorporated with the wreck of the
ocean liner? [2 marks]

b) Explain **briefly in your own words** the meaning of 'the floor of the
Atlantic is no longer so far away'. (line 7) [2 marks]

c) What has the company agreed not to sell from the wreck? [1 mark]

d) What steps has the company taken to inform the public about the
salvage operations? [4 marks]

e) Explain **briefly in your own words** what views have been expressed,
opposing the company's activities. [3 marks]

f) What **two** advantages may come from the study of the wreck? [2 marks]

g) Give **one** reason suggested in the passage for the enduring public interest
in the wreck. [1 mark]

---

2   Pausing only to whistle in apologetic salute to a French trawler which came
perilously close to being swamped by her bow-wave, the *Titanic* turned away
from land in the early afternoon of 11th April 1912, passing over the
horizon in an hour.

5   Ice-warnings for the north-western Atlantic notwithstanding, the weather
in the east and central regions of the ocean was delightful – mid-Spring at
its best.

From noon on Thursday the 11th to noon on Friday, the ship covered
464 sea miles and continued to accelerate. Meanwhile, the ice was closing
10 in.

At 11.30 p.m. on Sunday 14th the two lookouts on duty reported that a
slight but definite haze had appeared ahead of the ship. Ten minutes later,
one reached across and sounded the death-knell of the ship: three strokes
on the bell, meaning an object was straight ahead of the ship. Later, he said
15 he had seen 'a black mass ... more than fifty-five feet'. There was a faint
haze for ten minutes, then a collision. One passenger described it 'as though
somebody had drawn a giant finger along the side of the ship', another 'it
was just as though we went over a thousand marbles'. The ship did not hit

head-on; she struck the iceberg a glancing blow. An underwater ridge
20 scraped along the side of the hull, causing straggling damage some 300 feet
long but only a few inches wide. Ship and ice were in contact for a
maximum of ten seconds only.

The absence of a definitive list of all passengers and crew, when over
2,200 people were aboard the *Titanic*, is unfortunate but hardly surprising;
25 passenger lists remain just as unreliable in the computer age. There is no
need to labour the discrepancies between the people aboard and the number
of lifeboats. The saddest shortfall is the difference between the 705 saved
and the official capacity of the boats – 1,178. Apparently it was believed
among the officers that the boats were not strong enough to be lowered over
30 the side full – this was a tragic mistake.

The events that followed have come down to us as a confusing
kaleidoscope, a slow-motion bedlam; the enormous ship, lit up from stem to
stern, against a background of loudly hissing steam, rockets bursting
overhead, bandsmen playing familiar tunes and mysterious lights passing in
35 the distance. All witnesses agreed, even though their descriptions of it
varied wildly, that the ship emitted a terrifying and protracted death rattle.
There was a series of explosions or loud crashes, as boilers and other massive
items of equipment broke loose and smashed through the buckling steel
bulkheads. It is possible that the few boilers which had been kept going to
40 power the generators exploded on contact with cold water.

Many witnesses were clearly haunted by the noise. Those who survive
shipwreck often remember the extraordinary sound of a ship's final moments
more vividly than they recollect what it looked like afloat.

Adapted from *The Riddle of the Titanic* by R. Gardiner and D. Van der Vat

---

Questions

h) Why was the iceberg which struck the liner not clearly seen? [2 marks]

i) Explain **briefly in your own words** how the iceberg damaged the liner. [4 marks]

j) What, most probably, were the 'mysterious lights passing in the distance' (lines 34–35)? [1 mark]

k) Give **three** details of the 'confusing kaleidoscope' (lines 31–32) which has come down to us about the ship's last moment. [3 marks]

l) Give **in a single word or short phrase** the meaning of each of the following, as used in the passage:
glancing (line 19)
straggling (line 20)
definitive (line 23)
discrepancies (line 26)
buckling (line 38) [5 marks]

Section B (about I hour)

Imagine that a debate is being held between a director of RMS Titanic
Incorporated and a survivor. Using mainly material from the first passage, write
two speeches, the first justifying the salvaging of the ship and the second a brief
protest against it. Do not quote extensively or exceed a limit of 210 words.

Practice passage 12

The following passages and questions are taken from a University of London GCE O-level examination paper. All the questions were given before the three linked passages. In this book, the questions are given after each passage as a matter of convenience. The three passages and their questions were set in one examination paper.

Passage 1

We need more trees

Apart from obvious advantages such as the attractive flowers of some trees and the cooling shade that most provide, we all need trees for a much more fundamental reason if human life as we know it today is to continue on this earth.

5 Trees have a fundamental part to play in the preservation of our land and hence in our children's future. Secondly, trees play a vital part in preserving our present environment. Thirdly, trees help to clean the air we breathe and to replenish its oxygen supply. Let's look at these three aspects separately.

10 *1 Trees and the land*

In most parts of the world in primeval times large parts of the globe were covered with trees. As the human race increased in numbers these forests were regarded as major obstacles – to the development of agriculture and commerce and industry, and in the expansion of settlement. So we human 15 'pioneers' set about destroying the trees. Vast areas of tree cover and associated vegetation were wiped out and mostly burnt. No thought was given to the needs or wishes of future generations. We are now the unfortunate heirs to that process of indiscriminate tree destruction.

In many parts of the world trees are being lost for other reasons as well. A 20 large number are the victims of age, disease, the effects of dry land and irrigation-induced salinity, erosion, fire, grazing and cultivation. Relatively few are being replaced with young native trees.

We could regard a tree as a pump which every day removes about 400 litres of water thus playing a vital role in maintaining the water table at a 25 desirable depth along with its sub-soil salt. If you take away those guard pumps – the trees – then the water table rises and salinity is brought to the surface in quantities enough to destroy all but the most salt-resistant vegetation.

Thus dry land salting spreads and salinity increases in rivers and streams. 30 Of course excessive irrigation, over-use of fertilisers and inadequate drainage are prime contributors also; but all those lost 'tree pumps' would have reduced the problems considerably.

The Forests Commission of Victoria in Australia has studied water catchment areas and found that with 20% of its forest cleared the average 35 stream's salinity reading is about 40 mg per litre. But at 100% tree clearance the figure rockets to 500 mg per litre. This is severely destructive to dependent vegetation and very few plants can survive it.

The answer to this question is simple, straightforward, within the reach of each one of us: PLANT MORE TREES.

2 Trees in our environment

Trees in urban areas have a value far greater than their dollar unit. Trees alter our environment and the immediate vicinities of suburban housing.

We all know that the countryside, which has more trees, remains cooler throughout most of the day than the city, which has substantially fewer trees. This temperature difference is especially noticeable in the late afternoon unless there is a strong sea breeze. Studies in California, for instance, have revealed that while the centre of San Francisco was registering 21°C, a nearby forest reserve was as low as 12°. This doesn't mean that one tree will reduce temperature considerably – you need a group of them.

In a place like Western Australia group plantings of trees have a pronounced effect on human comfort.

Transportation and shade

Trees accomplish temperature reduction in part through the shade they cast and the large quantity of water they transpire. A large shade tree will transpire 400 litres of water a day; this consumes energy derived from the sun. Much of this solar radiation is trapped in the chlorophyll (the green part) of the leaf.

Controlling sound

Trees also help to control sound in cities. They don't actually absorb it; they merely break it up. Traffic-sound studies indicate that about 135 metres is needed to reduce highway noise to a comfortable level. This distance can be reduced to 100 metres by densely foliaged trees or high shrubs. But like the cooling effect you need more than one or two trees – you need a stand of them to do much good.

Of course there's the psychological effect of screening highways with shrubs and trees, which may be just as important as the actual breakup of sound.

3 Essential link in maintaining clean air

Trees also affect air purity. Small particles and gases, dust, fly ash, ozone, sulphur dioxide and many polluting nitrogen compounds are largely filtered out by plants. Particle matter is trapped in the very fine coating of hairs which most leaves possess though it may not always be recognised.

Gases are absorbed by leaves through their stomates (breathing pores) – sometimes to the detriment of the plant.

Trees also absorb carbon dioxide from the atmosphere, one of the major problems in the 'greenhouse' effect about which we hear so much these days. During sunlight hours, their leaves, along with all other green plants, shrubs and lawns included, take in carbon dioxide, combining it with water and converting them into sugars which they use for growth. During this process the leaves give off oxygen which we humans need in the air which we breathe.

Tests have shown in America that for every ton of timber in trees the air is enriched by one ton of oxygen, while one and a half tons of the harmful carbon dioxide is removed. Translated into practical terms this means that

85 ten trees would offset the pollution created by one motorcar travelling
50 km a day. If for no other reason, here is a case for planting many more
trees along our roadsides.

But of course all green plants help to counteract pollution and to
maintain the oxygen in the air which is vital to our lives. Therefore every
90 person can play a part in improving our environment by planting their
gardens. We should also encourage by all means possible the use of
reafforestation in areas under government control.

So, besides being effective air-conditioners, cooling your house, absorbing
dust, noise and other pollutants and giving you oxygen to breathe, trees can
95 beautify ugly areas in cities and add scale and restfulness to house and
garden.

Questions

a) How do trees control sound in cities? [1 mark]
b) List seven reasons for the loss of trees. [7 marks]
c) Salinity (or 'impregnating with salt') harms plant growth. What are said
to be the four main causes of too much salinity on the land? [4 marks]

Passage 2

How a campaign starting today hopes to save the snow-starved Alps and warn of the dangers of world pollution

Another snowless season of spoilt holidays, empty ski resorts and bankrupt
hotels is threatened in the Alps. But the greening of the pistes is only the
most immediately apparent of the environmental problems facing the
mountains which are Europe's backbone.

5   It is tempting to imagine that the Alps, standing thousands of feet above
the teeming cities and factories of the lowlands, are out of reach of the
pollution that afflicts them. But evidence is growing that the mountain
forests and pastures have already been gravely damaged by what is going on
below. And since four of Europe's main river systems – the Rhine, the
10 Rhône, the Po and the Danube – flow from the Alps, polluted mountains
mean a contamination of the well-springs of Europe's water supply.

If present trends continue, a third of the woodland in the Alps will be
dead by the year 2050, killed mainly by pollution from far-off traffic and
power stations. This will mean far more than a loss of picturesque scenery,
15 or even of earnings from forestry. The trees themselves influence the
climate, and they shelter roads and villages from avalanches. As they
disappear, ugly and expensive concrete shelters have to be built.

In spite of some disastrous skiing seasons, tourism in the mountains is
still growing fast. New motorways, hotels and ski-lifts are reaching up into
20 unspoilt areas. Deforestation and the tourist invasion are also helping
to undermine traditional agriculture. Every year, millions of tons of
freight traffic pass across the major Alpine passes, creating pollution
comparable to inner-city levels.

A campaign to save the Alps has been launched in Switzerland. A project
25 called Alp Action, to promote and sponsor initiatives, may help to stem the
tide. Working under the auspices of an environmental charity, the Bellerive
Foundation, it is designed to encourage business interests to take an active
part in the battle.

'If a company can get some mileage in terms of publicity from supporting one of our projects, that not only helps the project along, but also helps to make businesses and the general public more aware of the issues,' says a consultant working for the foundation. 'For some, there may be a conflict between their short-term commercial interests and their long-term interest in the health of the mountains. We want to see where their short-term and long-term interests merge.'

The campaign's promoters are anxious not to be seen as environmental utopians, hostile to commercial development or to recreation. They see the problems of the Alps as similar to those of the Mediterranean Sea. Both are areas of wilderness surrounded by large centres of population, traditionally thought of as inexhaustible but in reality highly vulnerable ecologically. Inevitably, trade-routes will flow across them, their natural resources will be harvested, and tourists will flock to enjoy their beauty. The challenge is to find ways of allowing all this to happen in a sustainable fashion.

Tourism is not the worst threat to the Alps. The biggest threats are to do with water. As towns and industries have needed increasing amounts of water, they have gone further and further up into the mountains, building reservoirs, and piping water down from them to the lowlands. Up to 95 per cent of the potential water resources in the Alps are already being exploited.

The land those pipelines run through dries out and becomes completely barren. Trees and other plants die, allowing the steep soil to be washed away by the rain, leaving bare rock behind.

The schemes being promoted by Alp Action are small-scale research projects, and efforts to encourage traditional agriculture and tourism which is environmentally harmless. Some are little more than photo-opportunities for companies wishing to polish their green image.

Alp Action rejects the suggestion that the campaign is a means of enabling exploiters to make a gesture of environmental concern while continuing their ravages. The idea is to be able to propose short-term projects which will bring visible results and show what can be done. One wants to get away from the usual syndrome of vast projects, vast ideals, a lot of conflict and interpretation and nothing much getting done.

There is a case for starting with the small and the specific. But the causes of many of the worst problems threatening the Alps are not local but continental in scope, and an effective remedy will need to be on the same scale.

Questions

d) A piste is a snow-covered track or path marked out for skiers. What is meant by 'greening' of the pistes (line 2)? [1 mark]

e) List **seven** similarities between the Alps and the Mediterranean mentioned in the passage. [7 marks]

f) In your own words explain the meaning in the passage of 'wishing to polish their green image' (line 55). [1 mark]

Passage 3

The Rift Valley

The forest itself evokes memories of Tarzan. It is green and cool. Among its trees, the magnificent figs and African mahoganies are taller than English oaks and beeches and far more luxuriant. The savannah just beyond the

forest grows many kinds of acacia. Near the lower part of the escarpment,
one tree dominates by size and stature, the baobab. Several African tribes
believe that the baobab is the home of night spirits. One legend declares
that God was angry with the tree and planted it upside down. Its trunk is
bulbous, and its branches do have an upsidedown look. Baobabs are
soft-tissued, fleshy, and frequently full of holes excavated by birds and small
mammals. They support and offer a temporary home to everything from
eagles to arboreal snakes. At night they are visited by bats that help to
pollinate their ghostly white blossoms.

Big-eyed bush babies creep around their branches in the dusk. It is small
wonder that the baobabs have found their way into legend as the homes of
ever-active night spirits.

The luxuriant forest supports a rich variety of animals. Lions lie idle along
branches, cooling in the breeze and escaping the attention of biting flies.
Baboons shake themselves from the trees like ripe fruits. Blue Syke's
monkeys swing and leap, using the creepers as trapezes. A heart-stopping
crash and tearing, close at hand, announces elephants; the dense ground
cover makes it impossible to see how many, even at 30 yards.

Where the springs cease, the dense forest ceases also. More open
savannah begins. It, too, is amazingly green, and its scattered stands of trees
are usually in leaf before the rains start. The run-off from the escarpment
makes its influence felt here, even if not in quite such an obvious way. The
soil, brought down over thousands of years from the highlands, is ready to
grow practically anything.

Among the trees of the savannah, *Acacia tortilis* is the one elephants like
to eat before all others. *Tortilis* is a beautiful flat-topped tree. Just before the
rainy season it blossoms with white flowers that baboons appreciate, and in
the dry season it is hung with yellow seed pods to which elephants are
addicted. At that season the elephants go on an *Acacia tortilis* binge, butting
the tree trunks with their four-ton bulk until the acacia sheds its pods in
golden rain. An elephant's trunk is a remarkably precise instrument. It can
pick up an acacia pod with a delicacy matching that of a sunbird selecting a
single blossom from which to sip nectar.

Though the elephants do much to destroy their acacia habitat, they also
perform a vital role in its regeneration. Their predilection for the tree's fruit
– a single elephant may contain in its intestines at any one time more than
10,000 *Acacia tortilis* seeds – provides *tortilis* with easily its most effective
method of propagation. Unlike other trees, such as the sycamore which
relies on the wind to disperse its seeds or the oak which enlists the burying
activities of squirrels, *Acacia tortilis* is regenerated through the guts and
droppings of elephants. There are two schools of thought about how the
cycle works, but both conclude that unless the seeds pass through the
elephants' alimentary canals, they are unlikely to germinate. One theory
places emphasis on the elephant's stomach. The acid in the digestive juices
eats away the seed's outer casing. By the time it reaches the ground encased
in a dropping, the seed is fully sensitized and ready to germinate. A more
recent theory argues that the key factor is the movement of the animal.
According to this, the seed is unlikely to germinate in the shadow of its
parent tree. What counts is not the eating away by acid but the dispersal of
the seed to places where there is adequate light.

The process of regeneration is continuous and lively, but by no means

55 sufficient on its own to keep pace with increasing demands from the
elephant population.

g) Baobabs are said to be thought the homes of 'ever-active night spirits' (line 15). Why, according to the passage, has this legend about the baobab grown up? [3 marks]

h) How are acacia seeds propagated with the help of elephants? In no more than 25 words state the two theories which seek to explain this. [4 marks]

Directed writing

Imagine that you are a journalist. You have been asked to write an article for a magazine about:

■ the benefit trees bring to the environment
■ the harm to the planet that might result from destroying them.

Use the material in Passage One particularly, but also anything relevant in the other two passages. Do not quote extensively. (You have no need to write more than 200 words.)

30 Practice passage 13

The following passages and questions are taken from a University of London GCE O-level examination paper. As a matter of convenience, the comprehension questions are given below each part here. In the examination paper, they were all given before the first part.

Passage 1

'Turtle and tourist at loggerheads' by James Sutherland

As Greece prepares for the annual migration of tourists to the island of Zakynthos, fresh attempts are being made to save the loggerhead turtles – also about to arrive on the island's sandy beaches. As many as 300,000 visitors are expected this year and it is feared they will eventually drive the
5 turtles away.

The problem lies in the development of the coastal areas around the beaches which serve as the turtles' breeding ground. Marine turtles, which come from as far away as Malta and Tunisia, have been nesting on the beach for thousands of years. Indeed, the first Greek coin, minted in Aegina
10 in the 6th century BC, bore the image of a turtle. Nowadays, Zakynthos has the greatest known concentration of nesting turtles anywhere in the Mediterranean, with 65% of the nests on two small, isolated beaches.

Over the past 10 years, the tourist industry has spawned a plethora of new hotels and tavernas – some built only yards from the shore – which
15 have caused such interference with the turtles' breeding habits that on the largest beach, Lagana, which stretches 3¼ miles along the southern bay of the island, there are now almost no turtles nesting any more. The increasing

number of speedboats taking holidaymakers water skiing and paragliding also poses a risk to the basking turtles, which congregate in the shallow waters in
20 the early evening before coming up to the nest.

Female turtles lay eggs only once every two or three years; however, about 800 come each year to make nests on the beaches. In the course of a summer, each turtle will make three nests containing an average of 100 soft eggs the size of a table-tennis ball. After 50 days, the small hatchlings –
25 about 2½ in. long – emerge from the sand and make their way to the sea during the cool of the night. Some go the wrong way, attracted away from the sea by the lights of the hotels and discotheques, making them vulnerable to such predators as stray dogs, or they simply dry up in the scorching heat of the Mediterranean sun. Although the plight of the turtles
30 was brought to the attention of conservationists in the early 1970s it was not until 1980 that a presidential decree outlawed the killing of adult turtles and the taking of their eggs. The first real sign of action came last year, when the government prohibited the construction of any building along almost eight miles of coastline up to 220 yards from the top of the beach.
35 The issue has split the islanders. Local people organised a conference on Mediterranean ecology last June, but many of those who own land in the protected areas oppose the law. Some of the most extreme hoteliers have threatened students carrying out research and have even urged killing turtles if the compensation they have been promised does not materialise.
40 Although conservationists welcome the new law, many feel that now the hotel companies know exactly where they are not allowed to build, they will simply build more and more furiously in the areas they are allowed to exploit.

Both the World Wildlife Fund and Greenpeace are concerned about the lack of protection and, especially, the ineffectual implementation of the
45 laws. A tourist boycott has been threatened if the new decree is not enforced.

Perhaps a more likely hope lies in the tourists themselves and their ability to influence the tour operators. As more holidaymakers take an active interest in the natural history of the places they visit, so it is hoped that
50 operators will begin to see the turtles as an exploitable tourist asset, providing some income for the local residents, while at the same time ensuring the species' continued survival.

<table>
<tr><td>Questions</td><td>

1 Write down a single word or phrase of not more than seven words which explains the meaning of the following as they are used in the passage:
a) annual migration (line 1)
b) materialise (line 39)
c) tourist asset (line 50) [3 marks]

2 Why do some newly-hatched turtles go in the wrong direction and not to the sea? [2 marks]
3 In what way may tourists themselves help to safeguard the turtle? [3 marks]

</td></tr>
<tr><td>Passage 2</td><td>

Wolves and domestic dogs share the same basic anatomy, physiology and patterns of behaviour; they are both generally long-bodied, large-eared, strong-jawed and possessed of highly developed senses of sight, hearing and smell. Most of the differences, such as colour patterns and the domestic

</td></tr>
</table>

5 dog's tendency to carry its tail erect or tightly curled, are a result of deliberate breeding by humans.

Barking once confused the picture, for it was widely believed that grey wolves did not bark. But detailed observations of wolves in the wild have revealed that, while their familiar eerie howling is associated with hunting
10 and territorial patrolling, they do bark when they are defending their dens. A dog barking noisily at the front gate is displaying the same kind of behaviour, and, as anyone who has tried practising grade-one violin or piano to the pet will have discovered, domestic dogs can howl too.

The main benefit that wolves derive from living in packs is that it enables
15 them to tackle large prey – and with this in mind it is worth speculating about the original man-wolf relationship. You might imagine the early hunter-gatherers – who, being omnivorous, opportunistic, far-travelling foragers and exploiters of large herds of hoofed animals had similar lifestyles to wolves – recognising the potential competitor.
20 In contemporary hunter-gatherer societies, women and children quite often tame wild animals, and studies of Bushmen have established that they hunt more effectively with trained dogs than without them. The development of the bow and arrow would have precipitated a rapid increase in wolf-dog-keeping, for their keen senses of smell and hearing would have
25 been perfectly suited to following up and locating injured prey. Then, with the switch to pastoralism and agriculture, dogs would have quickly gained value as herders of flocks and guards of crops. In fact, since domestication of the dog almost certainly pre-dated that switch, it can probably be said that dogs were the first creatures that man ever undertook to breed – i.e. to
30 manipulate genetically. And who knows – perhaps it was through dogs that man learnt that such domestication was possible. Moreover since agriculture is based to a large extent on domestication and Western civilisation is usually said to have begun with the discovery of agriculture, dogs could have a lot more to answer for than you might think.

Questions

4 Explain briefly the similarities and differences between dogs and wolves that are mentioned in the passage. Do not quote at length from the text.
   [6 marks]

5 Why does the writer suggest that it might be through dogs that man learnt that 'such domestication was possible'? (line 31) [4 marks]

Passage 3

Back to nature? Farewell to civilisation? It is one thing to dream of it and another to do it. I tried it. Tried to return to nature. Crushed my watch between two stones and let my hair and beard grow wild. Climbed the palms for food. Cut all the chains that bound me to the modern world. I tried to
5 enter the wilderness empty-handed and barefoot, as a man at one with nature.

My hair hung down to my shoulders and my beard was so long that my moustache could be seen from behind. I ran away from bureaucracy, technology, and the grip of twentieth-century civilisation. My only garment,
10 if any at all, was a flowery loin-cloth, and my home was of plaited yellow bamboo. I drew no salary, for I had no expenses; my world was free for birds and beasts and barefoot men to help themselves to what they needed, one day at a time.

I was still a high-school boy in Norway when I began to prepare myself for

15 this wild adventure. My home was a white-painted wooden house, covered with ivy, in a little coastal town at the mouth of the Oslo fjord – no smog, no pollution, no stress, nothing apparently to escape from. The largest buildings in the town were a wooden church and my father's brick-walled brewery. The air was pure and the river clean. It was safe to drink from any
20 running stream.

In the harbour the water was crystal clear, and little boys with long bamboo rods would sit in rows on the wooden pier watching shoals of fish wriggling up to nibble at their bait. There was nothing to see at the bottom but smooth boulders and gently waving seaweed. Further out lay large
25 whaling ships at anchor, with thousands of tons of blubber from marine giants which still roamed the southern seas in endless numbers. The little city of Larvik throve on its wealth of timber and its successful whaling fleet.

But there was something in the air. Modern whaling techniques had made the giant whales such an easy catch that there were real fortunes in
30 the whaling industry. This called for caution. The ocean was endless; it ran on with no beginning and no end, reaching beyond both poles. But man, too, was everywhere. Could he, with his technical progress, one day bring an end to nature's eternal supply of whales? No. That was unthinkable then. The world of whales was endless. The blue ocean was as infinite as the blue
35 sky, one merging into the other, and both being part of the boundless universe.

I feared the effect of technology in the world I knew; so I decided then to try living as nature intended.

Question	6 Why does the author:
	   a) crush his watch
	   b) mention the boys fishing
	   c) refer to the whaling industry? [6 marks]

Usage	7 (a) 'In the course of a summer' (Passage One, lines 22–23) If the writer had written 'the summer' instead of 'a summer', what would have been the difference in meaning?
	   b) What punctuation mark could be used instead of the semicolon after 'behaviour' in line 2 of Passage Two?
	   c) Write down the words that 'it' stands for in line 14 of Passage Two.
	   d) Why does the writer use 'i.e.' in the phrase 'i.e. to manipulate genetically'? (Passage Two, line 29)
	   e) 'marine giants which still roamed the southern seas in endless numbers' (Passage Three, lines 25–26). What is the significance of 'still' in the sentence?
	   f) 'Could he, with his technical progress ... whales?' (lines 32–33 of Passage Three). Re-write this question as a statement of fact, making as few changes as possible. Do not alter the meaning.
	   [6 marks]

Directed writing

8 Using material drawn only from the passages, write 150–200 words on **one** of the following:

Either: a) You are a journalist preparing an article on 'Nature'. Write two paragraphs for this article, one explaining how animals can benefit man and one showing how man can harm animals. (In this question 'animals' includes all living creatures.)

Or: b) What do the passages tell you about the differences between man's life in civilisation and in the natural environment?

31 Practice passage 14

Please note that in the original examination paper all the questions came at the end of the passage. As a matter of convenience, the questions are given here after the paragraph to which they refer.

A walk among giants

1 The story is told of a giant who waged war against the islands in the Pacific Ocean. Armed with a huge iron bar, he used it to lever up and gather together all the islands he came to. He then flung them back into deeper water, where they sank. Eventually he came to Easter Island. Although he
5 managed to break pieces off it to reduce its size, the remaining core was particularly hard rock which resisted all his efforts. His monstrous bar broke in his hands and he went away defeated.

Questions

1 a) What does 'resisted all his efforts' tell us about the giant's attempt to lever up Easter Island? (line 6)
  b) What fact does the fanciful story involving the giant tell you about the *nature* of Easter Island?
  [Total: 2 marks]

2 Easter Island is the most remote inhabited place in the entire world. No other is further away in any direction from the next nearest habitation.
10 Pitcairn Island lies some 2,200 kilometres to its west, and the South American coast some 3,700 kilometres to its east. All the rest is water. Not surprisingly, the island is difficult to get to. Indeed, until an airport was made in the 1960s, it was all but impossible, because the only connection with the rest of the world was a ship which visited the island once a year.
15 There is now something called a hotel on the island. Otherwise, many of the islanders, who number about 2,000, are keen to put up visitors: there is always a crowd at the airport to meet incoming planes and offer rooms and meals.

2 a) What fact does the fanciful story involving the giant tell you about the *situation* of Easter Island?
   b) Explain the meaning of the words in italics in:
      (i) '*inhabited* place' (line 8)
      (ii) '*all but* impossible' (line 13)
   c) 'There is now *something* called a hotel on the island'. What does the author want you to understand about the hotel in this sentence? (line 15)
   d) Explain fully why a hotel was unnecessary in the earlier years of the 20th century.
   e) Why has a hotel become necessary today?
   [Total: 7 marks]

3 What was I doing there? Like everyone else who comes, I had seen
20 photographs of the gigantic figures carved in stone, astounding and unique, which have made this island famous the world over. For years I had dreamed of a closer acquaintance with them, and now I had my chance.

3 'I had dreamed of a *closer* acquaintance'. What sort of *closer* acquaintance did the author want? [1 mark]

4 The first shock that I received had nothing to do with the stone figures I had come to see. It was the sight of the island itself that filled me with
25 astonishment. It was so barren: there were no trees, and it was apparent that scarcely any ground was good enough to support crops or even much grazing. Yet nobody looked hungry or unhappy. The second shock left me in a state of wonder. Many people have indeed seen photographs of the enormous stone figures, but the pictures show single statues or groups of
30 only three or four. What I now discovered was that there are hundreds: they are all over the island. The greatest concentration of the figures is near the eastern tip. Here lies the quarry from which the stone was taken. The imagination is stunned by the extraordinary number of the figures, in every stage of the making. There are fully formed statues, plainly ready to be
35 taken away to their resting-place, but there are also huge unshaped 'logs' of rock, waiting to be attacked with the stone adze, which was the only shaping tool the makers had; and there are figures in every stage between. To wander among them is a haunting experience. There is one in particular, lying on its back, staring for ever into the sky, that fascinated me. I felt that
40 if it had suddenly got up and walked, I would not have been surprised.

4 a) Explain *in your own words* why the author expected to see people on the island who were 'hungry'.
   b) What is unusual about the use of the word 'logs' (line 35) to describe the unshaped rock?
   c) What is meant by 'figures *in every stage between*'? (line 37)
   [Total: 4 marks]

5 Every visitor must be mystified as to how the figures were moved. They are massive, some more than ten metres tall, and weighing more than 80,000 kilos. Yet, it seems that the islanders, in the far-off days when these statues

were made, had not discovered the wheel. There was nothing with which to
45 make rope. They had no kind of lifting gear. Still they managed to move
these immense, silent creatures over rough and, indeed, unsmoothable
masses of volcanic rock until they got them to the stone bases prepared for
them. Often they had to be transported from the quarry over distances of up
to sixteen kilometres.

6 And here we must pause to consider these bases: some of them are almost
200 metres long and over seven metres high. The gigantic blocks which
make them up had been shaped with the same primitive stone tool as the
sculptors had used. With nothing that could help them in grinding the
stone smooth, the blocks were nevertheless fitted so perfectly that the blade
55 of a knife cannot be inserted between them.

7 Very well: the islanders had made the bases; they had got the statues to
them. How did they get a statue on to a base? And, above all, how did they
get it upright? Experts have deduced that the island's population could
never have been more than about 3,000, seemingly far too small for the
60 tasks involved. So did they do nothing all day, but carve and build and
haul? Was their entire existence the making and siting of statues?

8 Oh, if only the statues would get up and walk, provided that they talked as
well! For a start, we might learn who they were, these long-dead carvers of
stone. Did they come from an island to the west, or from South America to
65 the east? No one knows. And when? Surprisingly, the experts can only offer
us possibilities of dates extending from the seventh century to the sixteenth.
No one knows. But the further we get into the mystery, the deeper becomes
our ignorance. What were the statues? Were they gods to be worshipped?
Were they monuments to ancestors? Were they used in rituals, ceremonies,
70 offerings? No one knows. Beautiful and elaborately carved inscriptions
have been found on them all over the island and scholars have studied them
for many years without succeeding in deciphering the signs and thus learning
the language. What did these people want to say to us? No one knows.

Question	5 a) What first made the author wish that the statues would talk as well as walk?

5 a) What first made the author wish that the statues would talk as well
as walk?
   b) The author wants to know when the carvers of stone arrived on the
island. Why are the dates offered by the experts surprising?
   c) Beautiful and elaborately carved inscriptions have been found on the
statues. Say what scholars have tried to learn from the inscriptions
and give *two* reasons to show why their failure is unexpected.
   [Total: 5 marks]

9 But the innermost mystery is this: apparently on one single day, a sudden
75 destruction took place. In the quarry, tools were flung down; figures, from
the finished to the hardly started, were deliberately toppled over.
Throughout the island those that were in the process of being moved to
their resting-places were overthrown and abandoned at the point reached
on their journey. Many theories have been put forward to account for this:
80 invasion, apparition, mass hysteria, civil strife. The stone faces, with their
impenetrable expressions, lying just where they were when disaster struck,
still guard their secret. It seems that no amount of study will enable scholars
to extract it from them, just as the giant in the folk-tale failed to lever up
the island's core of rock.

6 a) (i) invasions
(ii) apparition
(iii) mass hysteria
(iv) civil strife

Each of the words or expressions above is a short way of giving a reason for the toppling over of the statues.

Without using any of the words themselves, write **four** separate and complete sentences to state what the four reasons might have been.

Number your sentences (i), (ii), (iii) and (iv) for each separate reason.

b) What are the two similarities between the story of the giant and the experience of modern scholars?

[Total: 6 marks]

10 Before disaster struck, the island was ringed right round the shores with those mighty stone bases, each bearing a line of statues. You could picture them as ranks of silent sentinels, placed there to defend the island from sea-borne foes. You would be wrong: every one of the figures – yes, every one – had its back to the sea.

Adapted from *Now Read On* by Bernard Levin

7 Choose **five** of the following words. For each of them give one word or short phrase (of not more than seven words) which has the same meaning as the word has in the passage.
(i) entire (line 8)
(ii) keen (line 16)
(iii) astounding (line 20)
(iv) apparent (line 25)
(v) scarcely (line 26)
(vi) concentration (line 31)
(vii) mystified (line 41)
(viii) deduced (line 58)
[Total: 5 marks]

8 The author encounters much that is mysterious on Easter Island. Write an account to show what is mysterious and amazing about the statues, the bases and their makers. Use only the material from line 30 to the end of the passage.

Your account, which must be in continuous writing (not note form), must be no longer than 160 words, including the 10 words given below. Begin your account as follows:

The author discovered that there are hundreds of statues which ...

[Total: 20 marks]

Practice passage 15

The Asphalt Pitch Lake of Trinidad

1   The Asphalt Pitch Lake of Trinidad suggests visions of bubbling tar and a
    Satanic atmosphere. In reality, it is not quite the witches' cauldron that one
    would expect. The earliest record of the Lake comes from Sir Walter
    Raleigh who, having left England in February 1595, reached Trinidad on
5   March 22nd where he visited a place called Parico. In his *History of the
    Discovery of Guiana* he wrote that he rowed to a place which the natives
    called 'Piche' where there was so much stone pitch that all the ships in the
    world could be filled with it. When his men tried it out for repairing their
    ships they found it most effective, since it did not melt in the hot sun like
10 Norwegian pitch, and was therefore very valuable to ships trading in the
    Caribbean.

2   Little more seems to be known of the Lake or its uses until the 19th
    century, when various attempts were made to show the British Government
    the vast industrial possibilities of Trinidad Lake Asphalt. In the 1960s over
15 120,000 tonnes a year were being shipped to the United Kingdom and
    Canada for their road expansion programmes.

3   Our first impression of the Lake was disappointing, for it appeared as just
    over forty hectares of emptiness; a drab, monotonous expanse lying under
    the tropical sun. Contrary to popular belief, the Lake showed no evidence of
20 violent disturbance, but despite the apparent stillness it is all the time in
    complex motion. A channel cut one metre deep closes completely in eight
    hours. Buildings as far as a kilometre away are slowly being sucked towards
    the centre, causing foundations to twist and gaping cracks to appear in
    concrete walls. The Lake is covered by a thin, wrinkled skin, which
25 frequently develops a soft spot where the surface oozes into a treacherous
    black treacle. Even where the skin is hard enough to take the weight of a
    truck, one must keep driving, since many a vehicle left stationary for several
    hours has sunk out of sight. Walking on the Lake gave me the impression of
    trying to cross an enormous rice pudding. At times, the smell of sulphur is
30 quite overpowering, and escaping methane, carbon dioxide and hydrogen
    sulphide gases produce enormous bubbles which burst with a loud sucking
    sound.

4   Another strange phenomenon is the sudden appearance of trees, which
    often come through the surface in a perfectly upright position and continue
35 to rise until the trunks stand many feet high. In 1928 one of these trees
    emerged to a height of fifteen feet before the movement stopped. For a
    number of days afterwards it remained perfectly still before beginning to tilt
    eastwards. The tilting continued until the trunk reached an angle of thirty
    degrees, when once more it was sucked to the grim depths below. Before it
40 sank again, however, wood samples from it were examined by experts who
    estimated that it had been buried for five thousand years. Skeletons are also
    found frequently, but this is not surprising, for many years ago the Lake was
    used as a natural burial ground.

5   Many people believe the asphalt to be inexhaustible, but this is not the case.
45 In the past ninety years the level of the Lake has fallen by about twelve
    metres, and measurements in the centre have shown a depth of only one

hundred metres. At the side of the Lake the level is considerably less. Since there is an ever-increasing demand, the supply is by no means unlimited. Already the amount of asphalt taken exceeds 18 million tonnes. There is
50 also some doubt as to whether the whole Lake consists of asphalt, or if the asphalt is merely a crust. Indeed, the origin, formation and resources of the Lake have baffled geologists since the 18th century.

6 There is something strangely frightening about this freak of nature, situated where the sun beats down without mercy, making the pitch even hotter, so
55 that it burns the foot through rubber soles. I was quite prepared to believe the legend which says the Pitch Lake was created by the Carib Gods to satisfy their anger with a tribe of Chayama Indians who were killing for food the sacred Humming Birds. Ancestral souls were supposed to live in the Humming Birds, and so the Gods turned the whole area into bubbling tar
60 under which everything sank forever.

7 Before leaving the sulphurous fumes for good, we met an employee of the Trinidad Lake Asphalt Company, who several years ago had the terrifying experience of almost losing his life in an unexpected soft spot. It happened late one night while he was taking a short cut across the Lake, along his
65 usual route to the village of Vessigny. Suddenly he was engulfed up to his knees, unable to move. It was several hours before someone heard his cries for help, and by this time the pitch, with its relentless clutch, had sucked him down as far as his shoulders. With the aid of mobile emergency lighting and eight strong men, he was slowly pulled from an untimely grave. Apart
70 from crushed ribs, severe pressure bruising and slight burns, he suffered no really dangerous injuries.

8 We were introduced to a calypso singer called Melodius Philly who had composed a calypso about the event. He needed very little coaxing to give us a special performance of 'The Man in the Lake', which originally won
75 second prize in the yearly village calypso contest. Afterwards he gave us the words on a duplicated sheet, but set down on paper they lacked much of the initial charm. The words on their own were nothing without the soft flexible Caribbean voice, the clipped musical pronunciation, the tapping foot following the rhythm and the flashing gold teeth of the singer.

Adapted from *Tropical Quest* by Derek Townsend

Questions

Answer the following questions.

Section A [10 marks – 1 mark for each question]

Answer the questions in this section very briefly, wherever possible in a word or phrase.

1 Give two words or one phrase which suggests something evil about the Asphalt Pitch Lake of Trinidad.
2 Which of the following is nearest in meaning to 'cauldron' (line 2): mixture, house, dance, cooking pot, curse?
3 Name one advantage of the pitch from Trinidad.
4 Which of the following is nearest in meaning to 'monotonous' (line 18): flat, dull, wide, hazy, steaming?
5 Write down a phrase from the third paragraph which gives a general warning to those who take a vehicle on the Lake.

6 Which of the following is the nearest in meaning to 'phenomenon' (line 33): adventure, story, observation, marvel, sight?
7 Name one unexpected object which might be found in the Lake.
8 What does the fourth paragraph tell us about the age of the Lake?
9 For how long have geologists been studying the Lake?
10 Give the title of the calypso written about the Lake.

Section B [15 marks]

11 Give **three** reasons why the Asphalt Pitch Lake was so important in the 20th century. [3]
12 Explain briefly the meaning of the underlined words:
   a) 'where the surface *oozes* into a treacherous black *treacle*' (lines 25–26) [2]
   b) 'it was *sucked* to the grim depths below' (line 39) [1]
   c) 'this *freak of nature* (line 53) [1]
13 What aspects of the Lake have been studied by geologists? [2]
14 How does legend explain the creation of the Lake? [3]
15 Why did the words of the calypso about the Lake lack charm when they were set down on paper? [3]

Section C [25 marks]

16 Using material from paragraphs 3 and 4 of the passage, describe the appearance and activities of the Lake. Start your answer with the words: 'The Lake appears ...' and use no more than 120 words. [15]
17 The Lake seems very frightening to the reader. Using no more than 90 words, write an account of why this is so. You should take your material from paragraphs 6 and 7 only. Begin your answer as follows: 'The Lake is strangely frightening ...' [10]

33 Practice passage 16

The following passage is taken from a GCE exam paper set by the University of Cambridge Local Examinations Syndicate. In the original question paper, the questions were separate from the passage. In this book, the questions have been put after a few paragraphs as a matter of convenience for the reader. The numbers in square brackets are paragraph numbers.

Taki

The author remembers the experiences he had as a boy when a young fisherman, named Taki, took him sea-fishing at night. There are 11 paragraphs in the whole passage.

1 In the darkness, Taki rowed us out from the beach into deeper water, humming quietly to himself. Inside the boat lay a pole two metres long, armed with three fierce-looking prongs at the end. It was indeed a savagely-barbed trident. The boat carried a lantern up front which lit up the
5 sea bottom for three metres in every direction. In the bows I could see a little bottle of olive oil. This was a necessary aid to a fisherman, for if a slight wind should blow up, a sprinkling of the oil would have a magically calming effect on the ruffled waters. Slowly and steadily we rowed along, and I was eager to see how Taki fished with his massive trident.

2 Taki bent over his oars and we made our way along the edge of a reef. Here the sea bed was sandy. He slowed the boat to a standstill and picked up his trident. 'Look,' he said. 'Octopus.' My stomach gave a clutch of excitement, because the only octopus I had seen before was one that had been sold for its meat in the town. That surely bore no resemblance to the living creature.
15 But, peer as hard as I could, the sandy bottom of the sea bed appeared to be completely lifeless.

3 'There, there,' said Taki, lowering the trident gently into the water and pointing. 'Can't you see it? Did you leave your eyes behind? Look, I am almost touching it.' Still I could not see it. He lowered the trident another
20 half-metre. 'Now can you see it, foolish one?' he chuckled. 'Just at the end of the prongs.' And suddenly I could see it. I had been looking at it all the time, but its round body was so grey and sand-like that I had mistaken it for part of the sea bed. 'It's a big one,' said Taki.

Questions

The number of marks is shown in square brackets.

From paragraph 1

1 a) What enables Taki to fish effectively in the darkness? [1]
   b) If a wind sprang up, it could spoil the fishing. What could Taki do to counter the effects of the wind? [1]
   c) Taki's trident was two metres long. Write down **one** word from the paragraph which later emphasises its size. [1]

From paragraph 2

2 Up till then, the author had only seen octopus sold as food. Explain **in your own words** why the thought of seeing a live octopus now made him so excited. [2]

From paragraph 3

3 a) Taki called the author 'foolish one' for not seeing the octopus. How do we know Taki was only teasing when he said this? [1]
   b) The following sentence needs **one** word to make it clear why the author had not seen the octopus. Write down the **one** word.
       'The author had not seen the octopus because it was so well ...' [1]

---

4 He shifted the trident only slightly in his grasp, but the movement was ill-
25 advised. Suddenly, in self-defence, the octopus turned from a drab, sandy colour to a bright and startling green. It squirted out a jet of water and, propelled by this, it shot off the sea bed in a swirl of sand. With its tentacles trailing behind it as it sped through the water, it looked just like a runaway balloon.

5 Taki threw the trident down in the bottom of the boat and, seizing the oars,

rowed swiftly in the wake of the octopus, which came to rest on the sea bed some twelve metres away. Once again, Taki eased the boat up to it, and once again lowered the trident carefully into the water. When the pronged head was within half a metre of the octopus's domed head, Taki plunged it

35 home. Immediately the sand boiled up in a cloud as the octopus's tentacles threshed and writhed. An ink-like substance spurted from its body and clouded the sand and water all around.

6 Taki was laughing now. He hauled the trident up swiftly. As the octopus came with it into the boat, two of its tentacles seized the side and adhered

40 to it. It needed a sharp tug by Taki to pull them free. Quickly, he grabbed the round slimy body of the octopus and deftly removed it from the prongs of the trident. Then to my astonishment he lifted its writhing head and put it to his face, so that the tentacles wound round his forehead, his cheeks and neck, their suckers leaving white impressions against his tanned skin.

45 Choosing his spot carefully, he suddenly buried his teeth in the very core of the creature, then gave a snap and a sideways jerk of his head. He had obviously bitten through some nerve centre, for immediately the tentacles released their grip on his head and fell limply. Taki threw the octopus into a large empty oil tin. He cupped a handful of sea water and swilled his mouth

50 out with it. 'You have brought me luck,' he said.

Questions

From paragraph 4

4 a) The octopus suddenly changed colour in self-defence. What do you think its purpose was in doing this? [1]

   b) Explain **in your own words** how squirting out its 'jet of water' enabled the octopus to escape Taki's first attack. [1]

From paragraph 5

5 Why do you think the octopus sent out an ink-like substance when it was attacked a second time? You must answer **in your own words**. [2]

From paragraph 6

6 a) 'Taki was laughing now' (line 38). Why do you think he was laughing? [1]

   b) The octopus was still alive as it came into the boat. How could the author clearly see the power of its suckers at that moment? [1]

   c) The author was astonished when Taki put the octopus's head to his face. What was he afraid its tentacles could do? [1]

   d) Explain why Taki's bite was immediately fatal to the octopus. [1]

7 We now edged our way round the biggest of the reefs, our lantern illuminating the strange underwater cliffs covered with pink and purple seaweeds. Suddenly Taki stopped rowing and dug his oars gently into the water to act as a brake. The boat came to an almost complete standstill as

55 he picked up the trident. 'Look,' he said, pointing to the sandy bottom under a great wall of cliff. 'Scorpion Fish.'

8 At first glance I could see nothing, and then suddenly I saw what he meant. Lying on the sea bed was a fish about half a metre long, with sharp spines all along its back, like a dragon's crest, and enormous fins spread out

60 on the sand. It had a tremendously wide head with golden eyes and a down-turned mouth that gave it a severe expression. But it was the colours that astonished me. It was decked out in a series of reds ranging from scarlet

to wine, emphasised here and there with white. It looked immensely sure of itself as it lay there on the sand. 'This is good eating,' whispered Taki to my
65 surprise, for the fish looked highly poisonous.

9 Delicately he lowered the trident into the water, easing the barbed prongs little by little towards the fish. Slowly, inexorably, the trident got closer and closer. I held my breath. Surely that great fish with its gold-flecked eyes must notice its approaching doom? A sudden flip of the tail, I thought, a
70 swirl of sand, and it would be gone. But no, it just lay there gulping proudly and methodically to itself. When the trident was within half a metre of it, Taki paused. I saw him gently shift his grip on the shaft. He stood immobile for a second. Then, so speedily that I did not actually see the movement, he drove the three prongs swiftly and neatly through the back of the great fish's
75 head.

10 There was a swirl of blood and sand; the fish twisted and writhed on the prongs, curling up its body so that the spines along its back jabbed at the trident. But Taki had driven the trident home too skilfully and it could not escape. Quickly, hand over hand, he pulled on the pole, and the fish came
80 over the side and into the boat, flapping and writhing. I came forward to help him get it off the prongs, but he pushed me back roughly. 'Take care,' he said. 'The Scorpion is a bad fish.'

11 I watched him as he cautiously levered the fish off the trident with the aid of the oar blade. It lay on the deck, still wriggling and falling, and trying to
85 drive its spines into the side of the boat. 'Look, look,' said Taki. 'You see now why we call it Scorpion. If he stabbed you with those spines you would have to go to hospital quickly.' Then with the aid of the oar, the trident, and a dexterous bit of juggling, he managed to lift the Scorpion Fish up and drop it into another empty oil tin where it could do no harm. I wanted to
90 know why, if it was poisonous, it was supposed to be good eating. 'Ah,' said Taki, 'it's only the spines. You cut those off. The flesh is sweet, sweet as honey. I will give it to you to take home with you.' He laid the trident down in the bottom of the boat, and the oars squeaked musically as he rowed us home.

Adapted from *Birds, Beasts and Relatives* by Gerald Durrell.

Questions

From paragraph 8

7 Write down the two expressions from the paragraph which give the Scorpion Fish a human attitude. [2]

From paragraph 11

8 a) Lines 83–84 emphasise the caution with which Taki removes the fish from the trident. Explain fully why he was so cautious. [2]

b) 'The oars squeaked musically' as Taki rowed home. What impression is the author trying to create here? [1]

From the whole passage

9 Choose **five** of the following words or phrases. For each of them give one word or short phrase (of not more than seven words) that has the same meaning as the word or phrase in the passage.

standstill (line 11)	core (line 45)
in the wake of (line 31)	decked out (line 62)
writhed (line 36)	ranging (line 62)
buried (line 45)	dexterous (line 88) [5]

10 Taki was clearly a very skilful and experienced fisherman. **Using your own words as far as possible**, summarise the actions which show his skill and experience in his encounter with the Scorpion Fish. **Use only the material from line 51 to the end of the passage.**

Your summary, which must be in continuous writing (not note form), must not be longer than 160 words, including the 10 words given below.

Begin your summary as follows:
Taki stopped rowing, and then used his oars skilfully to... [25]

In the original examination paper, the questions were given at the end of the following passage. As a matter of convenience, they are given here after the paragraph to which they refer.

In 1854, Florence Nightingale was appointed to lead a group of nurses to assist with the wounded in the Crimean War. Before this, female nurses had never been allowed in military hospitals, and the army did not welcome them.

1 The doctors in the hospital at Scutari received the news of Miss Nightingale's appointment with disgust. Although they were understaffed and overworked, it was the last straw that a young lady from the upper class should be forced on them with a pack of nurses. Of all Government
5 foolishness, this was the worst example. However, they had no choice but to submit; open opposition would be dangerous, for Miss Nightingale was known to have powerful official backing. Opinion was divided as to whether she would turn out a well-meaning, well-bred nuisance or a Government spy. Army officers received the news without enthusiasm. Colonel Sterling
10 wrote in November 1854: 'I do not wish to see, neither do I approve of, ladies doing the grim tasks of nursing.'

Question

1 a) What was it about Miss Nightingale's appointment that disgusted the doctors? [1]
 b) What was the doctor's opinion of the Government? [1]
 c) Explain **in your own words** why 'open opposition' to Miss Nightingale would be dangerous. [2]
 d) 'Opinion was divided.' What is meant by calling **any** opinion divided? [1]

2 However, on November 5th, 1854, Miss Nightingale and her party were welcomed into the hospital at Scutari with every appearance of flattering attention and escorted in with compliments and expressions of goodwill.
15 When they saw their quarters, the picture abruptly changed. The rooms

were damp, filthy, and unfurnished except for a few chairs. There were neither tables nor food. It would in future be a warning to them about the flowery promises of those in authority back in England.

Question

2 a) The nurses were received 'with every appearance of flattering attention'. What does 'every appearance' tell you about this flattery? [1]

b) Explain why the nurses felt that the picture had 'abruptly changed' when they saw their quarters. [1]

c) What would they be warned not to do in future [1]

3 The hospital itself was totally lacking in equipment; it was hopeless to ask
20 for furniture: there was none, not even an operating table. There were no ordinary necessities of life, let alone any medical supplies. The nurses had to use the same tin basins for everything – washing, eating and drinking – and queue in a corridor for their daily ration of a single pint of water. They went to bed in darkness (for the shortage of lamps was acute), but they tried to
25 console themselves by thinking how much greater were the sufferings of the wounded in the ships bringing them across the sea from the battlefield. As the rats scurried about all night long beneath the wooden platforms on which the nurses had to sleep, in rooms alive with fleas, the spirits of every nurse sank.

Question

3 a) How could the nurses console themselves by thinking of the sufferings of the wounded? [1]

b) What is meant by 'the spirits of every nurse sank'? [1]

4 Almost every doctor ignored Miss Nightingale; only one would use her nurses and supplies, for the army medical authorities felt that to accept help from civilians would be to admit failure. They knew that their activities were secretly reported to their army superiors and that anyone who accepted such help would be a marked man.

Question

4 From the evidence of this paragraph, state in your own words why the doctors were afraid to 'accept help' from Miss Nightingale. [3 marks]

5 To accomplish anything, she realised that she must first win the confidence of the doctors. She determined not to offer items from her stores or the assistance of her nurses again, but to wait until the doctors asked for help. She would demonstrate that she and her nurses wished neither to interfere nor to attract attention, that they were prepared to accept without question
40 the authority of the doctors. It was a policy which demanded self-control; the nurses were to stand by while they saw troops suffer, yet do nothing until officially instructed. Though Miss Nightingale could accept the hard fact that she would never succeed without first overcoming official opposition, she inevitably came into conflict with her nurses. The cries of
45 the wounded were to go unanswered: instead old linen was counted and mended. This was not what the nurses had left England to accomplish. They blamed Miss Nightingale.

5 Give two reasons why the nurses disagreed with Miss Nightingale's attempts to win the confidence of the doctors. [2 marks]

6 She was first able to gain some influence in the hospital through the kitchen. A state of starvation existed in the hospital: to cook anything
50 properly was practically impossible, so that the food was almost uneatable, even by healthy men; as a diet for those with cholera or dysentery it produced agonies. 'I have never seen greater suffering,' wrote one observer. Miss Nightingale began to cook 'extras' to supplement the inadequate rations supplied by the hospital; she also provided a special invalid diet from
55 her own stores, although she was always careful to obtain a doctor's permission before giving any patient such nourishment.

6 There was food – but the patients were starving. Give two reasons to show why this was so. [2 marks]

7 Cooking was all she had managed to accomplish when, on November 9th, the situation completely changed. A flood of wounded men poured into the hospital at Scutari on such a scale that a crisis of terribly urgency arose. The
60 previous prejudice and resentment of the doctors were for the moment forgotten. Through necessity, they at last allowed the most competent of the nurses to attend to the daily dressing of wounds and fractures. As the wounded filled the building, men were forced to lie on unwashed floors because of the shortage of beds. With desperate haste, the nurses sewed up
65 great bags and stuffed them with straw. The bags were then laid down in the wards and corridors with just enough room to pass between them. Even so, the rats still scampered to and fro among them. One of Miss Nightingale's first acts was to obtain a screen so that men might be spared the sight of the intense suffering of others during operations, a suffering they
70 themselves were doomed to undergo. But they were not spared the risk of infection in such a crowded hospital.

7 a) Explain the 'crisis' which made it necessary to call on the nurses for help. [2]
   b) The 'crisis' also included a threat to hygiene. List three examples of how hygiene was threatened. [3]
   c) What made the operations performed in the hospital at Scutari a more terrible ordeal than those performed today? [1]

8 In all the misery and confusion it began to dawn on the harassed doctors and overworked officials that there was one person in Scutari who could take action – who had money and the authority to spend it – and that was
75 Miss Nightingale. She had a very large sum at her disposal, derived from various charities, and nearby was one of the great ports of the world where almost anything could be bought. Each day she found out what necessities and comforts were lacking; these were fetched from the port and issued by her, but only when officially requested by a medical officer. Gradually the
80 doctors ceased to be suspicious and their jealousy disappeared.

8 a) Miss Nightingale used her money tactfully in helping the hospital authorities. What is the evidence in this paragraph that she employed this tact? [1]

b) 'Gradually the doctors ceased to be suspicious.' What does 'gradually' mean here? [1]

9 Her first purchase was of two hundred hard scrubbing brushes and sacking for washing the floors; then, under her supervision, the wards and lavatories were thoroughly cleaned. Her next step was to reorganise the poor laundry facilities; before her arrival, shirts were either not washed at all or washed in
85 cold water, and came back as filthy as when they were sent. She rented a house where washing of clothes might be done by the soldiers' wives, and arranged for boilers to be installed to heat the water. She supplied 2,000 thick flannel shirts, as well as other clothes, utensils, towels and soap, and she caused an entire regiment which had only thin tropical kit to be re-
90 fitted with warm clothing. She also arranged for the repair and cleaning of two extra wards, damaged by a fire some years previously, and equipped them herself, so that they could accommodate nearly a thousand extra patients. One of the wounded described his sensations when he was provided by the nurses with clean bedding and warm food. 'We thought we were in heaven,'
95 he said.

9 Choose **five** of the following words. For each of them, give one word or short phrase (of not more than seven words) which has the same meaning as in the passage.

(i)	submit (line 6)	(ii)	grim (line 11)
(iii)	quarters (line 15)	(iv)	demonstrate (line 38)
(v)	inevitably (line 44)	(vi)	supplement (line 53)
(vii)	doomed (line 70)	(viii)	sensations (line 93)

[5 marks]

10 Explain the ways in which Miss Nightingale and her nurses were at last able to help and improve the conditions which existed in the hospital at Scutari.

Use only the material from line 48 to the end of the passage.

Your account, which should be in continuous writing (not note form), must not be longer than 160 words, including the 10 words given below.

Begin your account as follows:
She was first able to improve conditions through the kitchen. [20 marks]

35 Understanding situations

Understanding character from speech

In some examinations, students have to say what speech reveals about a person's character.

Example 1

You are a stranger in town and ask a police officer for directions to the post office. The officer says:

(i) 'Come along with me. I'm going that way too.'
(ii) 'Why did you come to town if you didn't know where you were supposed to go?'

In each case what does the statement reveal about the policeman's manner towards you? Number your answer separately, (i) and (ii).
We could give these answers:

(i) This shows that the policeman was courteous and helpful.
(ii) This shows that the policeman was unhelpful and unsympathetic.

If necessary, we could give longer answers – but these are not usually required in answer to this type of question.

Suitable responses

In another type of question, students are given a situation and asked to choose the most suitable/polite/reasonable response.

Example 2

Study the following situation and then choose the best response.

You are in a restaurant and want to get the bill for a meal which you have just eaten. You can say to the waiter:

a) Can I have the check, please?
b) Bill, please.
c) How much?
d) Let's have it, please.

In this example, there are two possible answers: a) if you use American English, and b) if you use British English. In an examination, you would not be given alternative answers.

One phrase, two meanings

Sometimes you may be asked to explain two meanings which a single response can have.

Example 3

Susan: Who's that stranger? Do you know him?
Peter: He looks suspicious to me.

Give two ways in which Susan may interpret Peter's comment.

In the answer, we can say:

(i) She may think that Peter suspects the stranger in some way.

(ii) She may think that Peter means that the stranger suspects that something is wrong.

Describing the speaker

A remark may show that the speaker is one or more of the following:

discourteous –	courteous	unsympathetic –	sympathetic
rude –	polite	aggressive –	helpful
envious –	pleased, glad	bored –	interested.
selfish –	unselfish	scornful –	praising
bad-tempered –	even-tempered, calm	mean –	generous

or sarcastic, ungrateful, excitable, self-controlled, persuasive, consoling, non-committal, cautious, unhelpful, guarded, and so on.

Intonation and emphasis

The meaning of a statement can depend upon the intonation or the emphasis put on individual words.

'What a fine thing to do!' can show praise, admiration, and so on.

It can also show sarcasm, criticism, condemnation, etc.

Exercise 1

Study each situation below. Then give brief answers to the questions.

1 Your young sister has fallen down from a mango tree and has bruised her knees. You say:

a) 'That will teach you not to climb trees.'

b) 'Are you sure you're all right? Please don't move. I'll carry you to the house.'

How will your sister interpret each of these statements? Give two separate answers.

2 You meet a friend of yours at a wedding. You are wearing a hat and she says:

'Where did you get that hat?'

Give two different reasons why your friend should say this.

3 Listed below are four situations and eight possible responses. Match each situation with one response which you think most appropriate to it. Write down the number only of the situation and against that number write out in full the appropriate response you have chosen.

Situations

(i) Seeing a friend for the first time since the death of his or her mother.

(ii) Asking for help from your head teacher.

(iii) Replying to someone who has dialled your number by mistake.

(iv) Turning down a cousin's invitation to a birthday party.

Responses

I would love to come, but I'm not feeling well.

This is not the number you want.

Excuse me, Mrs Sendall. I need help.
Your mother passed away. What a pity.
I'm sorry I can't come.
I'm afraid you've dialled a wrong number.
Excuse me, Mrs Sendall. Can you please help me?
I was sorry to hear that your mother passed away.

Exercise 2

Here are five situations, briefly described. Read the description of each situation carefully and then answer the questions which follow, briefly.

1 You have just been told your O-level results and you discover that you passed only two subjects. On hearing this your father says:
   a) 'You tried your best. Better luck next time.'
   b) 'What? Do you think I am made of money?'

   What does each reaction reveal about your father's attitude?

2 When you board a bus at the terminal you offer the driver a $20 dollar note instead of the exact fare of 33c. The driver reacts as follows:
   a) 'I am really short of change. Have you got anything smaller?'
   b) 'Stop showing off and give me the exact fare.'

   What does each statement show about the driver's manner towards you?

3 Your friend asks you how you spent your weekend. You say:
   a) 'What I do during weekends is none of your business.'
   b) 'I read that novel you recommended by L. Nikosi. It was fantastic.'

   How will your friend react to each of these replies?

4 You have spent $35 on a T-shirt. You show it to your father and he says: 'You tell me you've spent $35 on this piece of junk?'

   Give two different reasons why he should say this.

5 A customer in a shoe-shop wants a type of shoe that is out of stock. The salesman says:
   a) 'We've none in stock. You'll have to try elsewhere.'
   b) 'I'm sorry, we don't have it. But let me show you something else that is equally as good.'

   In each case, say what sort of a salesman you think he is.

Exercise 3

Listed below are five situations, briefly described. Read the description of each situation carefully and then answer the questions which follow, briefly.

1 A member of your class hears that you have failed a test. He comes up to you and says:
   a) 'I must congratulate you on your brilliant performance!'
   b) 'Don't worry. Work harder next time.'

   What does each statement reveal about his attitude towards you?

2 You have applied for a job and you have just learnt that your application has been successful. You tell your friend about the good news. He says:

a) 'Well done! When do you start?'
b) 'You have too much luck. I never have any.'

What does each reply reveal about your friend's feelings?

3 You are having a discussion with someone else. He says something which you think is not true. You say:
a) 'Rubbish! You're talking nonsense.'
b) 'That's possible. But don't you think that the real truth is...'

What does each of your comments reveal about your manner?

4 A friend of yours, who has been in hospital for the past month, has returned home. You visit her at her home. You say:
a) 'You're looking much better now.'
b) 'You look terrible!'

What effect will each of these statements have on your friend?

5 You are with a group of friends working together in class. Your teacher has been dissatisfied with your recent performance. He begins to scold you and you are upset.

A friend says: 'But, sir, Peter has not been well lately.' Give two reasons to explain why your friend should say this on your behalf.

Exercise 4

Listed here are five situations, which are described briefly. Read the description of each situation carefully, and then answer the questions which follow, briefly.

1 During lunch break you offer your friend some food. He looks at it and says:
a) 'Do you call this lunch?'
b) 'Thank you, but I have eaten something already.'

What does each reply tell you about your friend's manner?

2 You want to leave home to find work in a nearby city. Your parents try to persuade you to stay and help them run their farm. You say:
a) 'Don't worry. If things don't work out, I'll come back. I won't let you down.'
b) 'You don't understand. There's no future for me here.'

What does each of these remarks reveal about the way you treat your parents?

3 You have taken your bicycle to the local shop for repairs. You go to collect it, but find it is not ready. You say:
a) 'I didn't realise it was such a long job. I'll call back again tomorrow.'
b) 'What? Isn't it ready yet? What have you been doing?'

Say what you think each of your remarks indicates about your attitude towards the delay.

4 You walk into a restaurant. The waiter walks up to you and says:
a) 'Stew only today. Do you want it?'
b) 'Would you like to try our stew today?'

How would the waiter's employer react in each case if he overheard what the waiter said?

5 You are riding around the garden on your motor-bike. You pick up speed and your father watches in horror as you screech to a halt, just missing the wall of the house. He says:

'You'll get yourself killed on that thing one of these days.'

Give two different reasons why your father should say this.

PART 3

Communication in Writing: Composition

Communication in writing

There are many forms of communication in writing. They include the forms shown below. We are interested mainly in the forms marked with an asterisk.

*Letters (friendly or business)
*Reports
 Email
*Applications for jobs
*Directed writing
*Argumentative writing
 Brochures and pamphlets
*Descriptions of people, places, etc.
*Factual accounts, e.g. explanations
*Stories and narrative writing
*Examination compositions
*Situational compositions
 Articles for magazines or newspapers, etc.
 Rules, regulations and instructions

GENERAL SKILLS AND SPECIFIC SKILLS

The first few units in this part of the book deal with general skills which apply to nearly all forms of written work. The later units deal with the specific skills needed when you write a letter, make a report, describe something or do another task.

Length

We are concerned here mainly with writing in an examination. Depending on which examination you take, you may have to do one of these things:

Directed writing

Write 80–220 words on a topic which is related to a passage. For example, the passage may describe agricultural life. You may then have to write 100 words describing how you think town life differs from agricultural life.

Situational writing

You may have to write a letter, a report or an article based on given information, for instance, notes, a picture, statistics, a letter, an advertisement or other details. This type of composition is often about 200 words long (but it can be any length).

Practical writing

You are asked to write 200 or 300 words for a given situation. The question may explain the situation but give you no notes or other information.

Essay topics

You may have to write up to 500 words about a traditional topic such as 'Leisure' or 'An Amusing Incident'.

Very roughly, a student at this level should be able to write 400–500 words in 1–1¼ hours. He should be able to write about 200–300 words in 30 minutes when given notes or data to use.

It is not essential to count the number of words in a composition. Draw three horizontal lines 16cm (6¼″) long. Copy any three lines from this book. Count the number of words in the three lines. Work out the average per line. Then write the correct number of lines in an exam. For example, if you usually write ten words per line, you should write about twenty lines for a composition of 200 words. It is a waste of time to count every word in the whole composition.

Handwriting

If an examiner cannot read your composition easily, he will fail to understand the development of your ideas. He may think you have made many spelling mistakes.

Talk to candidates who have failed already. You will find that most of them write badly.

1 Copy this: 'What's the date today?'
   a) Did you put the apostrophe before the 's' or on top of it?
   b) Did you write 'd' at the start of 'date' or 'cl'?
   c) Did you cross the letter 't' in each word – or did you just put a dash above the 't'?
   d) Did you form the letter 'a' correctly – or does it look like an 'e'?

2 Copy this: 'The archaeologists explored the ruins. It was a hot day.'
   a) Is the ink in your pen pale blue or dark blue? Use dark ink in an examination. It is easier to read.
   b) Did you make the full stop very clear after 'ruins'? If it is not clear, a reader may think you have not finished the sentence.
   c) Are your capital letters ('T' and 'I') at least twice as high as your small letters? Then they will be easy to see. An examiner will know that you have started a new sentence.
   d) Look at your letters 'g', 'p' and 'y'. Have you put unnecessary tails on them? Don't do that.
   e) Look at your word 'ruins'. Did you put a dot above the 'i' or above part of the 'u'? Be careful in future. Careful people succeed in life. You know what happens to careless people!
   f) Did you form the letters 'r', 'o', 'l' and 's' clearly? Change books with another student. Ask him (or her) to check your writing.

Read regularly and widely

Regular reading will improve your knowledge of tenses, sentence patterns, use of articles, prepositions, and so on. It will improve your vocabulary and increase your knowledge.

Your target should be 5 to 10 pages a day. If you have not got time on one day, read twice as much the next day. If you follow this method, your English will definitely improve within three months – but you may not notice the improvement yourself. However, your work will be of a higher standard.

Read anything interesting: detective stories, love stories, travel books, technical books about electronics, books about dressmaking or cookery – anything which you find interesting.

Choose your essay topic wisely

a) Some topics force you to use a difficult tense. For example, what tense will you use to write about 'What would you do if you won the first prize in a lottery?'?

b) Some topics may make you angry, bitter or rude. Your essay may be marked by a man or woman who may be of a different race. Be polite, logical and fair.

c) Some topics have several parts. Answer all parts or choose an easier topic.

d) Some topics are vague or not clear. Avoid them.

e) Choose a topic you know something about. If possible write about your own country and not about an overseas one which you have not visited.

Exercise 1

Which tense(s) will you probably have to use when you write about each of these topics?

1 The next ten years
2 The women of my country
3 Changes in fashion
4 Write a story to show that impatience can lead to trouble
5 If you were in charge of roads and transport in your country, what improvements or changes would you make?
6 Describe a time when you had a pleasant or an unpleasant surprise.
7 Trees
8 Traditions – should we preserve them or reject them?

Exercise 2

Think about each of these topics carefully. Which ones are dangerous because they might make a candidate write something rude or offensive?

1 Discuss the role of women in modern society.
2 Money
3 My favourite game or sport
4 Is tourism a good or a bad thing?
5 What can you learn from visiting new places?
6 Do you agree that Science students usually have more ability than Arts students?
7 Patriotism – a unifying factor or an indirect cause of wars?
8 The generation gap
9 Examinations
10 To what extent do you think the education system in your country is suited to the needs of students?

Understand your topic

Look at these two topics:

a) Films
b) Write about a very good or a very bad film you have seen

Note:

The topic 'A public holiday' allows candidates to choose which tense they will use. For example:

a) We can refer to a public holiday which occurred last month. Writing in the past, we can give the reason for the holiday and show what different types of people did then.

or

b) We can mention a public holiday which will occur next month. Writing in the future, we can say what people will do on that day.

or

c) We can write generally about how different classes of people (for example, shopkeepers, students, parents, manual workers, etc.) are affected when there is a public holiday. Then we can use the Simple Present tense most of the time.

In a) we must write generally about many films. We may wish to explain how they are made. We can classify them and write about different types of films. We can write generally about what makes films good or bad.

In b) we must write about one film only. It is thus clear that the two topics are different. If you described only one film when writing about the topic 'Films', your answer would be irrelevant and you would lose many marks.

Read these extracts from examiners' reports:

- ' "Myself in twenty years' time" was often misunderstood to mean "Myself twenty years ago".'
- ' "The future of my country" led some candidates to write mainly about the past.'
- 'Essays on "Trees" were dull, shapeless lists ... mentioning wheat trees, wool trees and potato trees.'
- 'Attempts to deal with "Traditional" stories were colourless and seldom kept to the point; many essays dealt with one story only.'
- 'The first essay, "A public holiday", was frequently taken as an opportunity to present a prepared essay as, for example, an account of a visit to an exhibition or to the seaside. Many candidates used it as a basis for narrative, telling a story with little reference to a holiday. Very rarely was there any emphasis on "public" and most essays were accounts of a visit to the beach, or a picnic, with no suggestion whatsoever of there being a "public" holiday. Some candidates wrote on holidays in general, having missed the point of the indefinite article at the beginning of the title.'

Exercise 3

Look at the following essay topics. Below each one, there are themes which past candidates used when writing about these topics. Say which of the themes were good and which were unsuitable. Say why some were unsuitable. Be careful. Sometimes all the themes may be good or all may be unsuitable.

1 **Topic** The machine in modern life
   a) I will describe the history and development of machines.
   b) I will describe the nature and importance of the Industrial Revolution.
   c) I will write about the boring life of factory workers.
   d) I will show the importance of machinery in different aspects of a modern community.
   e) I will show how machines have affected the lives of different types of modern people.

2 **Topic** The pleasure of cooking
   a) I will describe traditional ways of cooking.
   b) I will compare old and new ways of cooking.
   c) I will write about a time when I tried to cook some food and did not succeed.

3 **Topic** Growing up
   a) I will give an account of the problems of old people.
   b) I will explain how I grew up and what problems I had.

c) I will write a general account of the pleasures and problems which young people meet between the ages of about 10 and 20.
d) I will describe different ways of growing vegetables.

4 **Topic** It's never too late to mend
a) I will discuss the importance of being punctual.
b) We should not throw old things away if we can repair them.
c) I will show that a bad person can reform if he wants to do so.

5 **Topic** Strange customs
a) I will describe an unusual custom which I know about.
b) I will discuss the difference between western culture and my own culture.
c) I will try to explain why most western customs are strange.
d) I will write about some strange customs which I have heard of.
e) I will show why smuggling is bad for a country's economy.

6 **Topic** Man's treatment of animals
a) I will consider the ways in which people use animals.
b) I will consider people who keep pets and neglect their own children.
c) I will consider changing attitudes to animals throughout the ages.
d) The human race is superior to animals and everybody knows this.

Exercise 4

Consider each of the possible themes below. Say whether it is good or bad. Give reasons for your opinions.

1 **Topic** How I earn my living
a) I will explain how I spend my money.
b) I will give details of my job.
c) I will write about my life at home with my family.
d) I am a student, so I will write about studying at school.

2 **Topic** Describe an important event which you attended and at which you were very happy.
a) I will write about the funeral of my grandfather.
b) I will describe a time when I appeared in court and was fined for a traffic offence.
c) I will write about a friend's wedding which I went to.
d) I will describe a Speech Day at school, when I was awarded two prizes for good work.

3 **Topic** My favourite game or sport
a) I will write about the game I most enjoy playing.
b) I will describe the popular games and sports of my country.
c) I will explain the rules of football, which I like to play or watch.
d) My favourite sport is underwater swimming, so I will write about it.

4 **Topic** My best friend
a) My mother is my best friend, so I will write about her.
b) I will show how friends should behave to each other.
c) I will explain how to get friends and treat them properly.
d) I will describe the appearance, character and conduct of Peter, because he has always been my best friend.

5 **Topic** My home
   a)   I will describe the inside of my home.
   b)   I will describe the outside of my home.
   c)   I will explain where my home is and then describe the outside and inside of it.
   d)   I will write about my country.
   e)   I will show the importance of patriotism.

6 **Topic** Money spent on space exploration is a waste (Discuss)
   a)   I will show why this statement is right.
   b)   I will explain why I disagree with this statement.
   c)   I will consider both sides of the argument.
   d)   I will show why it is important to learn about the oceans.

37 Composition – basic points

These were the main points in Unit 36:

1   Check your handwriting. Improve it if necessary. For some students, this is the most important point in the whole book. An illegible communication is a bad one.
2   In an examination, count the number of lines, not the number of words.
3   Read regularly and widely.
4   Choose your topic wisely.
5   Understand your topic. Irrelevant answers are common and fatal.

Rough work

a)   You are advised not to write all your composition out in rough and then to make a final copy. There is not enough time for this in an examination or in adult life.
b)   Cross out (very clearly) all rough work so that you do not annoy an examiner by making him think the rough work is your final composition.

Find a clear theme for your topic

A 'theme' is a major idea for your whole composition. It is like the skeleton of an animal. It gives shape and unity to your work. It shows the writer what to look for when he makes his plan. It is impossible to make a plan before you have decided on your theme.

In many cases, the theme is shown clearly in the topic, as in the following examples.

Topic   Write a report of about 200 words on what your school or college has achieved during the past year.

Theme   I will write a report of about 200 words on what my school has achieved during the past year. (I can arrange my facts in time order – from the start to the end of the year – or under such headings as Sport, Drama, School Societies, and so on.)

Topic	Describe, for a visitor, some outstanding feature(s) of your town or country.
Theme	I will describe (for a visitor) some outstanding features of my country. (I will not write about my town and country together.)
Topic	Imagine you are showing a friend a family photograph. Your friend asks what kind of person your brother/sister is. Write what you would say to give a true impression of the character of your brother/sister.
Theme	I will write an answer to give a true impression of my sister. (I will briefly describe what she looks like so that he can get a clearer impression. Then I will describe her character and actions.)
Topic	Transport in my country
Theme	I will write about transport in my country. (I will probably deal with transport on land, by sea and in the air.)
Topic	The pleasure of craftwork (for example, carving, pottery or weaving) or cooking
Theme	I will write about the pleasure of cooking (and not about cooking in general).
Topic	Describe a day in the life of one of the following: a miner, a fisherman, a farmer.
Theme	I will write about a day in the life of a farmer (in my country).

In some cases, the theme is not clear, and there are many ways of writing about a topic. Then you can restrict the scope of your topic and use one of the methods shown by DAFTI. (In colloquial English, 'daft' means 'foolish' and a boy may call a friend 'dafty', meaning 'a fool'.)

The letters DAFTI show you five ways of finding a theme when one is not clearly given. Study the following explanation. Then learn the five ways of DAFTI by heart.

D = Different types, attitudes, reasons or factors
A = Advantages and disadvantages of a topic
F = Factual account
T = Time or historical approach to a topic
I = Importance of a topic in the life of man

Thus the five letters in DAFTI show us five ways of finding a theme if the theme is not already made clear in the topic. Below are some examples.

D = Different types, attitudes, reasons or factors

Topic	Trees
Theme	I will describe different types of trees.
	or
	I will describe different attitudes to trees..

Topic	Accidents in the home
Theme	I will describe different common reasons for accidents in the home (and perhaps how to prevent them).

Topic	Money
Theme	I will describe some of the different attitudes which people have to money.

Topic	My country in the next twenty years
Theme	I will take different aspects of my country (economic, social, political, military, etc.) and try to discuss what they will be like in the next twenty years.

Exercise I

Use D to find a clear theme for each of these topics:

1 Traffic accidents
2 Films
3 Television
4 Pollution

A = Advantages and disadvantages of a topic

Topic	Examinations
Theme	I will describe the advantages and disadvantages of examinations.

Topic	'Homework should be abolished.' Discuss.
Theme	I will discuss both sides of this statement, i.e. reasons why homework should or should not be abolished.

Topic	'International sport encourages goodwill amongst the people of different nations.' What is your opinion?
Theme	I will write about points which support and do not support this statement.

F = Factual account

This method is more suitable for topics such as these:

a) The importance of fertilisers to farmers
b) Modern methods of producing rubber
c) Radar

T = Time or historical approach to a topic

Give a historical account of the development of something.

Topic	Farming
Theme	I will give a historical account of the development of farming from early times up to the present. Then I will consider possible farming methods in the future.

Topic	Homes
Theme	I will give a historical account of people's homes, showing how these have changed from caves to huts, to houses, to flats in large housing blocks. (It is almost a complete circle.)

I = Importance of a topic in the life of man

Topic	Farming
Theme	I will describe the part which farming plays in the life of man and show how it has fallen in importance throughout the ages.

Notes

a) You must find a clear theme before you prepare your plan.

b) You must make your theme very clear to the reader. One way of doing this is by stating your theme in your opening sentence.

Sometimes we can combine two methods when dealing with a topic, e.g.

Topic   The development of industry in your country
Theme   I will give a historical account of the development of industry in my country and either show its importance or describe the different types of industries we have now.

Exercise 2

In each case give a possible theme for the topic. Your theme should consist of one or two sentences which summarise your main idea. They will be the 'skeleton' for the whole of your answer.

1. How does the climate affect the people of your country?
2. Loneliness
3. An election
4. Write a description of a vehicle or boat or aircraft used for carrying passengers, giving information about the journeys it undertakes, the kinds of people who use it, and the driver or other person who controls it during its journey.
5. Tell the story of an incident that changed the course of a real or imaginary boy's or girl's life.
6. Dancing
7. Pens or shovels?
8. Last year
9. What makes a good friend?

Exercise 3

Give a possible theme for each of these topics.

1. An interesting place I have visited
2. Discipline, at home and in school
3. Unwelcome visitors
4. 'Paying college students or school pupils wages to study would be as foolish as paying mothers wages to do work at home.' Discuss.
5. Smugglers
6. Memories of winter
7. Collecting things
8. In what ways have you enjoyed helping people in the past, and to what extent will your education enable you to help others in the future?
9. Safety in the home
10. Write a long letter of about 450 words to a pen-friend abroad describing your personal pleasures.

38 Composition – making a plan

There are three main steps in planning a composition.

Step 1 Find a clear theme for your topic.

Step 2 Think about your theme, ask yourself questions, and make notes of the important points.

Step 3 Arrange your points in a logical order. Sometimes step 3 comes before step 2. We can look at a theme and see ways of arranging the major points. Then we look for details.

You can use one of these ways of arranging your facts – or you can use any other logical method.

a) Advantages – disadvantages
    Good factors – bad factors
b) In time order
c) In place order
d) In order of importance, starting with the most important
e) Different types of something, also arranged in order of importance or commonness
f) Cause – event – results
g) Preparation – events – clearing up

Here are some examples:

Topic Safety in the home
Theme I will write about the need for safety in the home.
Plan   (types) safety for: the very old
                                      the very young
                                      children
                                      all people
or   (places) safety in: the kitchen
                                      the living-room
                                      bedrooms
                                      the garden (if you have one)

Topic Write a long letter of about 450 words to a pen-friend abroad describing your personal pleasures.
Theme I will write a letter describing my personal pleasures.
Plan   outdoor pleasures: athletics
                                     games
                                     picnics and outings
                                     travel
           indoor pleasures   watching television
                                     eating
                                     reading
                                     stamp-collecting

Topic Smugglers
Theme I will write about different types of smugglers.
Plan   Amateurs: tourists, travellers, ordinary people
           Professionals: by land, by sea, by air

If you look at the examples, you will see that the key word is **classify**. After you have decided on your theme, classify your facts in any logical way. This is very important because it helps you to think and write fluently. You can express yourself clearly – because you know what to say. For the same reason, you will make fewer mistakes in your English.

Here are further examples. Perhaps you can suggest alternative themes and plans for some of them.

Topic   Dancing

Theme   I will describe the historical development of dancing from the earliest times to the present.

Plan   Perhaps religious significance at first – or simple exercise.
Became formal gradually, e.g., waltz and other formal dances.
At the same time, folk dances remained, e.g. at Spring and the harvest.
In modern times, less formal – all sorts of ways of dancing.
Rather free and uninhibited.
But some formal dancing (ballet) still remains.
(Don't bother to think about the future – it is too difficult.)
or

Theme   I will describe some different attitudes to dancing.
a)   Young people – very keen; recreation and a way of meeting friends and people of the opposite sex.
b)   Older people – less keen; for formal occasions only.
c)   Very old – critical of new methods of dancing.

Topic   Last year

Theme   I will write about the major events in my country last year.

Plan   I will follow a time order, and list the events in order of time.
or

Plan   I will follow a good-and-bad order, starting with the good things.
or

Plan   I will arrange the events in order of importance, starting with the most important.

Topic   Loneliness

Theme   I will write about different types of loneliness, i.e. different reasons for it.

Plan   Sad (or bad) types: old people, divorced/separated people, ex-criminals, etc.
Better types: loneliness needed for thought, study, meditation, religious purposes, etc.

Exercise 1

Choose a topic. Write out your theme and your plan. Make a slightly longer plan than the examples given on the previous pages but use DAFTI or any other method to find a theme and the headings for your plan.

1 Water
2 Electricity
3 The fascination of railways
4 Describe either a market or a railway station at two contrasting times of the day.
5 How can we best deter young offenders from repeating their crimes?

As in Exercise 1, choose a topic, write out your theme, and then write your plan.

1 Which do you prefer, playing games as a member of a team or as an individual?
2 Inventions that I hope will soon be made
3 The place where I was born
4 Describe some interesting or amusing characters met on a journey by land or sea.
5 Write an account of a time when you had to take charge.

As in Exercise 1, choose a topic, write out your theme and then your plan.

1 Some problems I have met in learning English.
2 Consider the effect which inflation has had on your community.
3 'It is better to travel safely than not to arrive.' Do you agree?
4 An overseas friend is coming to stay with you for a week. Write an account of interesting places you can take him (or her) to, or of interesting things for your friend to do.
5 Pollution

39 Starting a composition

REVIEW

These are the important points from Units 36–38:

1 Write very clearly. Form each letter properly.
2 In an examination, count lines and not words.
3 Read regularly and widely.
4 Choose your topic wisely.
5 Check that you fully understand your topic.
6 Use DAFTI to find a theme if one is not given.
7 Your plan should be based on your themes. Arrange your facts in a logical order.

You can spend about 20–25 per cent of your time on thinking and planning – that is 12–15 minutes if your total time is one hour. This is the time recommended by examiners. Compare these candidates:

a) Matthew spent 5 minutes on his plan. He did not find a theme. His points were in no special order. He started to write after 5 minutes. He wrote quickly for 20 minutes. Then he had to stop. He could not think of anything more to write about. He wrote too few words and failed.
b) Sarah spent 15 minutes studying the questions, choosing a topic, finding a theme and making a detailed plan. She wrote for just under 40 minutes.

Then she spent 6 minutes carefully checking her essay and correcting mistakes. She passed.

Which type of candidate will *you* be?

WAYS OF STARTING A COMPOSITION

Go straight to the point as soon as possible. Do not waste time and effort with an introduction. That is an old-fashioned way of writing.

Try to show the reader your theme as quickly as possible. Then he knows what your essay, letter or report is about.

Do you know what soap is? Put a letter 't' in it and make STOAP (or change the letters and make A STOP). Then the five letters show you five ways of starting a composition. Learn these ways by heart.

S = Speech

Start with dialogue that is related to your theme.

Topic	Reading books
Theme	I will describe some of the different ways in which I read books, e.g. very fast, at my average rate or very slowly and carefully.
Plan	very fast: very exciting or I am looking for something
	average: the normal speed for something interesting
	slowly: study speed or for a very difficult but important book
Start	'Here, you'll enjoy this book,' my brother said, 'It's all about ghosts and mysteries.'

T = Theme

State your theme in your opening sentence. This is a common and useful method because it tells your reader what you are writing about.

Start	I have three speeds for reading books: fast, average and slow.

O = Opinion

Start with an opinion about your topic. This may or may not be your theme.

Start	Reading books is my favourite occupation when I have spare time, and I enjoy it very much.

A = Action

Describe some action which is related to your theme.

Start	I went into a library and looked for a book by Barbara Cartland. A friend had recommended her books to me, so I wanted to read one.

P = Proverb or quotation

Find a suitable proverb or quotation.

Start	'All round my room my silent servants wait – My friends in every season.'

I remember seeing this quotation some years ago, and it seems a good way to stress the value of reading. I have three main...

Here are some more examples. The letters S, T, O, A and P refer to the methods shown above.

Topic   The market
Theme   (I think most other candidates will write about a market for meat, fish, vegetables, fruit, etc., so I will describe a different type of market. It will be interesting for the examiner and probably get me a higher mark because it is more original.) I will describe a money market: the Stock Exchange of Hong Kong.
Plan   Chronological approach – from 10 a.m. to 12.30 p.m.

Ways of starting

S   'What's that? Fifteen thousand or fifty? Oh, five oh. What price? $10.50? Yes, I think I can get them at that price. OK. I'll ring back when I've bought them.'
    Mr Chan made an entry in his book: '50,000 Land at $10.50 – Peter Jackson.'

T   One of the most interesting markets in Hong Kong is the money market, the Stock Exchange. On busy days, more than a billion dollars' worth of shares change hands on it.

O   There are many different kinds of markets but the one which fascinates me most is the money market. I know about it because my brother works in the office of a stockbroker.

A   Mr Chan walked to the 'Buyers' column for Hong Kong Land shares. He picked up a piece of chalk and wrote '10.50'. Then he added his number '69'. Almost immediately a seller shouted at him ...

P   'A market is a place where buyers and sellers meet,' say economists. In fact, it is something much more interesting than that.

Topic   My most vivid dream
Theme   (I have forgotten all my dreams but this is the only topic I can write about, so I must invent a dream.)
    I will describe my most vivid dream – about a time when I learnt to swim in a dream.
Plan   fear of the water
    constant dreams of drowning, rivers and the sea
    the time when I learnt to swim in a dream

Ways of starting

S   'No, thank you,' I said in my dream. 'I'd rather not go swimming. As a matter of fact, I can't swim.'

T   My most vivid dream was also my most astonishing one. After numerous nightmares, I actually learnt to swim – in a dream.

O   I suppose I must have had thousands of dreams or nightmares in the past fifteen years, but there is one that I shall never forget.

A   I was half way across the flooded bridge. The water continued to rise until most of the bridge was covered. I was trapped – and the water continued to rise steadily. I watched in horror as it began to lap at my feet.

P   'Dreams are often the reflection of reality,' somebody once said. 'They show us the world as we want it to be – or as we fear it may become.'

That may well be true because I can vividly remember one dream I had when I was younger...

These examples show you that an introduction is quite unnecessary. You will save time and help your reader if you go straight to the point in your opening sentences.

Exercise 1

Show two different ways of starting the following essay. In each case, write the opening one or two sentences.

Topic Are modern inventions making us lazy?

Theme Yes and no. Yes – in the physical sense; no – in the intellectual sense. (= I will consider both sides of the statement.)

Plan Yes (physical): communication – telephone, email, letter, space satellite – easy to communicate
entertainment – watch it instead of play it
food – not necessary to grow it; get from supermarket
travel – no walking; bus, train, plane, etc.

No (intellectual): greater intellectual effort needed to handle modern inventions
driving a car (flying a plane; sailing a ship) repairing machines; using computers etc.

Exercise 2

Show two different ways of starting the following letter. In each case, write the opening one or two sentences.

Topic An overseas friend has written to ask you about the ways in which English is used in your country, and any local varieties of it. Write a suitable reply.

Theme I will describe the ways in which English is used in my country and describe the main local varieties of it.

Exercise 3

Choose one of these topics. Write out a) a suitable theme, b) a rough plan based on the theme and c) any suitable way of starting.

1 Television programmes or radio programmes
2 The advantages and disadvantages of being the age that I am now
3 Music
4 Happiness
5 Write about a club or organisation you belong to, describing its aim and activities, and showing what benefits you obtain from membership

40 Paragraphing and developing ideas

There are two approaches to the use of paragraphs. We can call them 'theory' and 'practice'.

THEORY

In theory, each paragraph deals with a single topic (or aspect of a topic). It usually contains a topic sentence which gives the theme of the whole paragraph. The topic sentence is usually near the beginning of the paragraph.

PRACTICE

If you look in a newspaper or in any novel, you will find that writers do not necessarily follow the description given above. For example, in many newspapers each paragraph consists of one or two sentences only. This is done so that a news report will be easy to read.

In Victorian novels, many paragraphs are very long. They may deal with two or more topics or parts of a topic, and may have no topic sentence or several.

These guidelines are useful when you write an essay in an examination:

a) Make each paragraph 6–12 lines long.
b) Use too many paragraphs rather than too few. Examiners complain if candidates do not start a new paragraph. They rarely complain that there are too many paragraphs.
c) Start a new paragraph when you write about a new part of your topic and each time you make somebody speak.
d) Link your paragraphs. Do not write about the Geography Society in one paragraph and then start to write about frying sausages or buying a pair of shoes. Ideas are linked in your mind, so show the reader the link.

Linking paragraphs

At the start of a new paragraph, there should be a word or expression which links it to the preceding paragraph. The table on page 126 shows you common ways of changing from one topic to another. The column headed 'Words' shows you words that may occur at the start of a new paragraph.

There are many other ways of linking paragraphs (or getting continuity). Your main aim should be to make a smooth change from one point to another when you start a new paragraph.

If you are not sure whether or not it is time to start a new paragraph, start one. You will probably be right and nobody will complain. On the other hand, long paragraphs look boring, so avoid them.

Ideas	Words
1 A change of time	After this Later on The next day Fifty years earlier
2 A change of place	In the next room In other countries Not far away
3 Similarity	Similarly In a similar way Much the same applies to
4 Contrast	On the other hand Despite this, it seems that
5 Modification	However, Nevertheless,

Exercise 1

Choose any passage earlier in this book. Study the author's use of paragraphs.

1 See whether he is following the theoretical method of paragraphing. If he is, find the topic sentences.
2 If he is not following the theoretical method, try to explain why he has started a new paragraph.
3 Look at the first sentence of the new paragraph. What words (if any) link it with the ideas in the preceding paragraph?

Developing ideas

In some ways, writing an essay is like building a house.

Step 1   You must decide what type of house you want, e.g. costing $500,000, $50,000 or $5 million; with two bedrooms or six; with no garden or a large one.

Step 2   An architect will produce a plan, based on your theme. This is the important stage. If there is no plan, you may find a bath in the middle of your dining-room. When you turn on a light switch, water may come out of a tap.
This is like the planning stage in writing a composition.

Step 3   Now the builder starts his work. He does not put the roof up first. He digs the foundations and the channels for the drainage system. Then he works upwards, building the walls and putting in doors and windows (or leaving spaces for them). Next he puts on the roof. Then he starts to work inside the house until everything is finished.

Write an essay in a similar way. Plan it carefully. Then advance step by step, getting things in the right order. If you have made a good plan, there is no problem. If you have not made a good plan, you are in trouble.

<table>
<tr><td>

Exercise 2

</td><td>

Write a composition of 450–500 words on one of these topics. Before you start your composition, write down your theme and give your plan in rough. Do not spend more than an hour on this work.

1. Why I should (or should not) like to be famous
2. My first date
3. Write an article for an overseas women's magazine in which you give information about the ways in which the role of women in your society has changed in recent years
4. Give an account of the thoughts that went through your mind before, during and after any game or athletics event in which you took part
5. Things that annoy me in life

</td></tr>
</table>

41 Finishing a composition

Finish your composition skilfully. Leave a good impression on the reader. The final paragraph should have an air of finality about it and not leave the reader wondering whether the composition has finished or not.

Your final paragraph should not be a hurried few lines. It should be written as skilfully as your opening paragraph. Here are some ways of finishing. They are shown by the letters SCARF.

S = Sum up an argument or give a summary of your main points

C = Climax

This means that you reach the most exciting point in a story and then finish quickly.

A = Air of finality

Use any method which shows the reader that you have finished.

R = Repeat your theme and show that you have proved your point

F = Look into the future

After you have dealt with Pollution, Happiness, Rivers or Dancing in the past and present, consider what may happen in the future. This shows your reader that you have finished.

. . . and then check your essay carefully. Correct any mistakes in it.

Exercise

You have written an essay on a topic in Exercise 2 in Unit 40. Look at your essay again. Write a different final paragraph for it, using one of the methods shown above. Write from 6 to 12 lines.

Test

This is a test of points in Units 36 to 41.

1 In preparing to write an essay or a report, which comes first: the plan or the theme?
2 I have to write a composition in 60 minutes. How long can I spend on finding a theme and making a plan?
3 What is a reasonable length for a paragraph?
4 What can we use DAFTI for?
5 Use DAFTI to find a theme for each of these topics:
   a) Doctors b) Juvenile crime.
6 Mary has to write on the topic 'Describe an interesting building you have visited'. What percentage of her time should she spend on describing her journey to the building? Why?
7 Name three useful ways of starting an essay.
8 Name two useful ways of finishing an essay.
9 In an examination, what colour ink is most desirable? Why?
10 You have just written two paragraphs saying why you think examinations may be harmful. Now you want to start a paragraph giving reasons why examinations may be helpful to students. What words can you use at the start of the new paragraph to introduce your change of topic?
11 How many lines should we put in a final paragraph?
12 Give a possible theme for each of these topics:
    a) Water b) Clothes.
13 Write the opening one or two sentences for each of the topics in (12).
14 What is the quickest way of estimating the length of an essay while you are writing it?

Other basic points

1 Don't copy out the question on your answer paper. This is a waste of time and applies to composition and comprehension questions. Write the number or letter of your topic, and then start your essay. No title is needed.
2 Don't write on alternate lines in an examination. This is a useful method at school because it leaves a space for a teacher to put in corrections and comments. In a public examination, write on each line.
3 Remember to answer all parts of your question. Some topics have two or more parts.
   a) If a topic has more than one part, write the number of parts on the question paper as a reminder to yourself.
   b) Always look back at the original topic two or three times while you are writing your essay. This will stop you from wandering from the point.

4 Don't make a rough copy of your composition and then copy out a final answer. We have mentioned this point already, and so it is repeated as a reminder. It is a waste of time to make a rough draft of the whole of an answer.

5 Try to be original. Use your five senses. Describe what you can see, hear and smell. Give useful details which bring your answers to life and make it interesting. Please see the unit on descriptive writing for further information (Unit 45).

42 What kind of English shall I use?

1 CAN I USE MEMORISED MATERIAL?

a) No – not if you did not write it in the first place. The examiners expect to see the candidate's own work. If you write down an essay copied from a textbook or from the blackboard at school, another candidate may give the same answer. You will both get no marks. Don't memorise essays written by other people.

b) Yes – if it is your own work. You can memorise corrected essays and use extracts from them in an examination.

c) Yes – if you wish to memorise useful expressions like these:

Giving an opinion

It seems to me that . . .

In my opinion, the main reason is . . .

In spite of this, I still believe that . . .

Some people may disagree with me but I think that . . .

I find it rather difficult to agree with this statement because . . .

Introducing a factor or a reason

In addition to this, there is another important factor which we should take into account.

However, there are other reasons for this, and we shall now consider one of great importance.

There are many useful expressions which you can memorise if you want to. This method is helpful to very weak candidates but is not necessary if you are good at English.

2 USE SIMPLE, CORRECT ENGLISH

a) Do not use difficult or uncommon words in an examination. The examiners want to see simple, clear English. Use simple words which you can spell correctly.

b) Do not use too many main or subordinate clauses in one sentence. Put only one or two ideas in each sentence.

c) Form each complete sentence in your mind before you start to write it. Mistakes occur more often if you write half a sentence and then stop to think how to finish it.

d) Use sentences of different length so that there is a variety in your work. Some sentences can be short. Others can be longer but not longer than about two lines.

3 DON'T BE TOO CLEVER!

There are three stages in the development of a writer's style:

■ In the very early stage (at the age of 6–12), a person may write sentences like these:
'I can see a dead man in the road.'
'My uncle is a postman. He works hard.'

■ In the intermediate stage (from the age of 12 to death), we become long-winded because we try to be more accurate. Then we may write sentences like these:

> Although the sun is in my eyes and it is difficult for me to see with any certainty, it seems to me that there is somebody in the road – perhaps a man or youth asleep or perhaps it is a dead body of a male (or a girl wearing jeans), showing that somebody has fallen from a vehicle of some kind or has been involved in a traffic accident.'

> 'A family friend (who lives not far away and visits us quite regularly) is employed by the Post Office, and sometimes delivers mail although his normal work is to sort parcels and he delivers mail only when it is necessary to replace somebody who is on leave or ill.'

Most people are in the second stage. They try to be accurate when they write or speak. Their sentences are long and difficult to understand. If you are in this stage, don't be too clever. Control yourself when you write. Don't write down everything you know.

■ Some professional writers go through the second stage and return to the first stage. Their writing is simple but powerful. We can easily understand what they say. You can find examples of this style in the works of Somerset Maugham, John Bunyan, Ernest Hemingway and John Steinbeck.

Your aim is to try to write in an interesting but simple way. Avoid the dangers of the second stage.

Exercise

Each of these passages is taken from the work of students preparing for the GCE examination. Mistakes have been corrected but the sentence structure has not been changed.

Read each passage and then express the main ideas clearly in your own words. You can copy from the passages. You can leave out or put in words. Use sentences that are easier to understand.

1   (*About space travel*) I realise that scientists have managed to obtain some useful information from space travel but I think it may be a waste of time, money and effort because in most countries many people are unemployed, and the money could be spent on welfare projects which would benefit far more people and perhaps create jobs so that people could support their families properly, especially in rural areas.

2   (*About safety in the home*) There are many causes of accidents in the home and some experts say that the home is a more dangerous place than roads, especially since babies and very old people can be killed or seriously injured in their homes without even going on any bus or vehicle, and so it is necessary for the Government to find out the causes of accidents in the home, and to do something to educate people and reduce the number of accidents.

3   (*About useful hobbies*) This may be a surprise to you because I am a girl but I find woodwork a very useful hobby, and I have learnt a lot from my elder brother who is a carpenter and often brings home wood to make furniture for our family and his friends, so that I can watch him and learn how to make things myself, even if my friends laugh at me and say that this is not suitable work for a girl but I do not care about that because I enjoy my hobby.

AVOID SPEECH FORMS IN WRITTEN WORK

■   We use words such as 'don't', 'I'll' and 'can't' in dialogue or in informal work. In an examination, write the full forms, 'do not', 'I shall' and 'cannot' unless you are using direct speech.

■   Do not use colloquial or slang expressions in formal work.

Colloquial   I was fed up waiting, so I beat it back home.
Formal   I was tired of waiting, so I went home.

Colloquial   Lisa's kind of attractive.
Formal   Lisa is attractive in a way.

Colloquial   That's what I think, and well that's what a heck of a lot of other guys think too.
Formal   That is what I think, and that is what a lot of other people think too.

43 Further practice with basic skills

FINDING A THEME

It is vitally important to find a clear theme for any composition topic.

Exercise 1

Using one or two sentences in each case, give clear themes for two of these composition topics.

1 The uses of electricity
2 Photography
3 'One man's meat is another man's poison.' Can you think of any spheres in which this proverb is often true?
4 'You behaved like an animal,' a judge said to a convicted criminal. What did the judge mean? Was he right?
5 A time when I hurt my leg
6 Bureaucracy
7 Try to account for the tendency in modern times for groups of countries to form regional associations.
8 What lessons can students learn from history?
9 Charity
10 To what extent do clothes reveal a person's character?

MAKING A PLAN

Explain why it is impossible to make a good plan if you have no clear theme. Then answer Exercises 2 and 3.

Exercise 2

Choose one of these topics. Make a clear theme and a detailed plan for the topic. Do not spend more than 15 minutes on this work.

1 Should marriages be arranged or not?
2 Pollution and ways to combat it
3 What contributions can an international language make to international understanding?
4 Drought – its causes and effects
5 Bilingualism

Exercise 3

Choose one of these topics. Make a clear theme and a detailed plan for the topic. Do not spend more than 15 minutes on this work.

1 In which occupations are women better than men?
2 Diets and dieting
3 The importance of religion in the life of man
4 An ideal home
5 The sea

STARTING A COMPOSITION

Give five different ways of starting a composition. Then answer Exercises 4 and 5.

Exercise 4

1 *Choose any topic from Exercise 3. It can be one you have already considered or it can be a different one. Write two different ways of starting your composition. Write 2–5 lines only.*

2 *Choose any topic from Exercise 2. Write an opening paragraph of 6–12 lines.*

Exercise 5

*Choose **one** of the following topics. Write the theme, the plan and the opening paragraph.*

1 Ghosts
2 The pleasures and problems of cycling or hiking
3 Raising money for charity
4 How the police help the public
5 The kind(s) of music I like

---

44 Factual composition

COMMON TOPICS

In recent years, examiners have asked about the following topics. In each case, candidates were asked to write about conditions in their own country, so make sure that you know your own country well. In some cases, questions have been repeated. For example, a question on how news is spread (by radio, television, newspapers, gossip, and so on) has been set at least twice in recent years.

These topics give you a good idea of what examiners have asked about in the past and may ask about in the future.

Travel
Ways of travelling; people met on journeys; types of vehicles or ships; ferries and tunnels; transport generally – and its problems

News
Newspapers; how news is spread; television programmes

Social or living conditions
Your home; poverty; customs and traditions; ceremonies; place where born; facilities for disabled people; evening entertainment outside the home; overcrowding; multi-racial community

Recreation and sport
Pastimes; motor racing or rallies; riding a bicycle or an animal; games and athletics; a park or beach you know well; dancing

Economy and work

Farming and growing crops; cost of living; tourism; market; exports; use of land; occupations and the work of named people; craft and craftwork; features and way of life of the people; currency, gifts, advice to visitors; postal services

Other topics

Climate and its effect on people and their occupations
School or college, subjects, examinations, school societies
Fashions and the role of women
Crime, criminals, justice, punishment
Literature and music

These topics are not surprising. The GCE paper is taken by candidates in a number of countries, and so the examiners look for subjects a) which candidates know something about, and b) which refer to all or most countries. They make sure that there are topics for both male and female candidates.

ARRANGING YOUR FACTS

Check the exact wording of your question. You may expect a question asking about transport in your country but the question may ask only about ways of improving it. You may expect a question asking about the contents of a local newspaper but the question may deal with a different aspect, for example what the 'Letters to the Editor' say.

Find your theme and gather your facts. Then arrange them in a suitable order, as explained in Unit 38. Classify your facts. If necessary, search horizontally and vertically.

Topic   What evening entertainment (outside the home) is there in your district or country?

Horizontally   I think of facilities near my home and then farther and farther from it, e.g. restaurants (eating), cinemas, window-shopping, concerts, sport (playing and watching under lights), lectures and talks, etc.

Vertically   I check through society, working from the poorest social class to the richest to check that I have not omitted anything worth mentioning.

Now how can I classify all the types of entertainment? I can use one of these methods:

Importance   Put the most common or popular types first.

Place   Deal first with those nearest my home. This is not a good method here.

Cost   I can deal with all the free entertainment and then deal with entertainment people must pay for.

Can you think of any other method of arranging the facts?

Topic   Discuss the importance of tourism to your country.

This time I will write down ideas as they come into my mind:

- money spent in shops and hotels
- creates jobs in shops and hotels
- forces the Government to improve facilities – airport, taxis, water – leads to better facilities – parks, convention halls, attractions – for tourists but these are also available to local people
- helps trade; some tourists become interested in business opportunities
- broadens the horizons of many local people, more contact with foreigners

How can I arrange these points in a logical way? Perhaps I can put them in order of importance, starting with money first, since that is the major importance of tourism to my country.

Topic   Discuss the use of land in your district or country.

farming, housing, shops, factories, parks, depots for buses and trains etc., road, railways, reservoirs, industrial estates

How can I arrange all these uses in a sensible way?

a)   I could start at the centre of the business area and work outwards.
b)   I could start with farmers and work in towards the city area.
c)   I could use a historical approach, showing the gradual change of use. I prefer this method. It will be easy for a reader to understand, so I must re-arrange my facts in this way:

Originally   most land for farming; some for villages
Later   less land for farming; more for towns, cities, roads, railway, reservoirs
Now   very little land left for farming; development upwards in tall buildings; land very expensive; offices, factories, depots, and so on; small areas of land used as parks

With this plan, it will not be difficult to write the composition

Conclusion   When you write a factual composition, arrange your facts in a logical order.

Exercise

Write 300 words on one of these topics:

1   If you had a chance, how would you improve education in your country? (Be practical. Do not suggest changes which the country cannot afford to carry out.)
2   How do most people in your country earn a living?
3   The telephone
4   Shopkeepers
5   Ways of preventing or reducing accidents at home
6   A magazine I read regularly

45 Descriptive composition

In a descriptive composition, you usually know what your theme is. You know which person, place or thing you have to describe. The two main problems are:

a) How can I make my description interesting?
b) How can I arrange my points in a sensible order?

I Describing a person

This is one of several possible methods:

a) Give a general impression of the person, e.g. My best friend is a girl aged 17.
b) Describe the outside of the person, i.e. his or her physical appearance, clothes, ways of walking or sitting, etc.
c) Describe the person's character.
d) Say why you like or dislike the person, and perhaps mention some of the things he or she does or has done.

If a person's character is very striking, we can deal with it before we describe his or her appearance.

2 Look for significant details

There is usually something about a person which gives us a clue to his character. It may be his clothes, the way he speaks, his untidiness, wrinkles on his face, a look in his eyes, dirty finger-nails, shining teeth. Try to find and describe details which help the reader to imagine the person you are describing.

Exercise I

Write 5–10 lines on one of these topics:

1 Somebody's hair
2 Somebody's shoes
3 The way a person looks at you
4 Somebody's voice
5 A person's face
6 A person's hands

3 Describing a place

Either start from the centre of the place and work outwards or start from the perimeter and work towards the centre. One method is as follows:

a) Give a short general description of the place, e.g. Mary lives in a valley between two hills.
b) Then describe the place, working outwards from the most important point.

As in 2 above, look for details which quickly help a reader to imagine the place. Use as many of your five senses as you can. In addition to describing what you can see, describe what you can hear and perhaps smell. Sometimes you may be able to describe what food tastes like or what something feels like.

You may be asked to describe a place only at certain times of the day. In other cases, you may be able to describe a place, such as a market, from the time when it wakes up at 4 a.m. until the time when it goes to sleep at midnight. This method gives you more to write about and makes a more interesting composition.

The examiners are always pleased if you use 'local colour', that is, local details which may not be found in another country. You may be able to describe trees, buildings, vehicles or people who exist only in your part of the world. (One advantage of this is that most examiners will not know if you make slight mistakes with your facts.)

Exercise 2

Write for half an hour on one of these topics:

1 Describe the view from a high place such as the top of a hill or a tall building.
2 Describe the outside and inside of any rural shop you have been in.
3 Give an account of the room in which you are now sitting.
4 Write an account for a tourist brochure of any interesting place which you think tourists would like to visit.
5 Describe some of the typical people you see every day on your way to school or work and explain where you see them.
6 Your family is moving to a new house. You can have a room of your own. If you could furnish it as you wish, what would the room look like?
7 Describe any urban or rural scene either late at night or early in the morning.
8 Describe the layout and facilities at a library or community centre.

46 Argumentative (or controversial) topics

Here are examples of argumentative topics:

a) Discuss the factors for and against capital punishment.
b) Equal rights for women? What is your opinion?
c) Family planning

These topics are dangerous because a) some of your arguments may be irrelevant or unreasonable, b) the examiner may disagree with you strongly, and c) these topics are more difficult than writing, for example, about a person or place you know well.

It is easier to write a factual descriptive or narrative essay than to write an argumentative one unless you have had a lot of practice and experience in dealing with controversial topics.

Conclusion   Avoid argumentative topics if you can.

If you decide to write about a controversial topic, try to follow these guidelines:

a) Stay cool. Keep your temper. Sometimes a student starts his essay in a calm manner but he becomes too enthusiastic or interested after he has written for half an hour. Then he unintentionally becomes rude or unreasonable.

b) Don't attack people of a different race or religion. Don't attack people of a different sex. If you write rude things about the place of women in society, your work may then be marked by a woman.

c) Always try to consider both sides of a topic even if you do not agree with one side. It is your duty to be calm and objective.

d) Don't exaggerate. Don't make generalised statements which are untrue, for example:
   (i) Men always consider themselves to be superior to women but actually women are more intelligent than men.
   (There is no proof for either of these statements.)
   (ii) Throughout the world, money is the only thing which people are interested in.
   (This is untrue. Many people are very interested in other things. Not all people are very interested in money.)

e) If you make a claim or a statement, try to provide some proof or examples.

f) Avoid dogmatic words like *always*, *never* and *only*. It is wiser to use words such as *often*, *seldom* and *one of the things*.

Planning

In many cases, you can use this method:

a) Discuss the need for something, e.g. women's rights, capital punishment, family planning.

b) Consider (perhaps in order of importance) the factors in favour of something.

c) Consider the factors against it.

d) Sum up or give your personal view. Try not to introduce new ideas in your final paragraph.

Exercise

Write a composition on one of these subjects. Your teacher will tell you whether to write 200, 300 or 450 words. Remember to be calm and objective.

1. One-party rule as a form of government.
2. Should marriages be arranged by parents or not?
3. The future of the world depends primarily on the work of scientists.
4. 'Examinations should be abolished because they put too much pressure on students.' Discuss this point of view.
5. To what extent is it true to say that there are some jobs for which women are more suitable than men, and other jobs for which men are more suitable than women?
6. Are traditions worth preserving or not? What do you think?
7. Contrast life in a city with life in a rural area and say which you prefer.
8. 'A person's first loyalty should always be to his or her family, and then to his or her country.' Discuss.

9 'A major cause of juvenile delinquency is the increasing lack of discipline at school, at home and in the community.' Do you agree?
10 'Man's technical progress has far outstripped his moral progress in the past two thousand years.' To what extent do you agree with this?

47 Narrative composition

A narrative composition tells a story or gives an account of some event. These are examples of narrative topics:

a) Write a story about a person who helped an enemy or somebody he or she disliked.
b) Describe an attempted robbery at a bank or shop. Assume that you were an eye-witness.
c) Give an account of your first day at a new school.

Making up a plot

In c), we do not need a plot. We can either remember what happened or make it up easily. In b), we can also make up the events, perhaps by remembering a report in a newspaper or a film on television. However, in a) we may have to make up a plot. There is a plot in any original short story or novel.

Think about somebody in trouble. Perhaps he is too ambitious or jealous. Perhaps he has had a quarrel with a friend. Perhaps his house is on fire or flooded. Then the rest of the story is how the person gets out of trouble.

If you have to make up a story, start by putting somebody in a difficult position. Then explain how he or she got out of it.

Dialogue

A story is more interesting if you use dialogue. Remember to use speech forms. Make your characters talk naturally. Start a new paragraph each time a different person speaks. Here is an example, based on a) above;

We were just getting ready to go to bed when there was a knock on the door, and then another. The knocking continued, urgently and loudly. I guessed that somebody was in trouble.

I opened the door and saw a neighbour, Mrs Lee.

'What's . . .?' I started to ask.

She did not wait. 'Can you help me, please? It's my husband. I think he's had a heart attack. He's on the floor. I don't know what to do.'

I called my wife. 'Mary! Can you come, please? It's urgent.' My wife is a nurse, so I knew she would be able to help, much as she disliked Mr Lee.

Short descriptions

There is no space for a long description in a story. Learn to give short descriptions of people and places. To be able to do this, you must keep your eyes open and observe people and buildings carefully. Here are examples of brief descriptions in a story.

> The mugger was a small man, rather like a human rat. The fingers of his right hand were stained with nicotine. He was about 25 years old and wore shabby clothes. The long knife glinted in his hand but it trembled, so I knew the man was nervous.

> The muggers' car was a 2000 Honda Accord, number TZ 1968. It was light blue, in good condition, and with a plastic doll swinging in the back window. I suspected that it had been stolen.

Background

Perhaps you are going to write a ghost story or a detective story or a romance. The story will be more interesting if you can set it in an interesting background. Perhaps your brother or father works for a taxi company or in a bank. Then perhaps you have some special knowledge of how taxi companies work or what happens behind the counter in a bank. If possible, try to introduce some of this special knowledge in your story. It will make an interesting background for the reader.

Characters

In a story, we can describe a character. We can show a person's nature by what he says and does. Try to make your men different from your women. Try to make old women act and speak differently from girls. Try to bring your characters to life – but this is difficult when you have only an hour to write your story.

Exercise

Write about one of these topics. Your teacher will tell you whether to write 200, 300 or 450 words.

1 Write a story to show the importance of using an opportunity when it first comes.
2 A quarrel in the family.
3 Describe an accident which happened in your home or in the home of a friend or relative.
4 You arranged to meet a friend outside a shop or cinema. By mistake, you both waited outside different shops (or cinemas). Explain how this happened and what the result was.
5 Describe an important incident in your life and say how it affected you at the time and later on.

48 Situational composition (using given data)

EXPLANATION

Writing most kinds of composition involves four main tasks:

a) Finding relevant (and interesting ideas) to write about
b) Arranging your ideas in a logical order
c) Using correct English (or any other language)
d) Using the correct layout, e.g. for a letter, report, article, etc.

Most marks are awarded for a), b) and c) in an examination. However, traditional essay topics are sometimes unfair to candidates. One candidate might be lucky and see a subject he knows a lot about. Other candidates may not know much about the subjects. As a result, a composition test may become a test of general knowledge instead of a test of language skills.

To avoid this problem, situational topics are set in many examinations. You may be given information in any of the following forms and asked to use some or all of it:

notes   statistics   statements from witnesses   a map or picture
a diagram or a series of diagrams

In some cases, situational topics are compulsory. In other examinations, you have a choice between a situational topic and a traditional one. You may find that a situational topic is easier because you do not have to worry about finding ideas to write about. However, some situational questions have unintentional traps, so study the following sections carefully.

Exercise 1

Read this specimen question and then answer the questions about it.

Expand the following notes, which were taken from a statement by a witness, into a report of about 200 words which a policeman might write to his superiors. Use only the information given.

3rd March – About 2.30 p.m. – junction of Emendi St and James St – cart crossing junction slowly – blue car came down James St – fairly fast – unable to stop – hit cart – wheel came off cart – load of fruit tumbled on top of car – witness rushed to car with cart driver – passenger getting out – driver trapped – door damaged – witness and passenger pulled driver out of other door – unconscious – phoned police and ambulance – cart dragged to side of road – arrived 2.45 – ambulance arrived 2.47 – driver taken to hospital – witness made statement

Questions

(not given in the specimen paper)

1 How many words are there in these notes?
2 Will you be able to add any details to the information given (without adding new information)?
3 Are you allowed to add new information?

4 Are the short lines (in the notes) dashes or hyphens? Will you use them in your answer?
5 Can you change the order of the facts?
6 Will you use notes or complete sentences in your answer?
7 Which of these sentences shows the correct approach in writing the answer?
   a) At about 2.30 p.m. on 3rd March, I saw a cart crossing the junction of Emendi Street and James Street. Then I saw a blue car coming...
   b) At about 2.30 p.m. on 3rd March, a witness said he saw a cart crossing the junction of...
   c) At about 2.30 p.m. on 3rd March, a cart was slowly crossing the junction of Emendi Street and James Street. A blue car came down James Street fairly fast...

8 Can we use words from the notes or must we use our own words all the time?
9 Which should we write: St or Street?
10 Comment on this way of starting the answer:
   At about 2.30 in the afternoon on Wednesday, the third of March, there was a serious accident at the place where Emendi Street meets James Street. The weather was fine at the time, and the visibility was excellent. There was no excuse for the accident. It happened that a fruit cart was crossing the junction slowly at that time, pushed by an old man who had a boy with him...

   (70 words)

Now do not look at the answers until you have given your own answers.
Cover the rest of the page until you have written down your answers.

Answers

1 87. (This means that candidates cannot add very much. The examiners have given too many words. As a result, most of the answers will be the same, and it will be impossible to tell the difference between good, average and weak candidates. In future, you should expect fewer words – perhaps not more than a quarter of the final length of the answer.)
2 This is possible in theory but unlikely because we have to change 87 words into 200 words. By the time we add prepositions, articles and verbs, there will be no space for details.
3 No. The last sentence of the instruction says 'Use only the information given.'.
4 They are dashes. I will omit them when I write the answer.
5 Yes, this is quite all right.
6 Complete sentences. Notes will be marked wrong.
7 C is correct.
8 You can use words from the notes and your own words. Do *not* try to avoid using words from the notes.
9 Street.
10 The writer has taken about 17 words from the notes and used 70 words in his answer. His final answer will then be about 87 × 4 words = 348 words, which is much too long. In addition:
   a) The writer has added new information not contained in the notes.

b) He has given an opinion about the accident, which is not reasonable here.

Advice

1 Read the instructions very carefully. Underline key words. Make sure that you know who you are. For example, when you write this answer, are you the driver of the car, the person pushing the cart, a witness, a policeman, or somebody else?

2 Find out what you are writing. Is it a letter, a report, an article, a police statement, or something else?

3 Find out who will read your answer, according to the situation. In this case, it will be a police officer.

4 Ask yourself, 'Can I add details or extra information? What do the instructions say?'

5 Ask yourself, 'Must I use all the information in the notes? Can I leave out some points? What do the instructions say?'

6 Always use your own punctuation. Omit dashes. You can combine notes to put three notes in one sentence. You can do the opposite and use two sentences for one note. This is a matter of common sense.

7 Use complete, grammatical sentences. Do not use notes or abbreviations (except those normally used in formal writing).

8 Be prepared to combine notes and change the order of the facts if you think that this is necessary.

9 Write neatly and legibly. Copy accurately from the notes. Spell words correctly.

10 Check your work for careless errors.

Exercise 2

Read the question at the beginning of Exercise 1 again. Then write an answer in about 200 words.

WRITING DIALOGUE

In an examination, you may have to write dialogue (a conversation). The instructions in Exercise 1 could have been: 'Write a conversation between the owner of the cart and the passenger in the car after the accident happened.'

1 Each new speaker starts a new paragraph in dialogue.
2 Make sure that your punctuation is correct.
3 Use speech forms in dialogue.
4 Try to make the conversation natural. Speakers sometimes interrupt each other, make exclamations, repeat themselves, etc. Here is the start of a possible answer:

'It's your fault. You were driving too fast!' Mr Grant, the owner of the fruit cart said. 'Why didn't...'

Mr Brown stared at the man for a moment. 'You must be blind!' he said angrily. 'I wasn't even driving the car!'

'Well, it's your friend's fault!' Mr Grant snorted. 'Look at my cart! Who's going to pay for the damage? Who's going to pay for all my fruit? It was good...'

'Oh, get out of my way!' Mr Brown shouted at him. 'Can't you see there's an injured man there? And all you're worried about is your silly cart and a few rotten oranges!'

Try to find a natural ending for your dialogue. In this case, we could make a policeman appear and tell both men to stop arguing.

Exercise 3

This is a practice exercise to make sure that you know how to set out and punctuate dialogue properly.

Write a dialogue of 10–20 lines for one of these situations:

1 A tourist has just arrived at a hotel in your country. He is speaking to a receptionist at the hotel, and he wants to obtain accommodation for himself and his wife.
2 Mr Green is asking Mr Jones questions about a car which he wants to buy from Mr Jones. They are standing by the car.
3 You are discussing with an overseas friend (who is visiting you) television or radio programmes in your country.

WRITING ABOUT PICTURES AND OTHER MATERIAL

Instead of notes, you may be given one of the following to write about:

a) A picture of a bicycle, tape-recorder or something else. You may then be asked to give advice to a friend who is thinking of buying something similar to the object shown in the picture.
b) A picture of a scene, for example after a storm or accident, or a busy day at a market or airport. For example, the picture may show a flood scene. You may then be asked to pretend that you were held up by the flood, and you may have to say what happened.
c) A series of pictures which tell a story or show a process, such as the manufacture of shoes or some other product.
d) A diagram or a map. For example, you may be asked to describe an imaginary journey made across an island, crossing mountains and streams, etc.
e) Statements made by two or more people who were involved in a fire, a dispute, an accident, etc.

Look at the pictures opposite and then read the text.

If you have to write about pictures, you can follow these guidelines.

1 Give the people names. You can use male and female names suitable for people in your own country *or* you can invent names which suit the race of the people in the picture.

adults: Mr John Green, Miss/Mrs Mary Brown
or John Green, Mary Brown

children: Tom Smith, Susan Jones, Peter Wilson, Anne Taylor, etc.

It is easier to write about people when they have names.

2 Decide whether the actions refer to past or present time. If the pictures tell a story, you will probably need to use the Simple Past tense. If the pictures show a process such as an experiment, study the question carefully. See which of these methods you must use:

First put the mixture in a beaker and heat it.   (orders)
First I/we put the mixture in a beaker and heated it.   (Past)
First the mixture was put in a beaker and heated.   (Past Passive)

3 Quickly find out how much time you can use to describe each picture *or* how many words you must use (if a limit is given). If you are told the time for a question but *not* the number of words, assume that 500–450 words in an hour would be reasonable.

4 Make use of memories expressions, e.g.
Not long after this, ...
At first, Mr X was not sure what to do. Then he decided to...

Look at the first picture on page 145. We can write:

a)   One day last week Mrs Mary Brown decided to go to the market near her home. She wanted to buy many things for her big family. First of all, she decided to buy some oranges, apples and vegetables. She went to Mr Green's stall because she had bought fruit from him for several years. (54 words)

Exercise 4

Continue the story of Mrs Brown and the oranges, as shown by the pictures on page 145. Write for 20 minutes only.

Exercise 5

*Look at the top six pictures opposite. Pretend that you were **one** of these people:*

a)   a person in one of the vehicles held up when the road was blocked
b)   the policeman who arranged for men to move the tree
c)   one of the workmen who came and moved the tree.

In 30 minutes write an account of what you saw, heard and did.

Exercise 6

*Look at the bottom four pictures opposite. Pretend that you were **one** of these people:*

a)   the man who snatched a woman's bag and ran away
b)   the boy or the girl who saw the man take the bag.

Write an account of what you saw, heard and did. Base your account on the pictures opposite. You can add further details if you like. Write for not more than 30 minutes.

147

For several days the water supply has been irregular and some districts have had no water because of a strike by workers in the Water Department. The news editor of a paper asked you, as a reporter, to investigate and then write a report for the newspaper. You made the following notes. Use them as the basis for a news report of about 200 words.

You can omit material in the notes and add additional information.

John Blank

secretary WD staff union; men want 12% increase, housing allowance, pay for overtime; govt refuses discuss claims; strike will continue; public advised boil water

Peter Brown

chief engr WD – govt willing to discuss; men must return to work first; water safe but advises boiling; denies govt slow to take action

Mrs Smith

housewife, 28, two young children – action vital; men's claims fair; danger of disease; some areas no water 2 days; gangsters selling unclean water from lorries

You are a reporter and you interviewed people when there was a serious fire in a hotel. You made these notes. Use them as the basis for a news report of about 200 words. You can add details of your own.

George Brown (electrician)

on night duty – went to 11th floor to repair bell – smelt smoke – went down stairs to 10th floor – saw smoke and flames coming from storeroom – lift out of order – ran down to reception desk – gave alarm

Mary Lee (hotel clerk)

phoned Fire Station – sent porters to warn guests – forced to leave hotel – several guests missing, believed killed – two members of staff injured

Peter Franks (fire officer)

started about 2.30 a.m. – 10 fire-engines used – under control by 4.30 a.m. – seven killed – four injured (incl. 2 firemen) – cause unknown
(See also Unit 53.)

49 Friendly and social letters

You have probably written friendly letters in English before. The purpose of this unit is to check that you are familiar with all the layouts and methods of writing friendly letters.

1 Address

Always give your address at the top of your letter. Do not do what some people do – put it only in the top left-hand corner of the envelope or on the back of it. You can certainly put your address on an envelope if you like (although sometimes this is unwise). In any case, you must put it on your letter. Many people open an envelope and throw it away. A busy person may later find that he cannot reply to your letter because he has lost the envelope.

The British method of giving an address is to start with the smallest point, as in the following examples:

Flat 4D, 4th Floor,	Hut 1516,	946 Rowan Road,
Happy Building,	Farmers' Village,	London SW7 3BH
394 Market Street,	Anytown,	England
Anytown	South Province	

It is not necessary to put a full stop at the end of your address but you can use one if you like. Some people do not put commas in an address now. In the third example, SW7 3BH is the postal (or zip) code.

But be careful in an examination. You may be told that you are studying overseas and have to write to your family. Then you must remember to make up an overseas address, for example

# 5A, Happy Building	# = apartment, and is used in the USA
123 River Road,	CA = California
San Francisco,	
CA 94156	

Exercise 1

If there is space on the blackboard, four students at a time can write their home addresses clearly. The class can point out any mistakes. Another four students can invent overseas addresses in the USA, Canada, Australia and the UK.

2 The date

Put the date below the address or, if you like, to the left of it. Remember that British people put the day before the month. Americans put the month before the day. In some countries, people put the year, and then the month, and then the day. In a British examination, use the British method, for example:

13th March 2001 or 13.3.2001 or 13.3.01

3 The greeting

In an examination, these will be the normal greetings in a friendly or social letter, depending on how well you know somebody:

Dear Mary, Dear Mummy, Dear Miss Smith, Dear Mr Lee,

We never use 'Dear Mary Smith' or 'Dear Miss Mary Smith'. Use a person's given name or his family name (surname) but not both together.

4 The body of your letter

You can start your letter in either of these ways:

Dear Mary,
    Thank you very . . .

or

Dear Mary,
Thank you very much . . .

5 Language

In a letter to a friend or relative of your own age, you can use slang,
speech forms or colloquial expressions. An examiner may not like these,
so it is wiser to use ordinary formal English.

6 The ending

We can use 'Yours sincerely' when ending a letter to a friend. We can use any
of these endings to relatives:

| With best wishes, | With love, | With love to everybody, |
| Yours, | Mary | Peter |

7 Contents of a letter

a) Write simply and clearly.
b) Think about the things the recipient is interested in – not what you are
    interested in. Give details which may interest your reader.
c) Use correct paragraphing.
d) Plan your letter as you would when writing a composition.
e) In an examination, check that you have answered all parts of the
    question.

Exercise 2

In about half an hour, write one of these letters:

1 You were studying overseas and had a minor accident. You spent a week
  in hospital and have now been discharged. Write a letter to your family,
  explaining what happened. Thank them for a letter received just before
  the accident happened.
2 A pen-friend has written to ask you for information about marriages in
  your country because she has to write a paper on 'Marriage Customs' at
  her college. Write a suitable reply.
3 You left school four years ago. Write to a former teacher, asking him (or
  her) if he will kindly write a reference for you. Give details of your career
  since leaving school.

Exercise 3

In about half an hour, write one of these letters:

1 You promised to visit a friend in another part of your country but cannot
  go now because of a family problem. Write to your friend and explain
  why you cannot visit him (or her). Suggest a visit at a later date.
2 You have just arrived in a foreign country on holiday. Write to a relative
  at home. Briefly describe your journey and say that you arrived safely and
  are enjoying yourself.

3 You are the secretary of an alumni (former students) association. Write a letter which can be sent to former students, inviting them to take part in celebrations on the fiftieth anniversary of the founding of your school. Give brief details of the events which will be held. Give the date, time, place and nature of each event.

Exercise 4

Take the corrected form of the letter you wrote for Exercise 2 or 3. Expand it and write a longer letter on exactly the same topic. Spend about an hour on your work.

50 Applying for a job

I Prepare!

If you are going to apply for a job, prepare a month or two in advance. Get any necessary testimonials (or references) and referees.

A testimonial (or reference) is a letter which praises you and recommends you to a possible employer. If a testimonial is 'open' it is often addressed 'To whom it may concern'. It has no greeting or ending. You can read it. There is an example below:

(address)
(date)

To whom it may concern

Miss Mary Blank

Miss Mary Blank has been a student at this school since 1997 and will leave us in a month's time. She has done well in school examinations and is particularly good at English, mathematics and history.

Mary has played an active part in school life and has been a good influence on other students. She is an intelligent, mature and reliable girl who will prove to be an excellent employee. She has some athletic ability and has represented her school in several games.

I am glad to recommend Mary strongly and wish her every success in her future career.

C.M. Lee
(Principal)

A closed testimonial or reference is a confidential one. If it is written about you (or spoken on the telephone), you will not know what is in it. It may be more frank and less pleasant than an open testimonial. It is written in the form of a business letter and contains information about the good and weak points of a person.

A referee is a person who has agreed to answer questions about you if he or she is asked to do so by a future employer. The employer will write directly to your referee, and the reply will be confidential. You must get the permission of a person before you give his or her name as that of a referee.

Exercise 1

Write a letter to your Principal or form teacher, asking if he or she will kindly act as a referee for you when you apply for a job.

2 Get your documents ready

Do not send original documents when you apply for a job. Send photocopies. This means that you should get several copies of such documents as these:

a) Your birth certificate
b) Examination certificates
c) Testimonials.

You can send b) and c) with your application. You may need a) when you have obtained a job.

Using an application form

Government departments and some large companies make applicants fill in an application form. When you have completed the form, you can send it in with a short covering letter like this:

```
Dear Sir,

                Vacancy for an Audit Clerk

     I have pleasure in enclosing my completed
application form in respect of the above post, and
shall be happy to attend an interview at any time
suitable to you.


            Yours faithfully,


     (*Type or print your name)
```

*Put (Miss) if you are a girl. Sometimes it is not easy for a stranger to tell whether a person is a boy or a girl merely by looking at the name.

Exercise 2

Copy the following headings, which may appear on an application form. Then give the necessary information about yourself.

1 Surname (family name):
2 Given names:
3 Sex:
4 Age:
5 Date of birth:
6 Address for correspondence:
7 Telephone number (if any):
8 Education (give dates and names of last two schools attended):
9 Marital status:
10 Qualifications:
11 Nationality:
12 Name of legal spouse:

Preparing a curriculum vitae (CV) or résumé

On the next page is an example of a *curriculum vitae* (Latin for 'an account of my life'), also known as a CV or a *résumé*.

Consider the following points:

a) If you go to a college or university, you can omit details of your primary school from your CV. It is not important.

b) Some people prefer to give their list of schools and jobs starting with the most recent one and working backwards.

c) There may be other headings or details which you should add. A lot depends on the particular job. For example, you may be an excellent singer or musician. In some jobs, this is of no importance or should not be mentioned. In other jobs, this might be a vital factor which you should mention. You might know that the owner of a company is a keen swimmer. If you have won prizes for swimming, you should mention this.

d) Skills: for certain jobs, it may be necessary to mention any experience or qualifications you have in using computers, accountancy, driving, etc.

e) Testimonials: always send copies. Never send originals. Take originals to an interview in case anybody wants to see them.

If you use a CV when you apply for a job, you can send it with a short covering letter, as shown below.

Dear Sir,

Vacancy for an Audit Clerk

I have much pleasure in applying for the above post, and I enclose a copy of my curriculum vitae together with copies of testimonials.

I shall be happy to attend an interview at any time convenient to you.

Yours sincerely,

(Print or type your name)

Curriculum Vitae

PERSONAL DETAILS

Name:	Wilson, Peter John
Address:	84 Market Street, Busytown
Telephone:	123456
Age:	22 Born 14th March 1980
Sex:	Male
Marital status:	Single
Identity Card:	EX 489138

EDUCATION

1998–2000	Busytown Polytechnic
1991–1997	Busytown Secondary School

QUALIFICATIONS

1996	GCE O-level distinctions in mathematics, English, history and geography. Credits in four other subjects.
1998	GCE A-level passes in Applied mathematics, economics and history.

LANGUAGES

(If a knowledge of languages is important, give details of languages you can read, speak or write fluently.)

EXPERIENCE

2000–present	Sales representative, Cityville Computers
1998–1999	Audit clerk, Busytown Electricity Company (part-time)

SPORT

(If you think your employer may be interested in your athletic or sports achievements, give details if they **are good. Otherwise, don't mention them.**)

TESTIMONIALS

I enclose copies of testimonials from the following:
(Give the names of people whose testimonials you enclose.)

REFEREES

You are invited to contact the following for further information about my character and/or work:
(Give the names and addresses of your referees. Give their telephone numbers if you know them.)

When you write a letter of application for a job,

a) Don't ask for special consideration because you have to support sixteen brothers and sisters, four grandparents and other relatives. This approach is never successful.
b) Study the advertisement carefully. Decide what qualifications or experience an employer wants. Try to prove that you have them.
c) Type your own application unless the advertisement tells you to apply in your own handwriting.
d) If you are pretty or handsome and look cheerful, stick your photograph in the top right-hand corner of your CV.

Exercise 3

Type or write your own curriculum vitae. Give it to a friend to check. Then hand it in so that your teacher can check it.

51 Business letters

BASIC POINTS

a) Each company has its own way of writing letters, sending memos, preparing receipts and order forms, writing sales letters, etc. You cannot learn all possible methods from books. When you work for a company, look in the files. Follow the models already used.
b) In many business letters, reference numbers are given – usually near the top on the left-hand side, for example:

Our Ref: AKC/174/16
Your Ref: No. 8 in 1678

c) The name of the recipient of the letter is often put at the left, above the greeting or at the end of the letter on the left.
d) Some years ago, most business letters started 'Dear Sir', 'Dear Madam' or 'Dear Sirs' and finished 'Yours faithfully'.
Many companies no longer follow this method. They prefer to make their letters more personal and friendly, because this is good for business. Thus many business letters now start and end in these ways:

Greeting	Ending
Dear Miss Lee, Dear Mr Smith, Dear Mrs Jones,	Yours sincerely, (British) Sincerely yours, (American)

e) You can put a full stop after Mr and Mrs or you can leave one out. Follow the method used in your company.

Do not put a full stop after Miss or Ms (Miz). Some people use Ms to indicate that a person is a female. Like Mr, it does not show whether the person is married or not.

f) Always keep a business letter as short and clear as possible. State your point politely and then stop.

FORM LETTERS

A form letter is a standard letter which can be sent to many people in similar circumstances. For example, a mail-order company received many orders but was not always able to supply goods quickly. Customers complained when there was a delay, so the company prepared this form letter:

LEFT AND RIGHT LIMITED

Business Building,
City Street,
Anytown

Our Ref:

Dear Customer

Thank you very much for your recent order which we appreciate.

We hope to send you the goods within a few days. Meanwhile, we enclose details of our special offers and feel sure that these will interest you.

Yours sincerely

Manager,
Customer Relations

In this case, a clerk in the company's office can just write in the date, put the reference number and send the letter. The signature can be printed. The company does not bother to give the name and address of the receiver since this will be on the envelope anyway.

Exercise 1

You work for a book company. Design a letter which can be sent to customers who have ordered books. Inform them that the books have arrived and are ready for them to collect. Leave a space so that a clerk can write in the titles of the books.

ORDER LETTERS

There are many kinds of order letters. Some are quite simple, e.g.

```
Dear Sirs

Please supply:

IBM Correctable film ribbons              50
IBM Lift-off Correction Tapes             24
Blank tapes, TDK D-C60                     20

Yours faithfully
```

More complicated orders are not sent in the form of a letter. A special Order Form is used. Information on this type of form may include the order number, catalogue number of each item, exact details or specifications, the number or quantity ordered, the place and method of delivery, credit terms and other information.

COMPLAINTS AND REPLIES

This is the body of a complaint about a watch.

Notes
a) *The writer is annoyed, so he finished with 'Yours faithfully' instead of the more friendly 'Yours sincerely'.*
b) *There is a threat in the last paragraph that, if the company does not repair the watch, the writer will complain to the Consumer Association.*
c) *The writer has tried to give all the necessary information about the type of watch, when and where he bought it, etc.*

```
Dear Sir,

        On 23rd March of this year I bought a Speedo Mark
V watch from an authorised agent in Cityville. It had a
guarantee form which I completed and posted to you.
        Two days later, the watch stopped. I took it back
to the agent who at first tried to avoid responsibility
for repairing the watch. Eventually he accepted the
watch and kept it for two weeks. When he returned it to
me, it ran quite well for ten days. Then it stopped
again. This time the agent (Quick-Sell Watch Company
of 49 Tourist Street, Cityville) refused to accept the
watch, saying that it was not the responsibility of
the agent to repair watches.
        Before I approach the Consumer Association here,
it seems fair that I ask you to repair the watch and to
inform me whether or not your authorised agents should
repair faulty watches.


                        Yours faithfully,

                        J. Brown
```

Here is the reply which Mr Brown received from the makers of the watch. Notice that it is a much more friendly letter. The writer wishes to satisfy the customer and avoid bad publicity.

Dear Mr Brown,

Thank you for your letter of the 18th April. I am very sorry to learn that you are having trouble with your Speedo watch. This type of watch is normally very reliable, so I am puzzled about the trouble you have had.

Normally we expect our distributors and agents to service watches sold by them or under guarantee. I shall be writing to the Quick-Sell Watch Company to discuss this point with them. Meanwhile, I suggest that you take the watch to Central Suppliers, 6th Floor, Central Building, High Street, Cityville. They are our main distributors and will be happy to repair your watch for you promptly.

I apologise for the problems you have met but trust that you will in future get courteous and efficient service from our agents.

Please do not hesitate to contact me if I can be of further assistance.

Yours sincerely,

P.R. Samson
Services Manager

c.c. Central Suppliers
(Our reference 45/147)

Notes

a) When he dictated the final paragraph, Mr Samson was thinking, 'Let me know if you need any help again', but he changed this to the more dignified 'Please do not hesitate to contact me if I can be of further assistance.' He adjusted his language to suit the occasion.

b) Mr Samson has satisfied the customer by suggesting that he will warn Quick-Sell Watch Company, and by arranging for the customer to go to another agent.

Exercise 2

1 A company sent you a bill a month ago and you paid it. The company sent you a receipt. Last week, you received another bill from the company for the same amount. Write a letter of complaint, pointing out that you have already paid the bill.
Give full details of dates, the amount, the receipt number, etc.

2 Assume that you work for the company in (1). Write a courteous letter of apology, explaining what happened.

A ROUTING SLIP

Inside a large company, many matters are dealt with by using a routing slip or a memo (memorandum) of some kind. Here is an example:

WORLDWIDE TRADING COMPANY

ROUTING SLIP

To . . . .

From . . . . Date . . . .

Attach file	Prepare reply
Comment	Pay
For information only	Recommend action
Investigate & report	See me
For necessary action	Signature needed
Note and return	Check figures
Note and file	Estimate needed

Remarks:

Exercise 3

You work in the Accounts Department of Worldwide Trading Company. You have just received a bill from a local company for $3,500 for repairs to a salesman's car. You want further information before you pay the bill.

What will you write on a Routing Slip? Who will you send it to?

MEMOS

The singular word is 'memorandum' and the plural is 'memoranda', but most people use the short forms 'memo' and 'memos'.

A memo is an internal letter, sent by one person in a company to somebody else in the company. The reply may be written on the original memo or it may be on a separate memo.

Here is an example:

MEMORANDUM

```
To:    John Brown, Sales
From:  Peter Smith, Accounts              4 Oct 01

    Do you know anything about this bill for Wilson's
car? It looks as if he hit a tree!

              P.S.
```

MEMORANDUM

```
To:    Peter Smith, Accounts
From:  John Brown, Sales                  4 Oct 01

    This bill is in order, so please pass on to the N.Z.
Insurance Company.
    Wilson's car was hit by a lorry, and the lorry-
driver has admitted the blame. This will be covered
under our knock-for-knock agreement.
    No problem!

              J.B.
```

What is a 'knock-for-knock' agreement?

Exercise 4

You are just starting a small company with a friend.

a) Design a receipt form for use when people pay money to your company.
b) Find out and briefly explain what each of these forms is:
   (i)   an invoice
   (ii) an advice note
   (iii) a debit note
   (iv) a credit note

52 Reports

Reports in daily life

People who work in a government department, for the Police or the Armed Forces, in business or in almost any other field, have to make reports every day, week or month. Here are some common examples

- Teachers have to make reports on students, new textbooks, syllabuses, equipment, accidents in school, trainee teachers, and so on.
- Policemen have to make reports on traffic accidents, thefts and robberies, family quarrels, property lost or found, complaints from the public, gambling offences, and so on.
- Businessmen have to make reports on employees, competitors, new goods, damage to goods, loss through fire or theft, a site for a factory or a new branch, any unusual profit or loss, and so on.

According to legend, Julius Caesar sent a very short report back to the Senate at Rome when he was fighting in Gaul (modern France). He said: 'I came, I saw, I conquered.' Most modern governments would expect a longer report!

Common factors

A report can be a few lines long or can consist of hundreds of pages. All reports must contain this information:

- Who wrote the report.
- Who the report is for.
- What it is about.
- The date.

People who write reports must know the difference between facts and opinions. They must make sure that their facts are correct and in the right order.

A report nearly always has a heading. It often has sub-headings and numbered paragraphs. It may include an appendix or several appendices. It may include maps, diagrams, photographs or other material.

A report may contain no details or many details, depending upon the circumstances. For example, details are needed in a report on a serious accident or the death of a person. No details may be necessary when somebody wants to know only the total sales figure for a month or the number of soldiers wounded in a battle.

Format

A report may take one of these forms:

a) It may be a letter or part of a letter.
b) It may be a separate document, sent with a covering letter.
   (i) It may then follow a fixed format.
   (ii) The writer may decide on the format.
c) It may be a form, e.g. an annual confidential report on an employee.
d) It may be a news report on the radio, on television or in a newspaper.

Exercise 1

You work for a firm that buys and sells many used cars. Design a simple form which an employee can use when he is inspecting and making an offer to buy a used car.

Either follow the format shown below and complete the headings, or design your own form.

	CONDITION		
	good	*fair*	*poor*
tyres – front			
tyres – rear			
bodywork			

Exercise 2

Your company has a warehouse (or godown) which is too small. The manager has asked you to visit the warehouse, estimate future needs and report to him what type of warehouse will be needed, and where it should be. You have written your report. Do not write the report. Write a covering memo or letter (as you wish) to send with the report to the manager for his consideration.

Using headings

We could use these headings for the report in Exercise 2.

Warehouse Facilities

Existing warehouse
Future needs
Possible sites
Cost
Recommendations

The five sub-headings could be numbered 1–5 or given the letters A–E. If letters are used, we can use the numbers for points within each sub-heading.

Exercise 3

If you wrote the following four reports, what headings would you use? (This includes sub-headings.)

1 You are the secretary of the school Geography Society. The editor of the school magazine has asked you to write an annual report on your society.
2 You work in a government department. Somebody has asked you to write a report on the main causes of pollution in urban or rural areas, and to suggest ways of reducing pollution.

3 There have been several accidents at your school recently. Some were inside the school and others were in the playground. The Principal has asked you to write a report on the causes of accidents at school, and then to suggest ways of reducing the number of accidents.

4 You have been working for a company for five years. The company has just appointed a new office boy (or girl). You have been asked to watch the new employee and then write a report about his or her work and conduct.

Exercise 4

Choose one of the situations in Exercise 3 and then write a report without a covering letter. Remember to make clear the date, who is writing the report, who it is for, and a heading to show what it is about. You can use sub-headings if you like. You can number your paragraphs if you like. Use 35–55 lines in all.

53 Talking and writing about pictures

The pictures on the following pages will give you further practice in talking and/or writing about pictures.

169

PART 4

Vocabulary Development

GUESSING THE MEANING

In an examination, don't worry about very difficult words in a passage. You may be able to guess their meaning. There may be no questions about them.
Consider these examples:

■ In the middle of the gentle Indian night, an intruder burst through the bamboo door of the simple adobe hut.

'Adobe' is a difficult word, even for native speakers. It tells us that the hut was made of unburnt sun-dried bricks but if there is no question about this word, we do not need to worry about it in an examination.

■ Following the hospitality creed of his tribe, he walked over to the puzzled young Indian doctor whom his wife had bitten and handed him the cucumber.

Here, 'creed' means 'customs' or 'beliefs' but if there is no question about the word, it does not matter if a reader cannot fully understand it. He can guess the rough meaning from the context.

■ With great dignity, Mohan Singh stood ramrod straight.

We can guess that 'ramrod' is some kind of straight rod. It was once used to push things down firmly inside a gun but is no longer used.

Nearly all examination passages contain some very difficult words about which there are no questions. Guess their meaning or ignore them.

MORE THAN ONE MEANING

Many words have more than one meaning. If you have to explain the meaning of a word, check that you give the meaning which fits the situation.

Exercise 1

Briefly explain the meaning of each word in bold type below.

1 When she said this, the real reason for her visit **struck** me.
2 Be careful of him. He is a really **smooth operator** and will sell you things you don't need.
3 I watched a **minute** insect crawling up the wall.
4 She is an expert on the **culture** of mushrooms.
5 Companies which have a large land **bank** will benefit very much from the sharp increase in the price of land, and will be able to develop large estates.
6 We stopped to admire the neatly **stepped** fields, which reached from the valley nearly to the top of the hill.
7 I saw him raise his rifle. The **report** of the shot was deafening in such a small room.
8 I turned round and saw a **familiar** face in the crowd.
9 A doctor should not become too **familiar** with her patients.
10 Life in the bush is a placid **affair** in which very little happens.

11 According to village gossip, the doctor is having an **affair** with one of his patients.

12 We have discussed this problem for far too long. It is time for us to **get down** to work and find a solution.

13 It is always more difficult to climb up a mountain than to **get down** again.

14 The man spoke so quickly that the reporter could not **get down** everything he said.

15 Mr Brown hoped that he would be promoted manager, so he was rather **put out** when he discovered that somebody else had got the post.

16 It took the firemen two hours to **put out** the fire at the paint factory.

17 Every morning we **put out** our rubbish and a man takes it away.

18 We **pitched** camp on a sandy bank by a small stream.

19 The plane **pitched** and rolled alarmingly as we went through the storm clouds.

20 Zak **pitched** so well in the last game that nobody was able to score a run.

Reminder:
When you have to explain a word in a passage, always consider the exact meaning which it has in the sentence.

Exercise 2

Each of these sentences is ambiguous. Discuss what each sentence could mean. Pay attention to the words in bold type.

1 The **last** owner of the house moved to London a year ago.
2 No one had been manager of the firm **for a long time**.
3 The result of the marathon was **outstanding**.
4 Mrs Brimlow **stood by** her son when he was accused of theft.
5 Mary can **only speak** English.
6 **As** the lorry raced straight towards us, we jumped out of the way.
7 This is Mr Brown. He is a **late** arrival.
8 Peter! What a **fine** thing to say! I'm really surprised.
9 I can't afford to buy **all** these dresses.
10 I want you to **put down** the price.

Exercise 3

*Choose **five** of the words below. In each case, write **two** sentences to show the different meanings which the word can have.*

list   club   bracket   tender   post   conviction   with   late

Exercise 4

*Choose **five** of the following. In each case, write **two** sentences to illustrate the different meanings which the word or expression can have.*

quarry   comb   pay tribute to   take off   dead   fast   in time

Exercise 5

In the following pairs of sentences, the words in bold type are emphasised. Explain the difference between each pair of sentences.

1 a) My **aunt** wrote the second book.
    b) My aunt wrote the **second** book.

2 a) Mary did not vote **against** Peter.
    b) Mary did not vote against **Peter**.

173

3 a) **Trains** don't usually arrive on time.
  b) Trains **don't** usually arrive on time.

4 a) That shop only sells **Citizen** watches.
  b) **That shop only** sells Citizen watches.

5 a) I doubt whether **anybody** can play as well as John does.
  b) I doubt whether anybody can **play** as well as John does.

Exercise 6

Briefly explain the meaning of the words in bold type below. If possible, find a word or expression of similar meaning. Check that you give the right part of speech. Check that you understand the meaning of the word in each sentence.

1 There is an emergency at the moment, and so normal laws concerning the freedom of citizens are **in abeyance**. They will be restored when the emergency ends.
2 The rate of inflation has **accelerated** in recent years.
3 The orchestra played well but their performance was handicapped by the **acoustics** of the building.
4 People who can **adapt** to changed conditions are more likely to survive or to succeed.
5 She is a very obstinate lady and insists on **adhering** to the agreement made with the landlord twenty years ago.
6 Television sets, cars, washing-machines and refrigerators are signs of growing **affluence** in the community.
7 The situation is already bad. Don't do anything to **aggravate** it.
8 I'm not sure whose side he is on. His speech seemed rather **ambiguous** to me.
9 It often happens that the **amenities** of a new town are not very good.
10 Mary has a very **amiable** personality, and has very few enemies.
11 Both countries are building large numbers of **amphibious** craft.
12 We have received an **anonymous** complaint about the admission procedures.

55 Antonyms, synonyms and homonyms

ANTONYMS

Antonyms are words with opposite meanings. If you have to give an antonym for a word, make sure that it is the correct form, i.e. give an adjective for an adjective, an adverb for an adverb, etc. In some cases, you may be asked to give a short phrase. Check that it could be used in the given sentence.

a) Which of these words are acceptable antonyms for 'legal' in the following sentence?

In some countries it is **legal** *to buy and sell gold coins.*

bad   illegally   wrongly   unlawful   allowed   unlawfully   illegal   forbid

b) Which of these words are acceptable antonyms for 'realised' in the following sentence?

Before they **realised** *their danger, flames shot up into the air.*

understand   appreciate   understood   perceived   understanding
appreciating   appreciated   perceive

Exercise 1

Give antonyms for each of the words in bold type. Use a single word in each case.

1   This is an extremely **complex** problem.
2   They acted in a **barbarous** way.
3   Two of the men were found **innocent** of the charge.
4   Rebecca felt quite **nervous** when she attended the interview.
5   We were able to swim **with** the current.
6   Most of the players felt **exhausted** after the game.
7   She made the cake **with** flour.
8   Mara is a rather **innocent** type of girl and knows little about bribery in business.
9   He had some difficulty in getting a suitable post but now I am sure he will do **well** in his new job.
10 This is a **novel** remedy for toothache.

NEGATIVES AND ANTONYMS

Be careful with pairs of words which may look alike but which have different meanings, for example *disinterested* and *uninterested*.

uninterested means 'having no interest in something; not caring about it'.

■ I am **uninterested** in stamp-collecting.
■ I spoke to him about the plan but he was quite **uninterested** and declined to have anything to do with it.

disinterested means 'neutral; not favouring one side or the other'.

■ Can you give me your **disinterested** opinion of this plan?
■ We need somebody who is **disinterested** to give us a fair opinion of the scheme.

Exercise 2

Discuss the ways in which the words in each of these pairs are different in meaning.

1	a) dissatisfied	3	a) unqualified	5	a) unused		
	b) unsatisfied		b) disqualified		b) disused		
2	a) discover	4	a) dispossess	6	a) immoral		
	b) uncover		b) repossess		b amoral		

MAKING NEGATIVES

These are common negative prefixes meaning 'not', 'against', 'badly' or showing a meaning contrary to that of the word to which they are added:

anti anti-	Antibiotics can destroy bacteria. Anti-aircraft guns can shoot down aeroplanes. An anticlimax in a book or film is a part that is much less interesting or dramatic than the preceding part.
contra counter(-)	Mary is right, so don't contradict her. He is accused of being a counter-revolutionary. The assistant manager gave an order but the manager heard about it and countermanded the order.
dis	Susan disagrees with us. I tried to dissuade him from leaving but he refused to change his mind.
il im in ir	illegal, illogical, illiterate, illegitimate improbable, impossible, immoral, immortal, impure, impatient innumerable, inappropriate, inaudible, indecisive irrelevant, irrational, irregular, irresponsible
mal mis	malevolent, malformation, malpractice, a malcontent misbehave, misconduct, miscount, misjudge, mispronounce
non(-)	non-interference, nonsense, non-flammable, non-existent
un	unopened, uneducated, unintelligent, unsympathetic

Exercise 3

Add a prefix to each of these words to make a word of opposite meaning.

1	legible	5	logical	9	flammable
2	proper	6	responsible	10	agreement
3	honourable	7	defensible	11	climax
4	confirmed	8	rational	12	behave

SYNONYMS

Synonyms are words that are very similar or the same in meaning. For example, 'illegal' and 'unlawful' are synonyms.

In English, there are many words that are very similar in meaning but not many that are exactly the same in meaning and use. For example, 'thin' and 'slim' are very similar. However, a girl will object if you say that she is thin but she will not object if you say that she is slim. 'Thin' in this context means 'thinner than you should be' whereas 'slim' means 'suitably slim' and is a compliment.

If you have to give a synonym in an examination, make sure that you choose the correct part of speech.

Give words or short phrases similar to the words in bold type below.

1 Some men have come to **install** the air-conditioner.
2 The men walked about with the **sober** dignity of kings.
3 When he was not invited to the wedding, he considered it a personal **affront**.
4 She was mischievous but not **malicious**.
5 After the accident, he was **admonished** to drive with greater care.
6 The game will begin **forthwith**.
7 Who planned such an **audacious** undertaking?
8 I should have been more careful, **reflected** Peter, and then the accident would not have happened.
9 We discussed the **hazardous** journey ahead of us.
10 Then we made plans to meet any **contingency** which we could possibly foresee.
11 As the taxi went round the bend, it collided with an **oncoming** lorry.
12 The **advent** of television has had a profound effect upon people's lives.

HOMONYMS

Homonyms are words that are spelt in the same way but have different meanings. They have the same sound and spelling but are different in origin and meaning, for example:

■ The sea is usually rough in the **Bay** of Biscay and the **Bay** of Bengal.
■ Many people use **bay** leaves when they cook food.

■ Where are the **rest** of the girls?
■ You should have a **rest**. You look tired.

HOMOPHONES

Homophones are words that are spoken in the same way but which have different meanings and origins. They are spelt differently, for example:

■ Please **wait** for me.
■ What is your **weight** now?

For each of the following words write down a homophone. Then use each homophone in a separate sentence to show that you know how to use it.

Example   maize – maze

We soon lost ourselves in the maze of small streets near the main shopping centre of the town.

1	fowl	6	beech
2	fought	7	medal
3	stake	8	write
4	vale	9	taught
5	birth	10	gate

Briefly explain the meaning of the words in bold type.

1 This is part of the **heritage** which one generation **bequeaths** to the next.
2 We must find an **appropriate** way of settling this matter.
3 His action in cancelling the contract was very **arbitrary**.
4 The delays of **bureaucrats** are **notorious**.
5 The newspapers are urging housewives to **boycott** goods from that country.
6 **Camouflage** is an important means of defence for many smaller animals.
7 I admire your **candour** but advise you to be more **discreet** when you are talking to the manager.
8 Mary stared at the letter **pensively**. Then she said, 'I think it's a **forgery**.'
9 It is unwise to use **colloquial** expressions in formal writing.
10 Motorists caught smuggling goods across the border are liable to have their vehicle **confiscated**.
11 Most dogs seem to have an **implacable** hatred of cats but there are exceptions, particularly when a puppy has been brought up in a household containing cats.
12 Please note that the staff are forbidden to accept **gratuities**. A 10% service charge is added to all bills.

56 Pairs of words

PROBLEMS FOR NATIVE-SPEAKERS

Some native-speakers have difficulty with the following words, and you may find questions about them in an examination. The examiners perhaps think that these words are also difficult for non-native speakers. Check that you understand the difference between the words.

1	a)	affect	4	a)	stationary	7	a)	alternately
	b)	effect		b)	stationery		b)	alternatively
2	a)	compliment	5	a)	magnet	8	a)	economic
	b)	complement		b)	magnate		b)	economical
3	a)	eligible	6	a)	lay	9	a)	industrious
	b)	illegible		b)	lie		b)	industrial

Now check that you know the difference between these words:

10	a)	exhausting	12	a)	valuable	14	a)	illusion
	b)	exhaustive		b)	invaluable		b)	allusion
11	a)	ineligible	13	a)	non-flammable	15	a)	honorary
	b)	illegible		b)	inflammable		b)	honourable

16 a) proceeding	17 a) dissatisfied	18 a) concluding
b) preceding	b) unsatisfied	b) conclusive

SIMILARITY AND DIFFERENCE

How are a house and a flat or apartment a) similar and b) different?

They are both places where people can live. A house is a separate building but a flat or apartment is only part of a building.

Exercise 1

Explain how these words are a) similar and b) different.

1. thin, slim
2. yards, metres
3. seconds, months
4. a clock, a calendar
5. a fence, a hedge
6. a helicopter, an aeroplane
7. a female, a woman
8. a solution, a cure
9. a letter, an alphabet
10. a coach, a bus

PROBLEM WORDS

Non-native-speakers have many problems with vocabulary.

a) In some cases, words have a similar meaning but are used differently – that is, the structure of the sentence is different in some way.

able to; capable of ... ing
1. He is **able** to do the work by himself.
2. He is quite **capable of doing** the work by himself.

answer; reply to
3. Please **answer** my letter as soon as you can.
4. Please **reply to** my letter as soon as you can.

intend, intention
5. I don't **intend to interfere** with their plan.
6. I have no **intention of interfering** with their plan.

consists of, comprises, is composed of
7. Their team **consists of** five girls and six boys.
8. Their team **comprises** five girls and six boys.
9. Their team **is composed of** five girls and six boys.

There are many other pairs of words which have similar meanings but are **used** in different ways.

b) Some pairs of words may (wrongly) seem similar in meaning but are different in meaning and often in usage.

bring, take
Use 'bring' for movement towards where the speaker is or thinks he is.
Use 'take' for movement away from where the speaker is or thinks he is.

1 (Mary is at school.)
My father brought me to school this morning.

2 (Mary is at school but she is writing a composition about her life at home. She therefore imagines that she is at home.)
Every day my father takes me to school.

3 (Mary is at home.)
Yesterday my father took me to school. My mother brought me home.

come, go
Use 'come' for movement towards the speaker and 'go' for movement away from where he is.

borrow from, lend to
▨ I **borrowed** some money **from** my friend.
▨ Peter **lent** some money **to** one of his neighbours.

Exercise 2

In each case, choose the right word from the brackets.

1 Last week my cousin _____ (brought, took) us for a ride in her car.
2 Mary is a very _____ (conscious, conscientious) worker, so you can rely on her.
3 Can you _____ (recommend, introduce) a book on gems?
4 Please _____ (take, bring) this letter to the school office.
5 I _____ (hope, wish) Uncle comes tomorrow.
6 I _____ (hope, wish) Uncle would come soon.
7 Which dress shall I _____ (put on, wear) to the party?
8 Mary likes to _____ (watch, look) the news on television.
9 Two men were arguing in the street. The noise soon _____ (attacked, attracted) a crowd of people.
10 This ring _____ (worth, is worth) at least a thousand dollars.
11 My brother works very _____ (hard, hardly) and usually comes home late at night.
12 Peter has joined the Army _____ (as, like) his brother.

Exercise 3

In each case, choose the right word from the brackets.

1 The fire started _____ (during, while) we were asleep.
2 Two men _____ (stole, robbed) a lady and _____ (brought, took) her bag away but they were caught by the police.
3 Peter should _____ (spend, pay) more attention to his handwriting, and _____ (spend, pay) more time on planning his work.
4 Did somebody tell you to send the cable or did you act on your own _____ (initiative, initiation)?
5 We must find out the _____ (cause, reason) for his absence from the meeting.
6 What was the _____ (cause, reason) of the disaster?
7 There are many thorns on this path, so don't walk along with _____ (naked, nude, bare) feet.
8 When one of the players was injured, the manager _____ (replaced, substituted) him.
9 Can we _____ (replace, substitute) zinc for iron in this experiment?

10 Two people retired in June, and six retired in July. That means that eight people have resigned _____ (altogether, totally) in the past two months.
11 This drink tastes nice. I would _____ (very, much, very much) like to know how you made it.
12 There is no mistake. I _____ (ensure, assure) you that we have checked the invoice carefully.

Exercise 4

Choose the answer which best explains the meaning of the word in bold type.

1 Our company has just **acquired** two new tractors.
   a) bought
   b) purchased
   c) stolen
   d) obtained

2 He is a very **consistent** player and rarely has a bad game.
   a) maintaining the same standard
   b) experienced and skilful
   c) determined and aggressive
   d) courageous and ready to tackle obstacles

3 Mr Blank dislikes motorists, so he may be a **biased** witness whose evidence is not reliable.
   a) reluctant
   b) prejudiced
   c) unpleasant
   d) dishonest

4 When Mrs Brown heard that she had won first prize in the lottery, the news was almost too much for her. She sat down and stared at the floor, **oblivious** of the other people in the room.
   a) overcome by excitement
   b) regardless
   c) not trustful
   d) nervous

5 Mr Green is a **persistent** critic of the electricity company.
   a) sarcastic
   b) convincing
   c) continual
   d) unfair

6 Mrs Blank is coming here tomorrow to give the senior girls a talk on **deportment,**
   a) methods of banishing people
   b) how to walk and sit properly
   c) the reasons for exiling a person
   d) unloading goods from a container ship

7 Under the new regulations, the government can detain people without trial for 30 days **initially** and then indefinitely.
   a) at first
   b) voluntarily
   c) certainly
   d) definitely

8 According to the radio, several **mercenaries** took part in the rebellion, and three of them have been captured.
   a) men who are not satisfied with a government
   b) people who fight for anybody who pays them
   c) members of any opposition party
   d) poor peasants who want more land

9 This decision must not be regarded as a **precedent** for future problems of a similar nature.
   a) warning
   b) excuse
   c) reward
   d) model

10 There is a **cavity** in one of your front teeth.
   a) a filling
   b) a hole
   c) decay
   d) food

---

57 Phrasal verbs

In this unit we will consider some common verbs followed by a preposition, adverb or particle. There are often loosely called 'phrasal verbs' and are very common in English, particularly in speech. There are many different phrasal verbs. For example, there are fifteen different ways in which 'make up' can be used. Here are some examples:

1 We want to buy Mrs Brown a retirement present costing $100 but we have collected only $80 so far. We need another $20 to **make up** the amount required to buy the present.
2 Did you **make up** this story yourself?
3 We must **make up** these pages ready for printing.
4 A plant is **made up** of cells and other matter.
5 The dispenser will **make up** this prescription for you.,
6 Can you please **make** these files **up** into bundles which I can carry?
7 You can take your own cloth to a tailor and ask him to **make it up** into a dress or suit.
8 The fire is nearly out. Please **make it up**. (Put more fuel on it.)
9 We must **make up** regulations for the use of the swimming-pool.
10 Some unexpected guests came, so we **made up** beds for them on the floor.
11 Are you going to accept the offer? You must **make** your mind **up** quickly.
12 I'm sorry you didn't get the contract this time but we'll **make it up** to you by increasing our orders for plastic toys.
13 Don't hold a grudge against him. Shake hands and **make up**. (Become friends again.)

14 He is **making up** to the manager to try to get himself promoted.
15 Before you go on stage, **make** your face **up** properly so that you appear to be much older.

Match the following explanations with the sentences above. They are not in the right order now.

a) compile; devise and write down a list of
b) consists (of); is formed of
c) flattering and trying to impress; always agreeing with and pleasing
d) decide what to do
e) complete; reach the desired total
f) tie up neatly; sort out and tie up
g) put the ingredients together to make medicine; fill an order
h) prepare in an orderly way (for printing); decide on the layout
i) put cosmetics on your face
j) sew it and make a dress or suit
k) compensate you
l) prepared and got ready; constructed with sheets and blankets
m) invent; create
n) forget a quarrel and be friendly again
o) add fuel to it and make it stronger and better

Exercise I

In each case, find one word which we can use to replace the words in bold type. Check that you have used the right part of speech and the right tense or form of a verb.

1 I watched some men **pull down** some old huts.
2 The dentist told Bela that it was not necessary to **pull out** a tooth.
3 The patient is still seriously ill but I am sure he will **pull through** all right.
4 A taxi **pulled up** suddenly and two men jumped out of it.
5 We must all **pull together** to ensure that our team wins.
6 Peter is a popular singer, so he will **pull in** the crowds if we can persuade him to sing on Saturday evening.
7 I'm not sure whether or not we can get the contract but the managing director will be delighted if we manage to **pull it off**.
8 When you reach the drive leading to the next big house, **pull into** it and then stop.
9 We were losing 1–0 at half time but we managed to **pull back** the deficit and draw the game.
10 Don't try to **pull the wool over my eyes**!

SOME PHRASAL VERBS

Check that you know these expressions:

to put out a fire = to extinguish a fire
to put off a decision = to postpone making a decision
to put a speech across well = to impress the audience
to put food away = to put in a cupboard or refrigerator or to eat it
to put by (money) = to save

to put somebody down = to humiliate them or cause them to lose face

to put in a tender = to submit a tender

to put on airs = to become proud or think that you are superior to others

to put somebody's nose out of joint (colloquial) = to upset somebody

to put through a deal = to succeed in a business matter

to put through a telephone call = to make a call or connect somebody with another person

to put up the price = to raise the price

to put up with a person or thing = to endure or suffer

to put back the clock = to change ten a.m. to nine a.m. or to do something old-fashioned or which restores things to a previous condition

to put into a place (on a journey) = to visit or stop at a place

to put down your arms (weapons) = to surrender

to put up a proposal = to submit a proposal to somebody

to put out feelers (about a business proposition) = to make a cautious approach or enquire about a possibility

to put your name down for something = to join, subscribe or agree to do something

to put in for a rise = to ask for an increase in pay

Exercise 2

Find words which can be used to replace the words in bold type and which have a similar meaning. Not all the expressions use 'put'.

1. Why don't you **put up** a plan to expand the company?
2. We shall have to **put off** making a decision until Mrs Smith arrives.
3. Last year, the price of oil was **put up** twice.
4. I'm sorry about the inconvenience but you'll have to **put up with** it until the painters have finished their work.
5. You ought to **put** some money **by**. You may need it later on.
6. A taxi **ran into** the back of a bus.
7. 'I can understand laziness,' Mr Wilson said, 'but I won't **stand for** theft.'
8. On this map, the letter 'm' **stands for** 'metre(s)'.
9. My brother always tries to **get out of** washing up dishes.
10. We wanted to visit Uncle in Canada, so we felt very **let down** when he wrote to say that we could not visit him because he was very busy.
11. The younger wrestler **gave in** when his opponent caught him in a hold from which he could not escape.
12. We were **held up** by heavy traffic on our way to the airport.

VERB + PREPOSITION OR PARTICLE

Check that you know the meaning of these expressions and how to use them:

agree on a course of action
agree to/with a plan
agree to go/come/play
agree with a person
ask for a book
ask her the time/date/way
ask him about the plan
ask somebody to help you

back up (support)
bear out (prove)
blow up (explode)
book up (reserve accommodation)
break away from somebody
break down (stop; fail to work)
break down the cost of a scheme
break in (interrupt)
break into a building (as a burglar)
break into a conversation
break off (stop a friendship)
break out (start of a war)
break out in spots
break out of prison (escape)
break through a fence
break up a meeting (create a nuisance and cause it to finish)
bring about (make something happen)
bring evidence against a person
bring off a deal (succeed)
bring on a heart attack (cause it to occur)
bring out the best in her
bring somebody round (make them conscious again)
bring up children
bring up a query or point at a meeting
bring your friend along with you

call at a place (visit)
call by (visit casually)
call for something (collect it)
call in reserves (summon, bring)
call off (postpone or cancel an event)
call on (visit formally)
call on a person to do something (ask them to do it)
call round and see us tomorrow
call up money (require shareholders to increase the capital of a company)
call up reserves (summon, make use of)
carry on (continue)
carry out (do something)
catch out (detect)
catch up (overtake)
cheer up (console, comfort)
clear up (settle a misunderstanding)
clear up (put things away)
clear up (become better – weather)
come about (happen by chance)
come across (find by chance)
come along with me (accompany)
come at the truth (find out, reach)
come by something (obtain)
come into money (inherit)
come off (succeed)
come on (come with me)

come out (be published)
come round (regain consciousness)
come through an interview (survive, endure)
come to (regain consciousness)
come upon something (find it by chance)
crop up (occur)
cross out (delete)
cut out a picture

die away (a sound becoming fainter)
die down (become weaker)
die of cancer (or another illness)
die off (used to refer to a weed or plant)
die out (disappear or become extinct)
do away with (get rid of or kill)
do in (slang: kill)
do somebody down (colloquial: cheat)
do somebody out of something (coll.: cheat them out of it)
do up your coat (button)
do without (manage without a person or thing)
draw up a document (prepare it)
dress up (put on fine clothes)
drop off (fall off; fall asleep)

end up (finish)
enter a room (no preposition)
enter for a competition
enter into an agreement

fall among thieves (find yourself in bad company)
fall back (retreat in war)
fall back on (rely or make use of somebody when we have to)
fall behind with your rent
fall between two stools (be unable to decide which of two things to do)
fall for a trick (be cheated)
fall for somebody (be infatuated or be cheated by)
Fall in! (of soldiers getting into neat lines or ranks)
fall off (decline or decrease)
fall on a victim (attack him)
It falls outside our jurisdiction. (We have no power to deal with it.)
fall out with a person (quarrel)
fall upon bad times (become poor or in trouble)
find out the truth

get a message across to an audience
get about (manage to move)
get around (visit, travel)
get at somebody (criticise or attack)
get away (leave, escape)
get away with (avoid punishment or detection)
get back (recover something)
get behind with rent (fail to pay it)
get by (coll.: manage to do something)

get in a car
get into trouble
get off (escape punishment)
get on/off a bus/train/ship
get on (make progress)
get out of a car/taxi
get over an illness (recover)
get through a test (pass)
get up a group to go to a party or concert
get up in the morning
give away something
give in (surrender)
give into somebody (yield, submit)
It gives off a gas when heated.
give out (distribute) books
give over (slang: stop talking or arguing about something)
give up (abandon an attempt)

Exercise 3

Find words which can be used to replace the words in bold type and which have a similar meaning. All the expressions are taken from the lists in this unit.

1 We must all **pull together** to make sure that our team wins.
2 You must **put** your application **in** before the end of the month.
3 Mary has just **put in** for a transfer to the Accounts Department but she doesn't know yet whether she will be successful.
4 Our plane was **held up** because of bad weather.
5 While Mr Jones was speaking to a customer, a clerk suddenly **broke in** and said, 'You're wanted on the phone, Mr Jones. It's urgent.'
6 Mary has **broken off** her engagement.
7 Wayne collapsed and soon became unconscious but a doctor managed to **bring** him **round**.
8 Did you **call at** San Francisco on your way home?
9 If this rain continues, we shall have to **call off** the game.
10 When I was in London, I **came across** an old friend of yours.
11 We had to **give up** our attempt to reach the top of the mountain because of very strong winds.
12 'I'll **do** you **in**!' the accused man shouted at the judge when he was sentenced to ten years in prison.
13 'My brother is always **getting at** me!' Pauline complained.
14 'I'm sure you'll **get through** your driving test at the first attempt.'
15 Do you think we can **get up** a group of at least thirty to go on a coach tour next month?
16 Our company has just **entered into** an agreement to supply concrete for the new dam.
17 The strain of gardening **brought on** a heart attack from which Mr Wilson has never fully recovered.
18 If I were you, I wouldn't **stand for** that type of conduct.
19 I **came upon** these letters when I was looking in an old file.
20 How did he **come by** such an expensive watch?

MORE VERBS WITH PREPOSITIONS OR PARTICLES

Check that you understand these expressions and know how to use them

go against (oppose)
go by bus/rail/sea/air
go for a person (attack – often used of dogs or people)
go for a walk/ride/picnic
go in for (take part in)
go off (explode)
go on and on (keep on doing something, for example, criticising)
go through a newspaper (read or examine it)
go through an ordeal (endure)
go through luggage (customs officers go through the luggage of travellers)
go under (of a company – collapse)
go up (increase)
go without a person or thing (manage without him or it)
grow up (become mature or an adult)

hang on (don't let go; wait)
hold out (maintain your position)

join in (take part in)

keep back (stay back or away)
keep back (retain something)
keep in with somebody (act so that he will like you)
keep off the grass
keep on talking (continue)
keep out of trouble (away from)
keep somebody out (exclude)
keep to your left/right
keep up the good work (continue)
keep up with somebody (go at the same speed)
keep up with the Joneses (live at the same increasingly high standard of living)

leave off (omit; don't wear)
leave out (omit)
to be let off (unpunished)
let off a firework (ignite it)
let somebody down (fail to keep an agreement or obligation)
let out a dress (make it longer)
let out of prison (allowed out)
don't let up (don't stop or give up your efforts)
live down a bad reputation (manage to get over a bad reputation)
live off the land (manage with things growing or found around you)
live on another person (rely on)
live to be a hundred (reach the age of 100)
live up to his reputation (act as people expect him to act)
look after (take care of)
look down on somebody (despise or feel superior to a person)
look forward to meeting her (*Note:* use the gerund and not an infinitive)

look into (investigate something)
look round a flat (inspect it)
look through the files (search for something)
look up to somebody (respect and admire a person)

own up (admit, confess)

pass away (die)
pass out (faint; become unconscious)
pay off (succeed)
pay out money
pick out (select; identify)
pick up from the ground

ring up (telephone)
rule out (ignore; reject)
run a person down (knock down in an accident)
run a person down (say bad things about him)
be run down (feel weak or ill)
run in (colloquial: arrest)
run into a person (meet by chance)
run off with (run away with)
run out of (have no more left)
run over (knock down in an accident)
run through your money (spend it)

see about something (deal with it)
see off (get rid of; force away)
see through a person (know what his real motives are)
see through a trick (detect it)
see to it (attend to it; deal with it)
set off on a journey
set out for London
set up (establish) a company
settle down
show off (act in a way which draws attention to yourself and your ability)
show up (attend, reveal)
stand by a person (be reliable when somebody is in trouble and needs help)
stand out (be obvious or prominent)
stand up to a person (not retreat; be willing to defend your ideas or yourself)

take a dress in (reduce the size)
take a person in (deceive or cheat him)
take a person off (mimic)
take after (be similar to; look like)
take back a statement (withdraw)
take down (write down)
take him down a peg (do something to make a person less proud)
take him for Paul (mistake; think that somebody was Paul)
take him into your confidence
take in what somebody says (understand)
take off clothes
take off surplus weight
take on a challenge (accept)

take out (extract, remove)
take over (be in charge; assume control)
take to her (like her)
take up a hobby
tell off (scold)
think it over (consider it)
think it through (think deeply about something)
think up a scheme (make it up)
throw in your hand/the towel (surrender)
throw up (colloquial: vomit)
try on clothes
try out a new car
turn down (reject)
turn off/on
turn round
It will turn up. (You will find it eventually.)
He will turn up. (He will come in due course.)

use up all your money

wash up the dishes
wind up a watch
wipe out (destroy, remove)
work out a solution
write him off (forget or ignore him because he is no good or not available)

Exercise 4

Briefly explain the meaning of the words in bold type. Not all the words are taken from the lists in this unit but many of them are.

1 When we first met David we were really **taken in** by his smooth manner but later we found out how deceitful he is.
2 *Mrs Chan*: Mary, I think there's something wrong with this plan. I want you to **look into** it.
   Mary: Yes, certainly.
3 While Mr Brown is away, I want you to **take over** his department.
4 I didn't **take to** Mary at first but later on I grew very fond of her.
5 *Mary*: Do you do much swimming?
   Anne: No, I don't **go in for** that sort of thing very much.
6 Guess who I **ran into** when I was in London.
7 Well, I hope I never have to **go through** another operation like that again.
8 Don't try to **keep up with** your neighbours. It is a waste of time and money.
9 Since it was Peter's first offence, the magistrate **let him off** with a warning.
10 Mary really **takes after** her mother, doesn't she?
11 When Mr Lewis was accused of theft, not many of his friends **stood by** him.
12 Have you seen Peter **take off** the manager? It's very funny.
13 Don't **look down on** people just because they are poor or uneducated.
14 They **set off** on their journey as soon as it was light.
15 At the end of the lecture, Inspector Lee **touched upon** the need for young people to resist temptation.

Exercise 5

Find expressions containing 'get' which can replace the words in bold type in the following sentences without changing the meaning.

Example   We expect to **reach** Uncle's house by 7.30 p.m. (*get to*)

1 Please **proceed** with the discussion.
2 My brothers always **rise** at 6.30 a.m.
3 I hope you manage to **pass** your driving test at the first attempt.
4 Two men robbed a bank and managed to **escape** with a lot of money.
5 The police expect to **recover** most of the money when they catch the men.
6 John often tries to **avoid** the task of cleaning his room.
7 Don't bump your head when you **enter** the car.
8 Be careful when you **alight from** the ferry.
9 Shall we **organise** a group to go on a picnic?
10 Mary will soon **recover from** her illness.

Exercise 6

Find expressions containing 'make' which can replace the words in bold type in the following sentences without changing the meaning.

1 That ship is **going** to Manila.
2 Did you **invent** that story or did it actually happen?
3 We need another $50 to **complete** the amount required to buy Mary a present.
4 I can't clearly **see** what this word is. The writing is not clear.
5 If there is a storm, the fishing boats always **sail towards** the nearest port.
6 Strangers will soon **go away** when they hear our dogs barking.

Exercise 7

Write any suitable phrasal verb which we can use to replace the words in bold type. When there are alternatives, give one phrasal verb only. Use the correct tense or form of each verb.

1 Tell the soldiers to **surrender** the weapons.
2 I watched some men **demolish** an old building.
3 We are going to **postpone** the final for a week because of the bad weather.
4 It is not easy to **raise** children if you are very poor.
5 Peter **happened to meet** a friend of yours in London last week.
6 Mary has **abandoned** her plan to become a lawyer.
7 The manager promised to **investigate** our complaint.
8 When we got off the plane, a Customs officer **searched** our bags thoroughly.
9 If you propose it, we will **support** you.
10 A man offered Uncle a lot of money for his land, but Uncle **rejected** his offer.
11 My dentist always tries to avoid **extracting** a tooth.
12 Mr Blank is a very good man. We all **respect** him.

58 Prefixes and meaning

In Unit 55, we considered some prefixes which have a negative meaning or can be used to form the opposite of a word. A knowledge of prefixes is sometimes helpful when you want to guess the meaning of a new word – and when you have to answer this type of question:

What is the meaning of the prefixes (in bold type) in these words?

a) **bin**oculars
b) **semi**circle
c) **tri**angular

d) **bene**factor
e) **vice**-chairman
h) **sub**way

g) **tele**vision
h) **mal**adjusted
i) **pan**-African

These are the answers but they are in the wrong order.

1 all, the whole
2 two
3 in the place of

4 three
5 badly
6 half

7 under
8 well
9 far, a long distance

Study the list in the following table and check that you understand the examples. This is not a complete list of Latin and Greek prefixes. Only the most useful prefixes are given here.

Prefix	Meaning	Example
ab	away, from, off	abduct (take away by force)
ad	to, towards	adjoining (joined to)
ambi, amphi	both	ambidextrous (able to use both hands equally well)
ante	before	antenatal treatment (before birth)
arch	chief	archbishop, arch-enemy
auto	self	autobiography, autograph
bene	well	benevolent, benefit
bi	two, twice	binoculars, bicycle
bio	life	biology (the science of living things)
circum	around	circumference (the distance round)
co	together with	co-operate, cooperate
com, con	with	compete, compare
de	down	descend
demi	half	demigod
dia	across	diameter, diagonal
em, en	in, on	enclose, emplane
equi	equal	equilateral (equal sides)
ex	out	expel, exit
ex-	former	ex-international player
extra	beyond, outside	extraordinary
fore	before	forewarn, foretell
hemi	half	in the northern hemisphere

homo	similar	homophones (with a similar sound)
hyper	above, over	hyper-sensitive (very sensitive)
in	in	inject, invade
inter	among, between	interrupt, intermediate
mono	one	monolingual (speaking one language)
multi	many	multitude, a multimillionaire
ob	against	obstruct, objection
oct, octa	eight	October (originally the 8th month)
omni	all	omnipotent (all-powerful)
out	beyond, outside	outnumber, outlive
over	above, too much	an overdose, an overcoat
pan	all, the whole	pan-American, pan-Asian
penta	five	a pentagon (with five sides)
per	through	perspire (breathe through the skin)
peri	around	perimeter
phil(o)	loving	philharmonic (love of music)
poly	many	Polytechnic (with many technical skills)
post	after	postscript, postpone
pre	before	prehistoric, premature
pro	for, forward	promotion
proto	the first	protoplasm, proto-Arabic
pseudo	false	pseudonym (an assumed name)
quad	four	quadruplets (4 children born together)
re	again, back, down	reproduce, re-cover, recover
retro	back(ward)	retroactive, retrospective
semi	half	semicircle, semi-final
sub, sus	under	submarine, suspend
super	more than	superman, superlative
tele	a long distance	telephone, television
trans	across	transfer, transatlantic
tre, tri	three	triangle, tripod
ultra	beyond, extremely	ultra-cautious, ultra-modern
under	below	undergrowth, undergraduate
uni	one	unanimous (with one mind)
vice	in the place of	vice-chairman
with	against, back	withstand, withhold

Exercise 1

Look at the following words and then in each case:

a) write down the meaning of the part in bold type
b) briefly explain the meaning of the whole word.

1 **trans**-Pacific
2 to **ante**date

3 **anti**-revolutionary
4 the **ex**-chairman
5 an **auto**biography
6 **ambi**guous
7 **sub**normal
8 **under**nourished
9 **post**natal
10 **extra**mural (studies)
11 a **mono**tonous speech
12 a **bio**logist

Exercise 2

Follow the instructions in Exercise 1 for these words:

1 **ab**sent
2 **arch**angel
3 **bene**volent
4 **dia**meter
5 **tele**gram
6 **with**hold
7 a **bio**chemist
8 to **circum**navigate the world
9 a **co**operative
10 **equi**distant
11 **poly**gamy
12 an **octo**pus

WORDS FROM LATIN

Some experts estimate that at least 80 per cent of English words have come from Latin words. Sometimes it is useful if you know the meaning of a Latin word because you can then guess the meaning of a new English word.

Latin	English meaning	English words
amo	I like or love	amorous, amateur, amiable
duo	two	duet, dual, duel

Exercise 3

Look at these Latin words and their English meanings (given in brackets). Then say or write English words which are derived from the Latin words.

1 labor (work)
2 liber (book)
3 habito (I live)
4 magnus (large)
5 verto (I turn)
6 ager (field) + cultus (tilled, ploughed)
7 manus (hand)

8 manus (hand) + factus (made)
9 annus (year)
10 navigo (I sail)

Exercise 4

Say or write English words which are derived from these Latin words.

1 contra (against)
2 dictus (said, spoken)
3 cubile (bed)
4 femina (woman)
5 exspecto (I wait for)
6 occupo (I seize)
7 mare (the sea)
8 miser (wretched, unhappy)
9 septem (seven)
10 satis (enough) + factus (made)

Exercise 5

Can you guess the English meaning of these Latin words?

1 elephantus
2 barbarus
3 Britannia
4 captivus
5 confirmo
6 defendo
7 despero
8 difficilis
9 exclamo
10 expello
11 flamma
12 Germani
13 honestas
14 medicus
15 recito

59 Problem words and correct usage – 1

In this unit and the next one, we will consider some of the words which students at this level sometimes use wrongly. Study each example and, if necessary, make up sentences containing the words.

1 Pairs of adjectives ending in -ed and -ing (excited, exciting)

a) A useful (but not always accurate) rule is to remember '*ing* for th*ing*', for example:

an exciting book/game/film/fight/story
a boring book/story/tale/lecture
an interesting scene/sight/view/programme

Use an adjective ending in -ing when you refer to a thing. Then use an adjective ending in -ed to refer to a person, for example:

an excited witness/child/girl/customer/driver

a bored spectator/student/boy/member of the audience
an interested person/spectator/listener

b) A more accurate rule is to say that an -ed adjective shows what has already happened to a person or thing. The result may have no effect on somebody who sees the person or thing.

Examples

I saw a **damaged** car. We heard the **injured** man call us.
'I' was not damaged. 'We' were not injured.

Then an adjective ending in -ing shows the effect which a person or thing has on us.

Examples

We watched a **boring** film. Mary saw an **interesting** game.

The film made us bored. The game made Mary interested in it.

Exercise 1

Choose the correct word from the brackets.

(*bored, boring*)
  1 We agreed that the concert was rather _____ and so we felt _____ .
  2 The film was _____ and so we turned the television off.
  3 In adult life, work is often _____ but we have to do it.

(*excited, exciting*)
  4 I was very _____ when I heard the good news.
  5 The winner of the competition was so _____ that she started to cry.
  6 I've got some _____ news to tell you.

(*frustrated, frustrating*)
  7 Mary applied for a job but felt _____ when she was not even invited to attend an interview.
  8 It is _____ to go shopping and then discover that you have left all your money at home. You will feel very _____ if you return home and find that the keys are inside your home and there is nobody in.

2 Absent, absence

With the exception of 'equivalent' (which can be used as a noun or as an adjective), words ending in 'ce' are nouns, and words ending in 'nt' are adjectives (when dealing with pairs of words like 'absent' and 'absence').

■ Who is absent today? (adjective)
■ Can you explain your absence from work? (noun)

Choose the correct word from the brackets.

(*different, difference*)

1 What is the _____ between 'ago' and 'previously'?
2 Is there any _____ between these two words?
3 I don't like this watch. I must get a _____ one.
4 Mary can never understand the _____ between purple and mauve.

(*silence, silent*)

5 Please be _____ in the library.
6 _____ is necessary so that students can concentrate on their work.
7 When I asked him for an explanation, he remained _____.
8 His _____ seemed to be an admission of guilt.

3 Practice, practise

'c' comes before 's' in the alphabet. 'n' comes before 'v'. Thus:

ce – noun
se – verb (also '-sed' and '-sing')

a) You must **practise** more often. You need a lot of **practice**.
b) He is a **licensed** engineer. His **licence** is on the wall.

4 Problem words

the number – singular   The number of accidents is increasing every year.
a number – plural   There are a number of reasons for this.

(Learn the second example by heart. It will remind you that 'a number' has a plural verb. Then 'the number' must have a singular one.)

more than one – singular   This is illogical but it is a fact.

a) There is more than one way of doing it.
b) More than one of the boys is to blame for this.

dead – adjective   That man is dead. He has died.
die – verb   Every year people die in traffic accidents.

afraid – adjective   Are you afraid of mice? He is afraid of spiders.
fear – verb or noun   Do you fear mice? He fears spiders.

Remember to use a form of the verb 'to be' with 'afraid' and 'dead'. Don't try to turn these words into verbs.

injure   People are injured in accidents but not in war.
wound   Men are wounded in war or when attacked by robbers with a knife.
damage   Cars, buildings and other things can be damaged.

pass   If you use a subject and verb, never use 'past', which is an
passed   adverb or preposition
past   a) He passed me. I will pass him soon.
　　　　b) He walked past me. A cat ran past.

raise	We can raise things. Things rise by themselves.
rise	a) Please raise your left hand.
	b) Can you raise your eyebrows?
	c) Hot air rises.
	d) Prices seem to rise each year.

affect	normally a verb: How will this affect you?
effect	normally a noun: What effect will it have on us?

Words with no 's'

We do not add an 's' to uncountable nouns. We cannot add an 's' to any of these words:

information	behaviour	dirt	fun
knowledge	bamboo	dust	firewood
equipment	bread	drizzle	the following
apparatus	baggage	dictation	gold
laughter	luggage	punctuation	homework
attention	blame	evidence	importance
advice	make-up	rice	something
blood	mischief	rainfall	traffic
jargon	mud	rubble	thunder
slang	poetry	scenery	lightning
mail	charcoal	excitement	
music	conduct	furniture	

Words that keep their 's'

The expression 'to make friends with' is fixed. We cannot omit the 's' even when we refer to only one new friend. This is correct:

There is a new girl in our class. I have made friends with her.

Do not omit the 's' at the end of these words:

Singular words

a lens	The lens in this camera has a crack in it.
a means	It is a means to an end. One means of doing it is bad.
a summons	This summons is from the High Court, and so you must obey it.
a gallows	He was hanged on a gallows. The gallows was made of wood.
an innings	This innings is the most important one in the game.

Plural words or fixed expressions

odds and ends	Put all the odds and ends on the table.
grounds	She has no grounds for a divorce.
surroundings	The surroundings here are magnificent.
contents	The contents are shown on the first page.
take pains	She always takes pains to speak well.
regards	Give my regards to your sister.
congratulations	Please accept my sincere congratulations.
in low spirits	He is in low spirits because of his illness.
plastics	They work in a plastics factory.
make friends with	I will soon make friends with him.
barracks	Their barracks are some distance from here.
the proceeds	The proceeds are to be sent to a charity.
in other words	In other words, the organisation is a charitable on.

living conditions	His living conditions are not very good.
sometimes	Sometimes she helps me with my work.
as follows	The method is as follows....
earnings	His earnings will fall because of the strike.
belongings	Whose belongings are these?
in arrears	They are in arrears with their rent.
come to terms	You must come to terms with the problem.
last respects	We have to pay our last respects to the dead man.
nowadays	Nowadays not many people smoke cigarettes.
rudiments	I have some knowledge of the rudiments of first aid.
second thoughts	On second thoughts, I'd rather not go on Saturday.

60 Problem words and correct usage – 2

Check that you understand these words and know how to use them. Use any new words in your own sentences.

1 Common, popular

Common means *widespread, found everywhere.*
Popular means *liked by many people.*

a) The common cold is very common but it is not popular.
b) In some cities, robbery is common but it is certainly not popular.

2 Confidently, confidentially

Confidently means *feeling sure that we will succeed.*
Confidentially means *in secret; other people must not know.*

a) Emilio entered the competition confidently because he felt sure that he would win.
b) I gave you that information confidentially, so don't tell anybody.

3 Other + singular or plural noun, another

Another means *one other*; use it before a singular noun or as a singular pronoun.

a) Your other friend can have those other stamps.
b) Tell me another story, please.

4 Owe, own

To *owe* (money) is to be in debt; to *own* (property) is to possess something.

a) I owe you $5 and Peter owes me $20.
b) Who owns this shop? My uncle owns it.

5 The young, the poor, the disabled, the rich

We can use the above words (which are normally adjectives) as nouns. Then we do not add an 's' to them. We use a plural verb with them.

a) The rich are not worried about a small increase in income tax.
b) The elderly and the disabled need our help and affection.

6 Amount, number

Amount is used to refer to uncountable nouns; *number* is used to refer to countable nouns.

a) There is a large amount/quantity of tin stored here.
b) A large number of customers complained about the car.

7 Former, latter

Use a singular verb if these words refer to a singular thing. Use a plural verb when they refer to a plural thing.

Singular   John is 18. Paul is 20. The former is a student. The latter is a cashier.

Plural   There are both boys and girls in my class. The former are good at mathematics but the latter are better at English.

Exercise 1

Find and correct the mistake in each sentence. All the sentences are based on material in this unit or the previous one.

1 The delay was very annoyed because we were in a hurry to get to the office before it closed.
2 We were all disgusting by his behaviour and cannot understand why he acted like that.
3 There's not much different between these two colours until you look at them in daylight.
4 A good chess-player needs a lot of patient and the ability to concentrate on his game.
5 My friend advised me to practice until I could type without looking at the keys.
6 The amount of people in the stadium was really quite surprising.
7 There is a number of factors which we must consider in detail.
8 When I bent down to examine the cat, I was sorry to discover that it was died.
9 Take all the furnitures out of this room so that we can use it for a game.
10 Make sure that you clean all the apparatuses before you leave the laboratory.
11 We had a lot of funs at the picnic but Mary managed to lose her bag again.
12 Will the drought have much affect on the crops next month?
13 I can't go out tonight because I have lots of homeworks to do.
14 There are a few points I should like to rise at the next meeting of the committee.
15 I heard somebody shout and then a man ran passed me, nearly knocking me down at the same time.

16 Two men were seriously wounded when a crane collapsed on a building site this morning.

17 Does anybody in your family afraid of cockroaches? I know you're not scared of them.

18 What a pity! I left my belonging in a taxi and didn't take its number.

19 His income is insufficient to match his expenditure, and so he has to find an additional source of money. In another words, he is in debt.

20 Everybody knows that the youngs are very interested in modern music and that many of them can sing or play quite well.

8 Damage, damages

The plural form, *damages* is used only when we speak of compensation awarded by a court or as a result of a dispute. When we refer to damage caused by a storm or in an accident, we never use the plural form.

a) Have you repaired all the damage caused by the fire?

b) Look at all the damage caused by a single accident!

9 Reward, award

We can get a reward when we do something for other people, e.g. catch a robber, recover stolen property, find a lost dog or passport, give information about smugglers, and so on.

We usually get an award for service or skill. For example, a person may get an award (often a certificate) for public service, for bravery, or for skill as an artist, for rescuing a drowning person or for writing poems.

a) Mrs Lee will award the certificates at the annual Speech Day next Saturday.

b) The police have offered a reward for the capture of the men who robbed the bank last week.

10 Unemployed, under-employed

An unemployed person has no job. An under-employed person has a job but not enough work to do.

a) The number of unemployed persons always rises at the end of a school year because some school-leavers cannot get jobs immediately.

b) In some countries, the Government keeps unemployment down by creating two jobs when only one person is needed. As a result, some people are under-employed and productivity is low.

11 On time, in time

Sam was due to arrive by plane at 6 p.m.

a) His plane arrived on time at 6 p.m.

b) I reached the airport at 5.50 p.m. in time to meet him.

In many cases, 'on time' means exactly at a time or very near it. Then 'in time' means at a suitable time before the time of an event.

12 Every + a singular noun and verb

This is a reminder. Use a singular noun and verb with 'every':

a) Every tree has roots and branches.

b) Everybody wants one, don't they? Yes they do.

Notice that in the second example we use 'they' to refer to the singular word 'everybody'. This is because 'he' or 'she' sounds unnatural with a word which has a plural connotation.

13 Let + an infinitive without 'to'

Do not use 'to' in the infinitive after 'let'.

a) The driver let us get in the taxi.

b) Will your parents let you go camping next week?

14 Final -ed

Some students do not pronounce the final -ed at the end of a word. As a result, they forget to use it in writing as well.

Wrong We were very please with the result.
Right We were very pleased with the result.

15 Even if

This sentence is correct:

a) I'm not interested in music, and so I won't go to the concert even if you pay for me.

Here, 'even' emphasises the statement which starts with 'if'. We can put the 'if' clause first:

b) Even if you pay for me, I won't go to the concert.

Do not use 'even' by itself in a conditional sentence.

16 Unable to, incapable of

Do not confuse the above expressions. Notice the patterns of these sentences:

a) He was unable to walk 100 metres by himself.

b) He was incapable of walking 100 metres by himself.

17 Grateful, thankful

Use 'grateful' when somebody has done something for you.
Use 'thankful' when you have avoided something unpleasant.

a) I am grateful to you for your advice.

b) I am thankful that I don't live in the Arctic.

18 No matter whether

After 'no matter' we normally use a 'wh-' word or 'how'. Use 'whether' if there is an alternative. Do not omit it.

a) She won't sell the painting no matter what you offer her for it.

b) She won't sell you the painting no matter whether she likes you or not.

19 Memorise, learn by heart

'Memorise' means 'learn by heart'. Thus we do not add 'by heart' after 'memorise' because that means 'learn by heart by heart'.

a)   We had to memorise a list of words yesterday.
b)   We had to learn a list of words by heart yesterday.

20 Vocabulary, word

These two words are not synonyms. A vocabulary is a *list* of words. It is not a single word. We cannot use 'vocabularies' instead of 'words' in the sentences in section 19.

a)   She has a wide vocabulary. His vocabulary is not so good.
b)   Learn these words tonight.

21 Lower a standard, the standard is falling

Use 'lower' before 'standard'. Use 'fall' after 'standard'.

a)   Some manufacturers seem to have lowered the standard of their goods.
b)   The standard of courtesy seems to be falling.

22 Neglect, negligence

Negligence is more serious than neglect. A farmer may neglect to water his crop. Then the plants may die. That is the farmer's worry and responsibility. However, if a lifeguard falls asleep on duty and somebody drowns as a result, that is negligence. We can express this another way and say that – in most cases – 'neglect' means 'not doing something' but 'negligence' means 'not doing your duty'.

23 A lack of, he lacks, he is lacking in, there is a shortage of

These words often cause problems for students.
Do not use a preposition after the verb 'to lack'.

a)   He lacks experience. We lack information about her.

When using 'is lacking in' use a suitable form of 'to be' before 'lacking'. Then put 'in' after 'lacking'.

b)   In my opinion, they were lacking in experience.

When using 'a lack of' we can use 'There is ...' before 'a lack of' or 'a shortage of'.

c)   There is a lack of information about cloning.
d)   There was a shortage of food at the barbecue.

24 Refrain from, restrain + an object

refrain – deliberately not do something
restrain – stop somebody else from doing something

a)   Although she was annoyed by Peter's remark, Mary refrained from replying.
b)   When the accused man was sentenced to two years in prison, he took off

his shoes and tried to throw them at the judge, but two policemen quickly retrained him.

25 Renovation, innovation

Renovation means *making new again, making repairs.*
Innovation means *a new idea or method.*

a) After extensive renovations, the hotel looked much better.
b) In many parts of the world, television is still something of an innovation.

Exercise 2

Find and correct the mistake in each sentence. Some of the sentences are based on material in this unit but some are not.

1 My father complained that the standard of English is lowering.
2 Sometimes I cannot understand a passage completely because it contains difficult vocabularies.
3 In our history lessons, we have to memorise many dates and facts by heart.
4 His train was due to arrive at 10.30, and it pulled into the station at 10.30 – dead in time.
5 Yesterday there was a chain collision involving five vehicles. It caused a lot of damages but no injuries.
6 When there is a recession, some people lose their jobs and become under-employed.
7 Peter was very tire after the game, so he was glad when a friend gave him a lift home in his car.
8 They won't win the game even they have two international players on their side.
9 We are very thankful to you for the wedding present.
10 Don't wake Daddy up no matter Mr Brown phones or not.
11 My friend accompanied with me to the meeting last night.
12 Some people say that there has been a negligence of attention to grammar in the teaching of English.
13 I could not finish my work because time was not enough.
14 When Mary heard all the shoutings, she looked out of the window.
15 What are the underline causes of the recession? We must look below the surface to find them.
16 Facing with an unexpected increase in his rent, Mr Gomez did not know what to do.
17 Sometimes my father will not let me to watch television late at night.
18 I very agree with the movement to get equal employment opportunities for women.
19 Did you see the letter from Anne on today's newspaper?
20 At first I did not like living in a busy city but as time past I found it more interesting.

Exercise 3

Briefly explain the meaning of the words in bold type.

1 Mary was **dumbfounded** when she read the letter.
2 The meeting passed without **incident** and finished at about 5 p.m.
3 The ship rolled and **pitched** as it ploughed its way through the huge waves.

4 Before he sentenced the men, the judge scolded them for their **sinister** attempt to ruin the reputation of an innocent man.

5 Some workers complain that work in a factory is **monotonous** and should be done by machines.

6 Despite the heat and rain, the patrol advanced **doggedly** towards the hill where the enemy were believed to be waiting.

7 Koi carp are a Japanese **species** which are now very popular because of their beautiful colours.

8 Eels live in **crevices** and are difficult to catch.

9 When we attempted to catch an octopus, it quickly retreated into its **lair** and defied all our attempts to **dislodge** it.

10 When she was peeling some onions, Mary's eyes watered **copiously** until her mother told her to keep the onions under water.

11 When he reached the police station, the man's **belligerence** soon disappeared and he seemed **awed** by the procedures and appearance of the place.

12 During a drought, a forest is particularly **vulnerable** to fire, and this is the time when **arsonists** are most likely to attempt to cause trouble.

13 All members of the police and Parks Department are therefore expected to be particularly **vigilant** and to **interrogate** anybody seen to be behaving in a suspicious manner.

14 One method of containing a forest fire is by creating breaks. These **enable** firemen to move about more freely but their **prime** purpose is to prevent a fire from spreading.

15 Women are still **discriminated against** in many ways. When a party of educationalists was invited to Hong Kong not long ago, not one of the experts was a woman, despite the fact that half the students and most of the teachers are female.

61 Idioms and common expressions

Exercise 1

In one word or a short phrase, explain what emotion or state of mind a person shows when he does these things:

1 licks his lips
2 clenches his fists
3 scratches his head
4 raises his eyebrows
5 shrugs his shoulders
6 bites his lip
7 grinds his teeth
8 stamps his foot
9 winks an eye
10 shakes his fist at somebody

Exercise 2

Say what these expressions mean and when we can use them:

1 He leads a dog's life.
2 Let sleeping dogs lie.
3 He is a dog in a manger.
4 He's really gone to the dogs.
5 I'm dog tired.
6 He is the underdog in this case.
7 You lucky dog!
8 Every dog has his day.
9 It rained cats and dogs.
10 You haven't got a dog's chance.

Exercise 3

Say what these expressions mean and when we can use them.

1 She's like cat on hot bricks.
2 That was a catty remark.
3 He is only the cat's paw for somebody behind the scenes.
4 You silly thing! You nearly let the cat out of the bag.
5 My room is very small. There isn't room to swing a cat in it.
6 Let's wait and see which way the cat jumps.
7 When the cat's away, the mice will play.
8 Even a cat may look at a king, so don't be so proud.
9 That man is a well-known cat burglar and has a bad record.
10 The audience were disappointed, and they showed it with their catcalls.

Exercise 4

Say what these expressions mean and when we can use them.

1 Was there any **under-the-table** payment?
2 He is rather **under a cloud** at the moment as a result of a serious mistake he made last week.
3 There is a new hotel **under construction** not far from my home.
4 When we come **under fire**, keep your head down.
5 That company is **under new management** now.
6 Have you ever lived **under canvas** for more than a few days?
7 In that country, most of the young men are **under arms** now because the Government expects an attack from a neighbouring country.
8 A promise or agreement made **under duress** is not a legal one.
9 She is **under age**, so she must get the permission of her parents before she can marry anybody.
10 The man in charge of the department is **under investigation** as a result of charges made against him in a newspaper.

Exercise 5

Say what these expressions mean and when we can use them.

1 a red-letter day
2 red tape
3 caught red-handed
4 a red herring
5 like a red rag to a bull

6   It made me see red.
7   show the white feather
8   a white elephant
9   a white lie
10 a black sheep

Exercise 6

Say what these expressions mean and when we can use them.

1   to get out of bed on the wrong side
2   to hit the nail on the head
3   to see eye to eye with somebody
4   to kill two birds with one stone
5   to put your foot in something
6   to have a finger in too many pies
7   to have a bone to pick with somebody
8   to feel something in your bones
9   to put the cart before the horse
10 to get your teeth into something
11 to keep an open mind on something
12 to take the law into your own hands
13 to turn the tables on somebody
14 to pay somebody back (in his own coin)
15 to put all your cards on the table
16 to be in a person's good (or bad) books
17 to give somebody a wide berth
18 to get more than you bargained for (in a dispute)
19 to make short work of something
20 to be out of step with somebody

Exercise 7

Say what these expressions mean and when we can use them.

1   to turn a blind eye to
2   to turn a deaf ear to
3   to turn over a new leaf
4   to turn the other cheek
5   to turn the tables on an opponent
6   to turn up at a meeting
7   to turn down an offer
8   He turned up trumps.
9   He didn't turn a hair.
10 He is a turncoat.

Exercise 8

Say what these expressions mean and when we can use them.

1   He is dead right.
2   She was dead on time.
3   You are beating a dead horse.
4   That law is a dead letter.
5   He's waiting for dead men's shoes.
6   to foot the bill
7   to stand on your own two feet

8 The ball is at your feet.
9 He's got cold feet now.
10 He fell (landed) on his feet.

Exercise 9

Say what these expressions mean and when we can use them.

1 eyewash
2 soft soap
3 double Dutch
4 a busman's holiday
5 a fly in the ointment
6 a bad egg
7 a nest-egg
8 a hornets' nest
9 a mare's nest

Exercise 10

Say what these expressions mean and when we can use them.

1 It's like water off a duck's back to him.
2 Blood is thicker than water.
3 She's like a fish out of water in this job.
4 He's a square peg in a round hole here.
5 It's not easy to keep one's head above water with inflation so high.
6 In that case, you must learn to cut your coat according to your cloth.
7 You'll get into hot water if the manager finds out.
8 When she bought that used car, she really bought a pig in a poke.
9 It's about time we buried the hatchet.
10 He is very much under his wife's thumb.

Exercise 11

Say what these expressions mean and when we can use them.

1 to smell a rat (in a plan or what somebody is doing or saying)
2 to put all your eggs in one basket
3 to pull the wool over somebody's eyes
4 to look for a needle in a haystack
5 to take the bull by the horns
6 to give somebody a blank cheque
7 to play second fiddle to somebody else
8 to try to make both ends meet
9 to have too many irons in the fire
10 to take the wind out of somebody's sails
11 to read between the lines
12 to have your back to the wall
13 to make the best of a bad bargain
14 to tighten your belt
15 to get hold of the wrong end of the stick
16 to grease somebody's palm
17 to give somebody a run for his money
18 to be at loggerheads with somebody
19 to be a) thick-skinned, b) thin-skinned
20 to have a card up your sleeve

62 Common errors

In each of the sentences in the following exercises, the word in bold type is wrong. Correct each sentence by using another word or by altering the pattern of the sentence in some way.

Exercise 1

1 I spent a very **agreeing** time with some relatives in England.
2 Thank you for **organisationing** the concert last Saturday.
3 Most tourists find the pyramids of Egypt very **impassive** when they first see them.
4 Last week we went to visit my uncle. When we were **reversing** home, we had a puncture.
5 The sea was very rough, so some of the passengers were **illness**.
6 The shopkeeper was very annoyed with a customer. He waved his fist **angry** at him.
7 In recent years, there has been an increase in **violence** crime.
8 Letters to newspapers often **reflect** that people are dissatisfied with local conditions.
9 Sometimes it is difficult to **discriminate** between rumours and the truth.
10 The policeman **demanded** us to empty our pockets.

Exercise 2

1 I had never seen the man before, so when he spoke to me I did not **response**.
2 As I have pointed out in the **preceeding** paragraph, people have conflicting opinions of the merits of democracy.
3 Mary did not agree with the lecturer, so she could not **restrain** from asking some questions.
4 Are you **rather** sure that the last bus has gone?
5 We had to pay **quiet** a high price for our new house.
6 At most universities there is a shortage of **hostile** accommodation for students, so many of them have to spend a lot of time travelling.
7 Peter is a very good player. He has **shot** several goals for us this season.
8 In future, meetings will take place **alternatively** on a Wednesday or a Friday.
9 Please **assure** that this type of misunderstanding does not occur again.
10 The increase in the price of oil is not very great, so I doubt whether it will **effect** us very much.

Exercise 3

1 According to the radio, there has been a **break out** of rabies about a hundred kilometres away.
2 It is dangerous to **take over** a car on a bend.
3 Firemen wear **inflammable** clothes to protect them when they have to enter a building that is on fire.
4 This competition will **rise** the interest of our customers.
5 Make sure you take the right **root**. The wrong one leads to a disused quarry.
6 My brother has to get up early every morning to **own** his living.
7 Please **note** the bank if you change your address.

8   When I have any free time, I **look** the television with my friend.
9   Hong Kong is regarded as a shoppers' paradise. That is why Hong Kong **arrests** thousands of visitors each month.
10 Whether in a village or a city, a serious fire usually **hazards** the lives of several people.

Exercise 4

1   When we have dictation, the teacher reads out a passage and we **dictate** it down.
2   Susan **maybe** at the wedding on Saturday.
3   Mr Watkins has decided to **abandon** the post of Chairman because of his poor state of health.
4   When do you **anticipate** them to arrive?
5   When there is a sale, the shopkeepers usually **diminish** the prices of their goods.
6   They do this to **attack** customers to their shop.
7   The government has decided not to abolish corporal **penalty** since it is useful in certain cases.
8   You should pronounce the **ending** sound of this word correctly.
9   I must **remind** to bring you those stamps on Monday.
10 There was a severe storm during the night. **According to** it, several roads are blocked by landslides.

Exercise 5

1   I haven't seen Mary for more than six years, so I didn't **realise** her at first.
2   Somebody ran out of a shop and almost **crashed** me down.
3   Last night, a bus **collided** a lorry not far from my home.
4   My friend is very intelligent and does not **abide** fools easily.
5   Your written English is good but you must **spend** more attention to your spoken standard.
6   One of my uncles is very fond of fishing and **pays** a lot of his time to it.
7   We cannot **demand** students to speak English all the time.
8   This diamond is beautiful but I think there is a small **error** in it.
9   We were very **relieve** to hear that all the fishermen had been rescued.
10 There is only a **few** rain in November.

Exercise 6

1   Can you **introduce** us a good hotel in London?
2   **It** is no doubt about his guilt.
3   The thugs rushed into the shop and started to beat **against** the manager.
4   Most of the **machineries** in this factory were made locally.
5   Sometimes it is difficult for the police to **control** order at a popular football match.
6   John admitted that he had **done** a mistake in deciding to become an accountant. He was weak at mathematics.
7   Mary wanted to complain about the food, so she went to speak to the **runner** of the canteen.
8   Tomorrow somebody is going to give a lecture on **nowadays** art in the school hall.
9   **At the old time**, people often had very large families.
10 When my sister came in, I noticed that she was holding a fine **pack** of flowers.

PART 5

Language Practice

63 Word formation and parts of speech

This unit has two main aims:

a) To check that you understand the difference between the various parts of speech
b) to give you practice in making words.

Notice that 'fast' is only a word. It is not a noun, a verb, an adjective or anything else until we use it in a sentence. We can use it in these ways:

As a noun: One of the aims of a **fast** is to encourage people to think of poor people who have insufficient food to eat.
As an adjective: He is a **fast** runner.
As an adverb: She can run **fast**.
As a verb: They must **fast** from dawn until after the sun has set.

Many words which are often used as nouns can also be used as adjectives, for example:

a **factory** worker, a **shirt** factory; a **desk** diary; a **stamp** album; a **dress** shop; a **library** card.

THE PARTS OF SPEECH

There are different ways of naming the parts of speech. This is a traditional method which many people understand:

nouns pronouns adjectives[1]	verbs adverbs	conjunctions prepositions interjections (exclamations)

[1]Including articles

Nouns

Common Proper	a tree, a car, a road, an eye, dust, mud, blood John, Mary, Canada, Paris, Market Street, the Atlantic Ocean
Abstract Collective	laughter, happiness, hatred, wisdom, tolerance an audience, a team, a committee, a congregation

Exercise 1

Form nouns from these words:

1	long	6	simple	11	real	16	persuade
2	hot	7	provide	12	false	17	pronounce
3	conclude	8	deter	13	able	18	explain
4	destroy	9	divide	14	alter	19	inferior
5	explode	10	narrate	15	engrave	20	broad

Answer the following questions

1 When a collective noun like 'audience' or 'committee' is the subject of a verb, do we use a singular or plural verb?
2 Do abstract nouns usually have a plural form?
3 Do all common nouns have a plural form?
4 Which article (a, an, the) do we normally use before an abstract noun?

Plural forms

Check that you know these plural forms:

potato – potatoes[1]
piano – pianos[2]
Jones – the Joneses
spoonful – spoonfuls
passer-by – passers-by
son-in-law – sons-in-law
medium – media
baby – babies
monkey – monkeys
formula – formulae or formulas
thesis – theses
series – series
appendix – appendices or appendixes
bacterium – bacteria

[1,2] If we can eat a noun ending in 'o', its plural form probably ends in 'oes'. If we cannot eat it, the plural form ends in 'os'. An exception is 'pomelo' – 'pomelos'. (This is only a rough guide.)

Give the plural form of these words:

1	tomato	6	chairman	11	mouthful	16	curriculum
2	photo	7	index	12	life	17	octopus
3	radio	8	story	13	antenna	18	parent
4	mango	9	storey	14	museum	19	daughter-in-law
5	donkey	10	theory	15	pendulum	20	Smith

Pronouns

Personal	I know John. **He** lives near **me**.
Possessive	That's not my key. Ah, this is **mine**.
Indefinite	Would you like **something** to drink?
Relative	Anybody **who** wants a ticket must pay in advance.
Reflexive	Mary blamed **herself** for the mistake.
Emphatic	I know the story is true. Mary told me **herself**.
Demonstrative	**That** is Uncle's car. **This** is Mr Brown's.
Interrogative	**Who** told you that story?

In every case, a pronoun is a word used in place of a noun so that we do not have to mention the same noun several times. In some cases, you may be asked what a pronoun refers to, for example:

Peter was worried about the cost of repairs to his motor-cycle. Even if he went to a friend's garage, he reckoned that it would be at least $1,000.

Q. To what does 'it' refer in line 2?

A. cost

Adjectives

An adjective gives us information about a person or thing. Most adjectives are put before nouns or after the verb 'to be'. Some adjectives can be used after such verbs as 'feel', 'become', 'look' and 'grow'.

Unless you are very good at English, it is wise not to use more than two adjectives before a noun because you may not know the correct order.

a) He has an **old**, **battered** car. It is **slow** and **unreliable**.
b) He became **nervous** and looked rather **pale**.
c) When the weather grows **cold**, I become **uncomfortable**.

Form adjectives from these words:

1	danger	7	legend	13	race	19	fool
2	comfort	8	boil	14	horror	20	create
3	brute	9	freeze	15	cube	21	sense
4	suburb	10	absence	16	music	22	child
5	buoy	11	statue	17	walk	23	brother
6	circle	12	use	18	vice	24	omen

When you use a compound adjective, spell it correctly, for example:

■ He is a **middle-aged** man.
■ She is a **well-known** actress.
■ I tore my socks on a **barbed-wire** fence.
■ We need a **bell-shaped** jar.

Verbs

The most important thing to remember about verbs is that, in formal written work, there must be at least one verb in each sentence. It must be a finite verb (= a working verb with a subject) and not a non-finite form (e.g. an infinitive or participle).

Wrong	My brother very excited.
Right	My brother was (is/will be) very excited.
Wrong	I saw an elderly man. Crossing the road very slowly.
Right	I saw an elderly man crossing the road very slowly.
Wrong	There are many accidents nowadays. Because of the great number of cars on our roads.
Right	There are many accidents nowadays because of the great number of cars on our roads.

In this unit we are concerned mainly with vocabulary, so we will not deal with tenses and other forms of the verb here.

These are examples of verbs made from other parts of speech:

danger – endanger
short – shorten

terror – terrify
strong – strengthen
critic – criticise
diverse – diversify

Exercise 5

What verbs can we form from these words?

1	flame	6	joy
2	deep	7	sharp
3	wide	8	threat
4	horror	9	solid
5	belief	10	natural

11	general
12	gulf
13	knee
14	pure
15	popular

Exercise 6

What nouns can be made from these verbs?

1	explode	6	listen	11	seize	16	carry
2	pronounce	7	describe	12	choose	17	clear
3	explain	8	provide	13	know	18	decide
4	annoy	9	rob	14	apply	19	deliver
5	agree	10	burgle	15	behave	20	enclose

Adverbs

Some adverbs end in -ly but some do not. Some adjectives end in -ly.

Adverbs   The dog looked at the food **hungrily**.
                She speaks fast but very **intelligently**.
Adjectives   That girl with **curly** hair is very **friendly**.

We can use some adverbs to add to the meaning of an adjective, for example: unusually, extremely, rather, slightly.

Prepositions

Prepositions such as 'in', 'from', 'by' and 'at' are used before a noun or pronoun. They often start an expression which shows where, when or how something was done.

a) He lost his wallet **on** a ferry.
b) I met Mary **outside** the Rex cinema.
c) Grandfather came **by** train.

Most modern English words have come from German, Latin or French, and there are many prepositions in these three languages. For example, in early German, 'with' often meant 'against', so in modern English we say, 'He had a fight with John', meaning 'against John'.

Notice that prepositions can be used to make a phrasal verb. Please see Unit 57, page 182.

Conjunctions

These are words that link two other words or two expressions. Common examples include 'and' and 'but'.

Exclamations (interjections)

Examples of these include the following (some of which can have several different meanings, depending on the situation):

Oh! Ah! Eh? Ugh! Oy!

Exercise 7

Put in a suitable form of the words in brackets.

1 It will do John good to study overseas for a year. The experience will be the (make) of him and help to (wide) his horizons.

2 The (starve) man licked his lips (hunger) when he saw all the food on the table.

3 If you want to get a new (drive) licence, you must first report the (lose) of your old one to a police station.

4 Mary can play the piano (beauty) but she has to (practice) (hard) nearly every day and this (take) up a lot of her spare time.

5 Mr Smith was accused of (steal) a bicycle but he denied the (allege) and said that he had only (borrow) it (temporary).

6 I'm sorry. All the tickets are sold. Your only chance of (get) one is if there is an unexpected (cancel). Would you like me to put your name on our (wait) list in case some tickets become available?

7 Mrs Lee was horrified when she found that the brakes on her car would not work. (Luck) for her, she managed to turn into a side road, avoid a (collide) with a (park) car, and then come (gradual) to a halt when she came to a hill.

8 As soon as I heard somebody shout 'Fire! Fire!', I jumped up (hurry) and ran to the window. I saw smoke (pour) from a window of the house opposite ours and a very (excite) woman (scream) from the floor above.

9 For marathon runners, (endure) and (fit) are extremely important. The most (success) runners are (usual) over the age of 25.

10 (Impatient) and (care) are two major causes of traffic accidents. Until the (punish) for guilty drivers is more severe, the number of accidents is (unlike) to fall (drastic).

64 Adjectives

CHECK-LIST

Check that you know these points already:

1 Excited, exciting	Use -ing for thINGs. Use -ed for pErsons. (Please see Unit 59.)
2 Absence, absent	Words ending in -nce are nouns. Words ending in -nt are usually adjectives. (Please see Unit 59.)

3 The young	'The young' and 'the poor' are used with a plural verb. We never add an 's' to them. (Unit 60.)
4 Verb + adjective	We can use an adjective after verbs that need another word to complete their meaning, e.g. grow, become, look, seem, appear, turn. (page 214.)
5 How + adjective	a) How kind of you to come! b) How beautiful she looks!
6 As + adjective + as	a) Mary is nearly as tall as her mother. b) He turned as white as a sheet.
7 Adjective + infinitive	a) I'm happy to meet you. b) We were delighted to hear of his wedding.
8 Adjective + preposition	a) I hope she won't be angry with you. b) They are jealous of you. c) He was successful in persuading her to go.
9 Indefinite pronoun + adjective	a) I've got something good to tell you. b) Have you heard anything bad about him?
10 Don't omit final -ed	a) They were tired after the long journey. b) She was delighted with your present.

FORM

In some languages, the form of an adjective changes to agree with the number (singular or plural) and gender of the noun it refers to. With the exception of 'these' and 'those', we do not use plural adjectives in English. The form of adjectives such as 'big' and 'white' is unchanged, regardless of what noun they refer to.

POSITION AND ORDER

Normally, adjectives precede a noun. These are three common positions;

a) Mary has just bought a new cotton dress.
b) The sky was quite red this morning.
c) Your brother looks happy this morning.

When two or more adjectives are used before a noun, they are often put in this order:

determiner, epithet/quality, size, shape, age, colour, origin, nationality, material/substance, gerund/noun.

a) There is a beautiful red dress in the shop window.
b) That's an old Persian carpet.
c) Mary has a cheerful, cooperative attitude.

The order can be changed when we want to emphasise an adjective. In most cases, it is wise to use only one or two adjectives before a noun. Other adjectives can be put in phrases or clauses after the noun.

d) There's a beautiful red dress from China in the shop window. It is made of silk and gold thread.

PHRASES AND CLAUSES

Adjectival phrases and clauses usually come after a noun. Phrases often start with a preposition or a participle. Clauses contain a finite verb.

Phrases
a) The lady **in the back of the car** is Mary's aunt.
b) I picked up a wallet **lying on the floor.**
c) The dog **with the long tail** belongs to my neighbour.
d) Anybody **caught stealing goods** will be prosecuted.

Clauses
e) The lady **who is sitting in the back of the car** is Mrs Lee.
f) I picked up a wallet **which was lying on the floor.**
g) The dog **that has a long tail** belongs to Peter.
h) Anybody **who is caught stealing goods from this shop** will be prosecuted.

Exercise 1

Each of these sentences contains an error in the use of adjectives. Find the errors and correct them.

1 He is very concern about the high rate of inflation and its likely effects on the economy of the nation.
2 Margaret is a rather shy and reserve girl but you will find that she is kind and helpful.
3 I live in a peaceful rural area, so there are not many excited events to tell you about.
4 It may not necessary be a bad idea to ration petrol and restrict the amount used. In fact, it may be quite a good idea.
5 Mary: What's the weather like?
Anne: Well, we've got a blue bright sky and the sun is shining.
6 She can be very sarcastical when she wants to be, so be careful what you say to her.
7 The answer is expected to this type of question is 'No'.
8 When the weather is hot and the humidity is high, I often feel sleepily.
9 The engine of this lorry is useless. We need a complete new one.
10 A lawyer has to speak and write as accurate as possible.
11 I should be much grateful if you would send me a catalogue by airmail.
12 This scheme appears to be rational, inexpensive one.

Exercise 2

Correct any errors in these sentences.

1 When John went to bed, he was lazy to check that the doors were locked.
2 It is unable to live two weeks without water, so take plenty with you and follow the caravan routes across the desert.
3 We were surprised to see how bad he paints. We thought he was a good artist but apparently he is not.
4 Any increase in the price of basic materials is bound to have a harmful effect on the poors.

5 The below examples show common mistakes at this level.
6 Be careful! It is easily to cause an accident in a laboratory.
7 Mr Smith is getting old. He is less active now than previous but he still goes for a walk in the evening.
8 This type of fruit grows quickly and tastes sweetly, so it is very popular.
9 My uncle is a successful businessman, so some people jealous of him.
10 The Government has built an industrious site just outside the city, and many new factories have been built there.
11 Now I will give a brief account of the principal economical factors of my country.
12 Peter's family felt sadly when he left to study overseas.

<table>
<tr><td>

Exercise 3

</td><td>

Correct any errors in these sentences.

</td></tr>
</table>

1 Ants and cockroaches are unwelcomed visitors to our homes but it is difficult to keep them out or get rid of them completely.
2 My sister works in a shirts factory. She is a quality controller and has to check the quality of the finished products.
3 Living in the countryside has several serious disadvantages although it is more peacefully than conditions in a busy city area.
4 Don't worry about any trifle mistakes you find in the report. The editor will correct them automatically.
5 The sharp rise in unemployment is something that is unexpectable to most people – especially to those who cannot get a job.
6 The dentist gave me an injection, so I felt painless while he was drilling the tooth.
7 Be careful how you get the driver out of his seat. He is an injured, so you must be careful how you lift him.
8 I like both the dresses. This one is beautiful but the other one is more elegance.
9 Don't afraid of the dogs. They won't hurt you. Try to show them that you're not scared of them.
10 The kitchen walls were painted light green colour and look quite attractive.
11 He lay on the ground unconsciously until a passing motorist happened to see him.
12 My mother has just bought a white small car and finds that it is very reliable.

<table>
<tr><td>

Exercise 4

</td><td>

Correct any errors in these sentences.

</td></tr>
</table>

1 His comments were critical, surprising but we paid attention to them.
2 My father's friend is honesty and ability, so people respect him.
3 I couldn't hear what Susan said because all the people were talking noisy and joking about the game.
4 In most mountain countries, there is an abundant of rivers which can be used for hydro-electric schemes.
5 When people are oppressed, ill-treated, there is always a danger that they will rebel against the government.
6 As a result of this, most governments adopt a cautiously attitude when considering new laws.

7 When several hours passed without news of the rescue attempt, Mrs Smith became more and more anxiously about her husband.

8 Anne is very imagination and should do well in some kind of creative occupation.

9 The detective questioned Peter for a long time. He could not prove that Peter was guilty but his mind was full of suspected.

10 The number of youth offenders has great increased in recent years, and the Government is going to investigate the reasons for this.

11 Mr Smith is a very will-strong man and is not very tolerant when people disagree with him.

12 There may be a psychology reason for his strange behaviour, so perhaps we should get a medical report.

<h2>Exercise 5</h2>

Express these sentences in a different way. Start with the given words but keep the meaning of the original. You may have to omit words, add words or change the order or form of some words. The exercise does not deal only with adjectives.

1 Silence is necessary in the library.
   You must . . .
2 He managed to persuade her to go.
   He succeeded . . .
3 Nobody noticed that Peter was absent from the meeting.
   Peter's . . .
4 They were tired after the long journey.
   They found . . .
5 We had difficulty in finding your address.
   It was . . .
6 His athletic ability is well known.
   He is a . . .
7 We were very surprised by the news.
   We found . . .
8 The taxi was in front of the lorry.
   The lorry was . . .
9 A friend informed us of the results.
   We . . .
10 It was a cloudy day but we decided to go for a picnic.
   Although . . .
11 'Where are you going tomorrow?' Peter asked us.
   Peter asked us where . . .
12 'Shall we go for a walk?' my friend suggested.
   My friend suggested . . .

65 Agreement

CHECK-LIST

Check that you know these points already. Very elementary points have been omitted since you should know them already.

1 **Every**	We use a singular noun after 'every', and a singular verb after 'every' and its compounds (except in question tags). a) Every country has its own army. b) Everything is ready.
2 **More than one**	Use a singular verb and not a plural one. a) There is more than one hotel in this city. b) Sometimes more than one student is absent.
3 **... of the ...**	In an expression such as 'a bunch of bananas', the subject is the first noun, and the verb agrees with it. a) This bunch of bananas is too large. b) The captain of the team was injured.
4 **People, person**	When we refer to individual people (and not to races), 'people' is plural and we do not add an 's' to it. We can use 'person' as the singular form. a) There's a person standing by the tree. b) The people are waiting for the game to start.
5 **There is**	The verb agrees with the following subject. a) There is a mosquito in the room. b) There are some mosquitoes in the room.
6 **A number – plural** **The number – singular**	a) A number of people are waiting to congratulate you. b) The number of old people has increased in recent years.
7 **Collective nouns**	These can be singular or plural, depending upon the situation. Use a plural verb if the context requires this. a) The audience is a small one tonight. b) The audience are clapping their hands and stamping their feet.
8 **The rest, the remainder, all of, some of, a lot of, most of, the majority**	Use a singular verb when these words refer to an uncountable noun. Use a plural verb when they refer to a plural countable noun. a) The rest of the meat (rice, butter, milk, water) **is bad.** b) The rest of the men(people, cakes, apples) are bad.

9 **Subject – verb**	Sometimes a verb is separated from its subject by many words. When this happens, check back to see what your subject is. Make the verb agree with it. Be careful if you use two verbs with one subject. Both must agree with the subject. a) Sometimes my cousin, who works in a bank and is very accurate at figures, helps me with my homework. b) Mary lives in the same sort of house as most of her friends do but travels to overseas countries as part of her job.
10 **Pronouns must** agree **with the** words they **refer to**	a) The problem of what to do with the cows is a difficult one but it must be solved b) Sometimes a student cannot understand a word, and so he has to look it up in a dictionary or guess its meaning.

Exercise 1

Correct the mistakes in these sentences. They do not all refer to the ten points given above.

1 When students cannot decide on their careers, he sometimes takes the wrong type of job at first.
2 The people who lives near me are farmers.
3 If a town have no policemen, there will be trouble.
4 If someone feels ill, they should go to see a doctor.
5 Most people want to be a respectable man or woman.
6 When we reached the beach, we are surprised to see that the sands was white.
7 Now Tokyo have a population of over eight million people.
8 In most countries, the number of vehicles are increasing every month.
9 As a result, there have been an increase in the number of traffic accidents.
10 Everybody know that it is much hotter in a tropical country than in a temperate one.
11 Each of these pictures were painted by somebody in our school.
12 If there is an atomic war, our future are hopeless.

MORE AGREEMENT PROBLEMS

1 An implied subject

Sometimes a subject may be implied or understood.

a) Five hundred dollars is a lot to pay for a stamp.
   The implied subject here is 'an amount'. If we write the sentence in full, the subject becomes clear:
b) An amount of five hundred dollars is a lot to pay for a stamp.

2 A subject expressed in two ways

We use a singular verb when a subject is expressed in two ways or two nouns are taken together as a single subject.

a) The long and the short of it is that she is going to get married.
b) His son and heir is a man aged nearly fifty.
c) Eggs and bacon is the normal breakfast for most English people.

3 A parenthetical expression

In written work, we can use brackets or commas to mark off a parenthetical expression. In speech, the expression is spoken in a lower tone. Notice that we do not regard the parenthetical expression as part of the subject. It is often introduced by 'with', 'along with', 'together with', 'as well as' or 'in addition to'.

a) My sister (with one of her friends) often goes fishing in a river near my home.
b) The pilot, as well as two members of the cabin staff, was trapped when the plane sank but managed to escape.

4 Plural + verb + singular

The verb agrees with the subject and not with the complement in sentences like these:

a) The mistakes in his work are evidence of his carelessness.
b) Impatience and lack of care were the main cause of the accident.

5 None

Many native-speakers use a plural verb when 'none' refers to a countable noun, and a singular verb when it refers to an uncountable noun.

a) None of the girls have been to this museum before.
b) None of the meat is fit to eat.

Some native-speakers prefer to use a singular verb with 'none' at all times but this is not recommended by the OED or in Fowler's *Modern English Usage*.

6 A pair of socks

Use a singular verb with 'pair'. Use a plural verb if you use 'socks' without 'pair'.

a) This pair of socks is too small.
b) These socks are too small.

Follow the same principle when using 'a pair of' with trousers, spectacles, pyjamas, scales, scissors, shorts, pants, tweezers, gloves, shoes, etc.

7 Who?

We can use a singular or a plural verb after 'Who', depending upon the situation. If we are referring to more than one person, a plural verb will be necessary.

a) Who is that lady in the back of the car?
b) Who are those ladies in the back of the car?

Put in the right form of the verb in brackets.

1 The committee (have) been unable to agree and (have) postponed a decision until their September meeting.
2 The committee (have) given their final decision, so we must abide by it.
3 A large group of shopkeepers (have) asked me to act on their behalf in negotiations with the Government.
4 There (be) a large group of shopkeepers waiting to see you.
5 A large number of people (be) waiting to see you.
6 There (be) a number of reasons why I cannot sign the agreement.
7 The number of hotels (be) increasing every year.
8 We must arrange a meeting when everybody (be) free to attend.
9 Most of the news (be) good today. That (be) a pleasant change.
10 There (be) one or two things I would like to discuss with you when you are free.
11 Some people (say) that eating vegetables (be) better than eating meat.
12 Everyone (want) to live in peace, and nobody (like) wars.

Exercise 3

Put in the right form of the verb in brackets.

1 There (be) only a few important exceptions to this rule and they (be) not very common.
2 If a person really (like) you, he or she will help you when the need (arise).
3 Tell your sister she (need) not return my book until next week. There (be) no hurry.
4 Eggs and bacon (be) two completely different things.
5 Egg and bacon (be) a typical English breakfast.
6 Her friendliness and courtesy (be) definite proof that she will become a popular and useful member of our staff.
7 Singing and playing the guitar (be) what he does best.
8 Everybody in our class (take) part in our annual Sports Meeting in one way or another.
9 Here (be) the missing pieces of the puzzle. They were on the floor.
10 Where (be) the rest of the money? I hope you haven't spent it all.
11 Who (be) the two fastest runners in our relay team?
12 What (be) the names of those two girls?

Exercise 4

Find and correct any mistakes in these sentences.

1 These are some pills which the doctor gave Peter a month ago. We must keep it away from the children.
2 The threat of being late for school do not worry me any more because I have started my own business.
3 When one first start work at a new firm, one should not be too anxious to criticise and make changes.
4 Electricity were discovered during the nineteenth century, as far as I can remember.
5 According to that lady, both this lifts are out of order. She says they have not been working for several hours.

6 May would like to go to the dance but she dares not ask her mother for permission. Her mother is a very strict lady and does not approve of dancing.
7 A lot of the rubber grown here are exported to Japan, American or Europe.
8 Two fifths of forty are sixteen.
9 The price of vegetables have increased during the past year.
10 The news was bad, so Mr Smith looked worried.
11 We were brought up as good citizen, so we must try to do our duty.
12 What can we, as a student, do to improve living conditions?

Exercise 5

Put in the right form of the verb in brackets.

1 There (be) two main blocks in our school, and there (be) at least ten classrooms in each block.
2 Not many people (be) working at this time of night, so there (be) not a lot of traffic now.
3 What (have) caused all these changes? That (be) a difficult question to answer.
4 Rats (be) often found in areas where they can find rubbish or food, and sometimes spread disease from one area to another.
5 The supervisor in charge of a gang of workers (be) responsible for the work of the whole group and (have) to check that everything (be) done correctly.
6 Two of the links in this bracelet (be) broken, so I must get them repaired.
7 All the food (be) contaminated by flood water, so it (be) thrown away two days ago.
8 There (be) not a lot of holes in this road but there (be) too much mud.
9 Mathematics (be) a difficult subject for some students and so (be) physics.
10 Each of the bedrooms in these flats (have) windows facing the sea, so there (be) an excellent view.
11 Somebody (have) forgotten to turn the lights off. Electricity (be) being wasted.
12 What we are proposing (be) good for everybody, so I hope we can rely on your support.

66 Articles

Check that you already know the points under the headings in this unit.

1 Using 'the'

'The' is a weak form of 'this' and 'that' 'these' and 'those'. We use it to refer to particular persons or things.

2 Using 'a' and 'an'

'A' and 'an' are weak forms of 'one'. We use them to refer to any person or thing and not a particular one.

Use 'an' instead of 'a' if the next word starts with a vowel sound when it is spoken. You cannot rely on the spelling of a word.

A	An
a one-way street, a one-armed man	an orange, an octopus
a European	an Englishman
a united party, a union	an umbrella, an urban area
a large apple	an apple
You have left out a 'u'.	You have left out an 'r'.
a sharp bend	an S-bend
a hotel, a history book, a hill	an hour, an honour, an honest man

Exercise 1

Put in 'a' or 'an'.

1 We need _____ sharp axe for this job.
2 I heard _____ very interesting rumour this morning.
3 Did you give him _____ opportunity to explain what happened?
4 This is _____ unique idea and should be _____ instant success.
5 John is _____ orphan. Some relatives are looking after him.
6 Mary works for _____ European airline. She is _____ hostess.
7 That word is spelt wrongly. You have left out _____ 's'.
8 What _____ extraordinary story! It really is _____ horrifying tale.
9 He lives in _____ L-shaped building designed by _____ American architect.
10 It is _____ honour to meet you. I hope you will give us _____ honest opinion of our plan.
11 We are going to have _____ IQ test tomorrow.
12 I don't agree with you. That is _____ one-sided point of view.

3 Plural nouns

As a general rule, do not put 'the' before a plural noun unless you are referring to known or particular things. Compare these sentences:

a) We all know that rooms usually have windows.
b) You know that **the rooms in our house** have windows.
c) It is a fact that tourists buy souvenirs.
d) It is a fact that **the tourists who visit my country** buy souvenirs.

4 The names of countries

We do not put an article before the name of a country unless:

a) it starts with 'United', e.g. the USA, the UK.
b) its name contains the word 'Republic' or 'Union', e.g. the People's Republic of China.

5 Society, the community

'Society' is a very general word. We use 'the community' to refer to a particular community. Thus we often use 'the' before 'community' but not before 'society'.

a) One of my aims is to try to serve the community.
b) One of my aims is to contribute to society in some way.

6 Language

the English language – use 'the'
in English – do not use 'the'

a) It is difficult for us to be fluent in English.
b) It is not easy to master the English language.

7 No article is needed ...

a) after the verb 'play' when a game is mentioned, for example 'play football'.
b) before an uncountable noun which is not qualified, for example 'We can obtain both knowledge and experience by working during the vacation.'
c) before the names of meals (unless they are special ones), e.g. 'What time is lunch?' and 'Have you had dinner yet?'
d) before the names of most festivals and holidays, e.g. 'She came to stay with us at Easter and on Christmas Day.'

Exercise 2

Take out any unnecessary articles in these sentences:

1 It is a hard work to find the meaning in some articles about economics.
2 At the first sight, all cars seem similar but in some the engine is at the back and not the front.
3 Newspapers are useful for the educated people but not for illiterate people.
4 A country can usually make a better progress if it is rich in natural resources such as oil, coal or iron.
5 The expression 'Get lost!' is a slang and should not be used in formal written work.
6 Courtesy is very important because it encourages the customers to visit a shop again.
7 The correct use of prepositions is sometimes confusing even to the native-speakers of English and has been the cause of several arguments.
8 I like going to the beach because you can get the fresh air there and can enjoy the sunshine.
9 Mr Smith's speech brought a loud applause from the audience and a vigorous nod of approval from the chairman of the meeting.
10 A peaceful life is something that all the people want, whatever country they may live in.

Exercise 3

Put in any articles that are needed.

1 Today we are going to learn about the circulation of blood in human body.
2 There are no tenses in Chinese language or in Indonesian.

227

3   If you walk to work each day, you can save great deal of money and use it in an emergency.
4   In some months of the year, insects are real nuisance, especially mosquitoes.
5   In my opinion, the television has bad influence on young people.
6   There will be a lecture at City Hall this evening on the need for industry to diversify in order to cope with the recession.
7   I thought my sister would be surprised when she heard the news but she was as cool as cucumber.
8   After lengthy discussion with my friend, we decided not to go to the barbecue because we had urgent work to finish.
9   My father usually reads newspaper in the evening when he comes home from work. Sometimes he listens to the radio instead.
10 We use 'it' to refer to a baby when sex of the baby is unknown.

Exercise 4

Put in any articles that are needed.

1   According to the police, a number of crimes are committed under influence of drink or drugs. In other cases, the criminal wants to get money to buy alcohol or drugs.
2   Many people suffered from malnutrition when a severe drought struck parts of East Africa and led to serious shortage of food.
3   You will get chance to meet Mr Lee on Saturday because he is the umpire for our game against the High School team.
4   I agree with you to certain extent but not completely, so we will have to agree to differ on one or two major points.
5   Poets and writers often use simile to make a statement more vivid. The simile introduces a concrete statement or comparison to give us a more vivid idea of how some action is done.
6   Please look at the first column of the table on next page and fill in any blank spaces with suitable words.
7   It is duty of a sentry to keep alert at all times during a war or when a war seems imminent.
8   Talking on telephone is not easy if you are not a native-speaker of the language you have to use.
9   Throughout ages, men have tried to understand Nature and to live in such a way that they do not disturb the harmony which Nature has created.
10 After we had been walking for more than half hour, we came to the path that led to the village in which my cousin lives.

Exercise 5

Each of these sentences contains a mistake in the use of articles. Correct the mistakes. It may be necessary to take a word out, put one in or change one.

1   I have explained the regulations which apply to tourists who visit Mauritius, and same rules apply to visitors who go to Singapore or Hong Kong.
2   Cyprus is island near the east end of the Mediterranean and is of considerable importance to countries in that region.
3   Malta has very long tradition and is still a popular place for tourists, who often ask to visit the forts and other places built centuries ago.

4   This is the word for word translation of what the man said when he was accused of attempted robbery.

5   Sometimes we go for picnic when the weather is fine and we have a holiday.

6   My sister is a nurse in a large hospital, and my brother is an university student; he is studying engineering and hopes to be a mechanical engineer one day.

7   One evening when we were having the supper, somebody knocked on our door.

8   In some cities, air pollution has already reached the alarming state and the authorities are introducing laws to restrict the amount of smoke from factories.

9   However, a lot of the pollution comes from vehicles and no adequate way of reducing this has yet been found, despite efforts of scientists in many countries.

10   One solution may be to use vehicles that are powered by the electricity and which thus have virtually no exhaust fumes – and cause no pollution.

67 Cloze passages

A cloze passage is a passage with blank spaces in it. Sometimes every fifth, sixth or seventh word is left out. In other cases, the blank spaces occur at irregular intervals. Cloze passages are a common form of testing.

Here is a short example of a cloze passage.

Example 1

When I woke up this ___(1)___, the sun had only just risen, and ___(2)___ air was quite ___(3)___. There was a lot of ___(4)___, making visibility poor. It was impossible ___(5)___ see more than thirty ___(6)___ forty metres.

(1) morning (*Alternatives such 'afternoon' and 'evening' are wrong because the sun had just risen.*)

(2) the (*It is very difficult to find any other suitable word.*)

(3) chilly, cold, damp, unpleasant (*There are many alternatives but we need an adjective here and not a noun.*)

(4) mist, fog (*We cannot use 'low cloud' if we are allowed to put in only one word at a time. We could use 'smog' or perhaps 'pollution'.*)

(5) to (*Is anything else possible here?*)

(6) to, or

Guidelines

1   Use the right part of speech.

2   Check that your words fit the situation and the sentence pattern. Each word must be grammatically correct as well as situationally right.

3   Always test the word yourself to see that it fits the passage.

4 Sometimes you must read on a few words (or lines) before you know which word to use. We cannot be sure that 'morning' is the right word for (1) in the above example until we read about the rising sun.

5 Make sure that any verbs agree with their subject.

6 Look and see whether nouns should be singular or plural.

7 Make sure that pronouns agree with the words they refer to.

8 Look at the punctuation of the passage. This sometimes shows you what type of word is needed.

9 If you have no idea what type of word to put in a blank space, try each of the eight parts of speech in turn. Try any noun, adjective, pronoun, adverb, verb, preposition, conjunction or interjection. This will usually show you what part of speech to use. You can then look for a word that fits the meaning and situation.

Exercise 2

Yesterday morning I had an unusual ___(1)___ on my way ___(2)___ school. I heard somebody ___(3)___ me and saw a friend on the ___(4)___ side of the road. I knew he was ___(5)___ to school, too, so I decided to ___(6)___ the road. I had only just stepped ___(7)___ the pavement when I was nearly ___(8)___ down by a ___(9)___ which suddenly came racing round the corner. I jumped out of the way and then ___(10)___ to laugh when four men ran round the corner, vainly shouting ___(11)___ at the buffalo, which had apparently ___(12)___ on its way to the market.

(1) What do you suggest? It was not an accident, so we cannot use that word. We could put in 'experience'.

(2) Is it 'to' or 'from'. We can tell from line 3 that it must be 'to'.

(3) Alternatives are possible here. We can use 'call' or 'calling' but we cannot use 'called'. Similarly, we cannot use 'shout' because then we would need 'at' or 'to' as well.

(4) other. We cannot use 'another'. We can also use 'opposite'.

(5) going, walking, strolling

(6) cross. We cannot use 'across' because it is not a verb, and we need a verb here.

(7) off, from

(8) knocked. The Simple Past tense is necessary.

(9) No, not a car or a taxi, as one might expect. We cannot use 'animal' because the preceding word is 'a' and not 'an'. When we read on, we discover that the right word is 'buffalo'.

(10) started, began

(11) This is very difficult. The examiner might accept a suitable adverb, for example 'loudly' or 'angrily'. An alternative would be 'curses'.

(12) escaped

Now it is your turn to find suitable words in the following passages.

Exercise 1

Write the number of each blank space and then write a word which can be used to complete the expression or sentence. Check that each word is grammatically correct, and that it fits the situation and pattern of the sentence.

My brother is very fond of ___(1)___ music, particularly the works of Chopin, Beethoven and Tchaikovsky. A few weeks ___(2)___ he bought a hi-fi set, ___(3)___ that he could ___(4)___ to tapes which friends lent ___(5)___ .

At first, everything went ___(6)___ but after a few days my brother
5 complained ___(7)___ the sound was beginning to fade. After ___(8)___ two days,
the sound had almost ___(9)___ disappeared.

My brother was very annoyed. He ___(10)___ the heavy set back to the shop
and ___(11)___ bitterly about it. An ___(12)___ examined the set and said that
there ___(13)___ nothing wrong with it. He cleaned the tape heads and ___(14)___
10 rollers ___(15)___ a 'Q' tip dipped in alcohol. Then he put ___(16)___ tape in the
set and played ___(17)___. The sound was excellent.

'___(18)___ you study the instructions ___(19)___ you first bought this set?' he
asked my brother.

'No, I didn't,' my brother ___(20)___, 'but now I'm going to read them
15 thoroughly.'

Exercise 2

Write the number of each blank space. Then write a suitable word which we can use in the blank space.

When you have got toothache and cannot ___(1)___ to a dentist immediately,
keep cool. Researchers in Canada have ___(2)___ that rubbing ___(3)___ cubes on
certain parts of the hand will ___(4)___ the pain.

Get some ice ___(5)___ and wrap them in thin cloth. Rub the person's
5 ___(6)___ between ___(7)___ thumb and the ___(8)___ finger. Do ___(9)___ until the
area feels numb. You will then ___(10)___ that the ___(11)___ from toothache is
reduced by at least fifty ___(12)___ cent.

This method was ___(13)___ by a doctor at Montreal General Hospital. The
doctor ___(14)___ outpatients who were attending the dental clinic. About
10 forty people were chosen ___(15)___ random. They were ___(16)___ waiting to see
a dentist. The patients were ___(17)___ how to massage their hands with ice
cubes. Although they ___(18)___ doubtful at first, they soon ___(19)___ that the
treatment was successful and ___(20)___ the pain from toothache.

Exercise 3

In the following passage, there are some words missing in each line but there are no blank spaces. Put a stroke / to show where a word is missing. Then write down the number of the line and suitable words which we can put in.

These lines have been done as an example:

Doctors in / hospital in Plymouth, England, often had to send urgent samples of blood / a neighbouring hospital for analysis / experts.

1 a   2 to, by

1 The samples sent by taxi and this was expensive. In addition, the journey a
2 long time because the roads were usually very crowded. In an attempt to
3 overcome the problem, hospital decided to make experiment with pigeons.
4 The blood was put in small containers were strapped to the birds' legs.
5 The experiment proved be highly successful. The birds did their work
6 cheaply efficiently without losing a single sample. Indeed, doctors to extend
7 the experiment to include samples of skin or other material. Meanwhile,
8 representatives several other countries went to Plymouth to learn about new
9 system.

In the passage below, put a stroke to show where a word is missing. Then write the number of each line and words which can be put in.

1 A few years ago, the of oil rose sharply. In the following years there further
2 increases. Countries which supplied oil said that they had increased the
3 price because inflation. However, increased prices led to recession in many
4 countries had an adverse effect on developing countries and others lacked
5 their own fuel. Many countries could no longer afford to oil, so they looked
6 for alternative ways of running vehicles and machines. In cases, for example,
7 alcohol produced from sugar cane. This method was developed on a large
8 scale in Brazil. In other countries, less fuel was and coal was used instead,
9 thus foreign currency.

68 Comparison

Check that you already know the points under the following twelve headings.

1 Forms (adjectives and adverbs)

	Positive	Comparative	Superlative
short words	tall	taller than	the tallest
	fast	faster than	the fastest
longer words	sensible	more sensible than	the most sensible
	neatly	more neatly than	the most neatly
irregular words	bad	worse than	the worst
	good		
	well	better than	the best

2 Don't use a double comparison

Don't put 'more' before a word and '-er' after it. Don't put 'most' before a word and '-est' after it. It is easy to make this type of mistake, especially in speech:

Wrong　　　　This is the most difficultest problem I have ever had to solve.
Wrong　　　　She is more younger than I am.

What are the correct forms of the two examples?

3 Most = very

Normally we put 'the' before a superlative. However, when 'most' means 'very' and does not involve a comparison, we can use 'a'.

A comparison　　Mary is **the** most intelligent girl in the class.
No comparison　　Mary is **a** most intelligent girl.

4 Inferior to

Normally we use 'than' after a comparative adjective or adverb. However, after 'inferior', 'superior', 'junior' and 'senior', we use 'to' and not 'than'.

   a)   This camera is definitely inferior to the other ones.
   b)   Mr Brown is senior to me, but Mr Smith is junior to me.

5 Less, the least

We can make comparisons with 'less' and 'the least'.

   a)   Mary is less intelligent than her sister.
   b)   Of the four girls, Mary is the least intelligent.

6 Better or best?

Mary looked at two rings. We can call them A and B. Mary preferred A to B. Which of these sentences is correct?

   a)   A is better than B.
   b)   B is the best.

Some grammarians say that we should use a comparative adjective (better) when we compare two things. You can follow this rule in an examination. Then 'A is better than B' is right, and the sentence 'B is the best' is wrong. However, many native-speakers use sentences like 'B is the best', so we cannot really say that it is wrong in speech. Native-speakers often say:

   c)   Put your best foot forward. (We have only two feet.)
   d)   May the best man win. (Often only two men fight.)
   e)   This ring is the best.

In 'This ring is the best', they are not worried about a comparison of A and B. They are speaking about the best one, regardless of whether there are two or fifty things in front of them.

7 Compare like things

What is wrong with these sentences?

   a)   The population of Japan is greater than England.
   b)   Your work is better than Mary.

The first sentence suggests that we are comparing the population of Japan with the size of England. In the second we are comparing work with a person. The sentences should be changed to:

   c)   The population of Japan is greater than that of England.
   d)   Your work is better than Mary's.

8 Two comparisons

You may want to use 'older' and 'more intelligent' together. When this happens, put the -er adjective before the 'more' adjective.

Not so good   She is more intelligent and older than Anne.
Better   She is older and more intelligent than Anne.

9 Older, elder

We often use 'elder' and not 'older' when speaking about members of a family. Use 'elder' or 'eldest' when the adjective comes before a noun.

a) Mary is my elder sister. She is older than I am.
b) She is the eldest child. She is the oldest student in our class.

10 Less, fewer

We should use 'less' to refer to an uncountable noun and 'fewer' to refer to a countable noun.

a) There is less noise now than there used to be.
b) I am glad to say that there have been fewer accidents on this road in the past year.

However, native-speakers sometimes forget this rule, so we can see 'Use not less than 400 words' on an examination paper.

11 Can we say 'most perfect'?

Some people say that we cannot form the comparative or superlative of such words as 'perfect', 'unique', 'dead', 'favourite' and 'complete'. If something is perfect, there is no need to say 'most perfect'.

However, many native-speakers use 'more' and 'most' before these words. Then they mean 'more nearly' and 'most nearly'.

a) 'This is the most perfect diamond I have ever seen.'
   'This is the most nearly perfect diamond I have ever seen.;
b) 'This painting is more unique than the others.'
   'This painting is more nearly unique than the others.'

Perhaps we should not imitate this usage. At the same time, it is wise not to correct other people if they choose to say 'most perfect'.

12 Me, I

Compare these three sentences:

a) Mary is older than me.
b) Mary is older than I.
c) Mary is older than I am.

The last sentence is the best type to use. 'Mary is older than I', is correct but is not used by many British people. The phrase 'older than me' is often used by British people but is said to be 'wrong' by some grammarians, because it does not follow the pattern of Latin sentences.

Exercise 1

Choose the most suitable word from the brackets and then put it in its correct form.

1 Tigers are (*small, large*) than cats.
2 Motor-racing is (*dangerous, safe*) than playing football.
3 Gold is (*valuable, hard*) than steel, but steel is (*valuable, hard*) than gold.
4 Girls are (*honest, strong*) than boys but sometimes are (*tough, talkative*) too.
5 The Pacific Ocean is (*large, cold*) of all the oceans in the world.

6 Food and water are the two (*useless, vital*) things for living things.
7 A gale is much (*gentle, powerful*) than a breeze and it is (*destructive, welcome*) too.
8 Men are usually a little (*old, young*) than their wives.
9 In the eyes of the law, robbery is (*bad, good*) than theft. It is a (*friendly, serious*) offence and carries a (*small, great*) penalty.
10 Travelling by air is (*slow, fast*), (*safe, dangerous*) but (*cheap, expensive*) than travelling in a taxi.
11 Many people regard Sunday as (*busy, pleasant*) day of the week. This is the day when they have (*bad, good*) opportunity of resting or of enjoying themselves.
12 Mr Hall is recovering from his operation. He is much (*weak, strong*) than he was a week ago, and his general condition is much (*good, bad*).

Exercise 2

Put in less, more, the most *or* the least.

1 Gold is _____ expensive than silver. Therefore silver is _____ costly than gold.
2 Human beings have _____ advanced homes than wild animals do but their senses are usually _____ developed.
3 Modern cars are much _____ complicated than the very first models and they are _____ reliable, too.
4 In a desert, _____ valuable commodity is water, and _____ useful is sand.
5 When a country has a large number of unskilled people without jobs, it tends to prefer new industries which are _____ labour-intensive although it will still accept industries which are _____ labour-intensive.
6 Earl is one of _____ superstitious people I know. On Friday the 13th, he refuses to leave his home.
7 My father wanted to buy a new car, so he inspected three new cars: the Speedo (30 kilometres per litre), the Whizzo (25 kpl) and the Snail (45 kpl). He noticed that the Snail was _____ economical to run than the Speedo but in the end he decided to buy the Whizzo, _____ economical of the three.
8 There is a well-known saying: '_____ haste, _____ speed'.
9 In Europe, _____ pleasant months for foreign visitors are probably June to August, and _____ attractive (because of unpleasant weather conditions) are January and February.
10 The sea is usually _____ rough in the Mediterranean Sea than it is in the Atlantic Ocean.

Exercise 3

Correct any errors (concerning the comparison of adjectives or adverbs) in these sentences.

1 We moved to a more bigger house a few months ago.
2 Question 6 is the most difficultest in the whole exercise.
3 It is easier to learn one's mother tongue than it is to learn a foreign language.
4 The income of a doctor is greater than a farmer.
5 I caught a cold on Monday and it was worst on Tuesday, so I stayed at home.

6 Walking is much easier and natural for human beings than swimming.
7 It is much easy to understand printed English than to speak good English.
8 The most bad thing in my country is the increase in the amount of crime.
9 Mary is a best friend of mine. I like her very much.
10 My test result was worser than I had expected.

69 Conditionals and 'if'

When 'if' introduces a condition, there are four main types of sentences.

1 When we refer to habitual actions, we can use this pattern:

If + Simple Present tense + Simple Present tense

a) If anybody speaks to Daddy when he is listening to the news on the radio, he does not reply.
b) If I miss the bus, I have to walk to school.
c) If A = 4 and B = 3, 6AB = 72.

Read b) again. Then compare it with this sentence:

d) If I miss the bus, I will have to walk to school.

In d), the speaker is referring to something which may happen in the future. In b) he is speaking about a habit. He means 'Whenever I miss the bus, I have to walk to school.'

2 Referring to a specific situation or a likely event

In a sentence like d), this is the pattern:

If + Simple Present tense + $\left.\begin{array}{l}\text{Simple Future}\\ \text{Imperative}\\ \text{can/may}\end{array}\right\}$

e) If you stand on that chair, it will collapse.
f) If you don't apologise to Mary, she will never forgive you.
g) If you ride a bicycle on a busy road, you may be killed.
h) If you see John at school, please ask him to phone Mary.
i) That house will fall down soon unless the owner strengthens the wall.

Exercise 1

Complete these sentences in any sensible way.

1 If Uncle comes tomorrow, ...
2 If our house catches fire tonight, ...

3 If there is a flood tomorrow, ...
4 If anybody phones while I'm out, please ...
5 If you're going to the Post Office, please ...
6 If there is a severe earthquake here next week, ...
7 If the Government doubles the rate of income tax next year, ...
8 If the rate of income tax is reduced at the next budget, ...
9 If there is a war and atomic bombs are used, ...
10 If you lend me fifty dollars, ...

3 Referring to a less likely event or making a general statement rather then referring to one specific event

This type of pattern is common in composition when we are writing about what **might** happen in the future. The pattern is:

If + * Simple Past Tense + } Present Conditional tense
could/might

a) If the Government abolished income tax, everybody would be very happy.
b) If there were no criminals, we would not need a police force.
c) If you offered Mr Smith $3,000 for his car, he might sell it.
d) If all the roads were flooded tomorrow, we could stay at home.

*In this pattern, we use 'were' (Past Subjunctive) and not 'was', even with a singular subject.

e) If I were you, I wouldn't accept the invitation.
f) If Mary were a boy, she could play for our football team.

We also use this pattern when reporting a speech containing the type of conditional sentence in section 2, e.g.

Direct   He said, 'If I see John, I'll give him your message.'
Indirect   He said that if he saw John he would give him my message.

Exercise 2

Complete these sentences in any sensible way. Say what might, could or would happen.

1 If the Government doubled the pay of policemen, ...
2 If motorists drove much more carefully, ...
3 If I won a million dollars in a lottery, ...
4 If I were in charge of education in my country, ...
5 If creatures from another planet invaded Earth, ...
6 If the price of oil increased by 100% within the next month, ...
7 If I had to live in another country, ...
8 If you were more careful in your work and made a greater effort, ...
9 If I found a handbag containing a lot of foreign money, ...
10 If I could go to a university overseas, ...

4 Referring to past time

The sentences in sections 2 and 3 refer to future action. When we want to speak about past events, we can use the pattern below. Then we can comment on something that might have happened but did not happen.

If + Past Perfect tense + Perfect Conditional tense
   a) If that plane had crashed in an urban area, many people would have died (or would have been killed). However, it crashed into the sea.
   b) If you had asked me to lend you some money, I would have been happy to help you (but you did not ask me).
   c) If we hadn't moved to higher ground, we would have been trapped by the flood (but we did move, so we were not trapped).

5 Using 'even if'

We can use 'even' to emphasise a condition. Do not omit 'if' after 'even' in sentences like these.:

   a) I won't sell it even if you offer me double the amount.
   b) Even if we had tried to save him, we would certainly have failed because of the heat of the fire.

6 Conditional tenses

Using the verb 'to meet' as an example, these are the forms of the Present Conditional and Perfect Conditional tenses:

Present Conditional

non-continuous   **would meet**

   a) He said he *would meet* us at six p.m.
   b) If you went to more dances, you *would meet* more people, Mary.

continuous   **would be meeting**

   c) You told me that Uncle *would be meeting* us at the station but he wasn't there.

passive   **would be met**

   d) I thought we *would be met* when we arrived at London but there was nobody there to meet us.

Perfect Conditional

non-continuous   **would have met**

   e) I *would have met* you at the airport if I had known that you were coming.
   f) Mary *would have bought* the dress if she had had enough money.

continuous   **would have been meeting**

   g) When we got off the train, we were disappointed. We felt sure that somebody *would have been meeting* us but there was nobody there.

passive   **would have been met**

   h) You *would have been met* at the station if you had let us know that you were coming.

7 Elliptic expressions

An elliptic expression is a short one in which words have been left out. We can use 'if ever', 'if so' and 'if at all' as short forms of longer expressions.

If ever	We won't move to San Francisco for a few years, if ever. = We won't move to San Francisco for a few years, if we ever move there.
If so	That horrible man, George Smith, may be appointed manager. If so, I shall resign. if so – if that happens.
If at all	We won't move to San Francisco for a few years, if at all. if at all = if we ever move there.

Question

Read this short passage and answer the question about it.

I don't like the look of the weather. It may spoil our plans. It's probably going to rain tomorrow and, if so, we'll have to cancel plans for the picnic. Never mind. We can stay at home and watch television – or paint the kitchen.

Q. What does 'if so' refer to in line 2?
A. It refers to the possibility that it will rain the next day.

8 If/whether

We can use 'if' or 'whether' in indirect questions:

Direct	'Have you finished your work?' Mary asked me.
Indirect	Mary asked me if/whether I had finished my work.
Direct	'Will your sister be angry if I don't go to the party?' he said.
Indirect	He asked me if/whether my sister would be angry if he did not go to the party.

Exercise 3

Change these questions into reported (or indirect) questions. (If necessary, see Unit 74.)

1 'Have you found your watch?' Peter asked me.
2 'Will it rain tomorrow?' Peter said.
3 'Do you understand English?' the lady said.
4 'Can we enter the building?' we asked the police inspector.
5 'Have you any relatives living here?' the inspector said.
6 Susan asked me, 'Are you going to John's wedding next Saturday?'
7 'Is the Rex Hotel a good one?' the tourist said to me.
8 'Can you drive a car?' the lady said.
9 'Did you see the accident happen?' the policeman asked us.
10 'Is it raining? Will the Sports Meeting be cancelled?' Anne said.

9 It looks as if

We can express possibility by using 'It looks as if...'

It looks as if
$\left.\begin{array}{l}\text{Peter did not pass the examination.}\\ \text{Uncle has been delayed by traffic.}\\ \text{nobody lives in this flat.}\end{array}\right\}$

The examples show that we can refer to past, present or future events.

10 If only

We can use 'if only' in a complete sentence or in an exclamation. It introduces a wish about the past, present or future. Notice the tenses that we use:

Past events – Past Perfect tense
- a) If only we hadn't bought such an expensive car!
- b) We could have saved a lot of money if only we had not bought such a large and expensive house.

Present time – Past Subjunctive tense
- c) If only we lived in Australia! (The weather is better there.)
- d) If only Peter were here now! I'm sure he could help us.

Future time – Present Conditional tense
- e) Several of us are going to Canada for a holiday next year. If only you would come with us! I'm sure you would enjoy it.
- f) You would pass the examination easily if only you would be more careful.

11 Other ways of expressing a condition

We can use 'provided that', 'on condition that' or 'as long as' to introduce a condition.

The table won't collapse as long as you don't stand on it.
I'll lend you $200 on condition that you repay the money before the end of the year.
Motorists would be glad to leave their cars at home provided that public transport was available and of a good standard.

70 Connectives

Study the information given in this unit. Then make up sentences similar to the examples or using the given linking words correctly.

1 Use one linking word or expression at a time

In some languages, linking words are used in pairs. In English (except for either ... or and neither ... nor), we normally use one conjunction to join two statements.

These are wrong methods of linking statements:

because ...so	although ... but	since ... therefore
because ... therefore	if ... then	*as ... so
when ... then	after ... then	since ... so
as ... therefore		

*We can use 'as ... so' when 'as' expresses manner.

The following examples are correct.

after	a) After I had finished my work, I wrote to my friend.
although	a) Although it was raining, the Sports Meeting was not cancelled. b) Although my uncle is not an educated man, he is a very successful businessman.
as = since	a) As there is not much land, we must build large blocks of flats b) As yesterday was a holiday and all the schools and offices were shut, I went for a picnic with some friends.
as = when	a) As I was coming out of a shop, I heard somebody shout for help.
because	a) Because of an accident on a flyover, traffic was delayed for nearly an hour. b) Because my friend could not come with me, I had to go swimming by myself.
if	a) If Uncle comes tomorrow, we can go for a drive. b) If it doesn't rain this evening, we can play basketball.
since	a) Since the watch was very expensive, Anne decided not to buy it. b) Since I had promised to help my friend with her homework, I went to her home.
when	a) When you have finished your work, you can go out. b) When anybody is injured, an ambulance comes to the scene.

Exercise 1

Complete these sentences in any sensible way. There are many possible alternatives.

1 Because of a fire in a road near our school, ...
2 Although there are more police now, ...
3 Since the price of the camera was too high, ...
4 If the shoes are too small, ...
5 As I was waiting for a bus, ...
6 Although some people may disagree with me, ...
7 When the Suez Canal was closed some years ago, ...
8 As I live on an island, ...

9 Since the sea was very rough and looked dangerous, ...

10 If the population of the world continues to expand rapidly, ...

2 Thus

There are two different ways of using 'thus'. Try not to confuse these common patterns:

a) In most countries, men and women have equal rights and opportunities. Thus the position of women in society has improved.

b) In most countries, men and women have equal rights and opportunities, thus proving that the position of women in society has improved.

Either 'Thus' starts a new (grammatical) sentence (as in a) or we use the pattern, thus ... ing (as in b).

Make up sentences similar to the examples.

3 Therefore

These are two common patterns:

a) 2a equals 10. Therefore a equals 5.

b) 2a equals 10, and therefore a equals 5.

Do not write: '2a equals 10, therefore a equals 5.'
Make up sentences similar to these two examples.

4 Conclusively, at last

'Conclusively' means 'beyond any doubt'. It does not mean 'in conclusion'. At the end of an article or composition, you can start your final paragraph with these words:

In conclusion, ...   Finally, ...   Lastly, ...

Do not use 'at last'. This means 'eventually' and not 'finally'.

a) In 1519–22, some Portuguese men sailed round the world, proving conclusively that the world is round and not flat.

b) I spent an hour looking for a key and at last managed to find it.

5 On the contrary, on the other hand

These two expressions are different in meaning.

'On the contrary' indicates that a writer is going to give an idea which conflicts with something already said or which presents an opposite point of view.

a) *Mary:* Are you in favour of compulsory voting?
   Anne: No. On the contrary, I believe people should be free to vote or to abstain.

'On the other hand' introduces an alternative or a different point of view which is not necessarily an opposing one.

b) *Mary:* What's the best way of sending these things to New York?
   Anne: Well, you could send them by sea. On the other hand, you could send them by air but that's much more expensive.

6 Nor

After a negative verb, use 'or' (and not 'nor') unless you add a clause in which the subject comes after the verb. These are correct examples:

a) I can't play the guitar or the piano.
b) Mary can't play the guitar or sing very well.
c) John can't play the piano and neither can his brother.
d) She can't swim; nor can I.

7 In spite of, despite

Do not use 'of' after 'despite'. Write 'in spite of' as three words.

a) In spite of the storm, all the trawlers returned safely.
b) Despite the storm, all the boats returned safely.

8 Otherlinking words

These sentences give examples of the correct use of some common linking words:

nevertheless (= despite this fact)
a) Grace has a bad temper and is rather arrogant. Nevertheless, she is a brilliant engineer and is very useful to our firm.

however
a) Mary is very fond of cats. However, she dislikes dogs.
b) Anne is fond of cats. Her dislike of dogs, however, is well known.

moreover (= in addition)
a) The Columbia space shuttle is cheaper to build than the earlier type of spacecraft. Moreover, it can be used several times and is thus cheaper to operate.

thereby (+ an -ing word)
a) When charged with the crime, the man nodded his head, thereby admitting his guilt.
b) When the traffic lights changed to red, a taxi stopped suddenly, thereby causing a chain collision which involved five vehicles.

whereas (introducing a contrast or comparison)
a) John always drinks tea, whereas his sister prefers coffee.
b) America usually exports a huge quantity of grain, whereas Russia often imports a large quantity.
c) Russia is self-sufficient in oil, whereas the U.S.A. is not.

for example
a) If she likes, Mary can take up a career, e.g. accountancy, law or medicine.
b) If she wants to, Mary can take up a career as, for example, law, medicine or accountancy.
c) If she is good enough, Mary can prepare for a career. For example, she can be a doctor, lawyer or accountant.

Notice that the following type of 'sentence' is **wrong**. The second part does not contain a verb.

Mary can prepare for a career. For example, law, medicine or accountancy.

What connectives can we use in the blank spaces below? Are there any acceptable alternatives?

1 As you know, Peter hurt his left leg in a game a fortnight ago. _____ this, he played brilliantly yesterday and scored two goals.
2 I have no wish to criticise the Government. _____, I agree with most of its actions and am a strong supporter of it.
3 Water is essential for animals and plants, and it has many advantages. _____, we cannot deny that it also has some disadvantages.
4 In the average company, an accountant is not responsible for marketing arrangements. _____ is he involved in the techniques of production or the design of products. He is concerned mainly with production costs and related matters. _____, he is responsible for producing the final trading figures.
5 In my opinion, the plan to merge the two companies is very wise. It will reduce competition. _____, it will enable us to make the best use of technical staff. _____, I agree that some problems will arise but I am confident that we can solve them.
6 There is considerable evidence that smoking is harmful. _____, it may cause cancer of the lungs. It can cause heart failure. _____, it causes bronchitis and other respiratory diseases. _____, I must agree that it is difficult for a person to give up smoking after many years.

71 | Future action

1 Unplanned future actions

We cannot plan the weather, so we ask: 'Will it rain next Sunday?' We do not ask 'Is it raining next Sunday?' or 'Does it rain next Sunday?' We use the Simple Future tense for unplanned (and planned) future events.

2 The Simple Future tense

The forms of this tense are:

active, non-continuous:	will make	will stop
active, continuous:	will be making	will be stopping
passive:	will be made	will be stopped

Note: *We can use 'will' with all subjects except in questions. Then we must use 'shall' before 'I' and 'we'.*

There are special uses of 'shall' with other subjects but they are not important at this stage.

a) If you like, I **will make** a dress for you next month.
b) In ten hours' time, you **will be sleeping** happily.
c) We **will be arriving** at New York Airport in an hour's time.
d) If you drop litter in the streets, you **will be fined.**
e) The work **will be finished** by tomorrow afternoon.

Put in a suitable form of the Simple Future tense of the verbs in brackets.

1   The interview tomorrow (decide) my future.
2   I hope the Government (not increase) income tax.
3   The firefighters say that the fire (put out) in about an hour's time.
4   Uncle (come) at about nine o'clock this evening.
5   He (meet) at the airport by everybody in our family.
6   If you work hard, you (promote) to the post of supervisor.
7   Mummy (be) pleased when she opens her present.
8   One day I hope there (be) peace throughout the world.
9   Mr Lee (leave) for San Francisco next Thursday.
10 He (take) the draft agreement with him for discussion.
11 I think our team (win) the cup.
12 When (see) we Mary again?

3 Shall I/we ...?

We often use 'Shall I' with the meaning 'Do you want me to (do something)?'

a)   **Shall I** turn the light on? Can you see properly?
b)   **Shall I** wake Daddy up? It's nearly time for him to get up.

We can use 'Shall we' to make a suggestion in this way:

c)   It's hot today. **Shall we** go swimming?
d)   There's a good film on at the Rex Cinema. **Shall we** go and see it?
e)   **Shall we** invite Peter to the party?

4 Planned future action

We can use the Simple Future tense to express planned future action. We can also use three other methods:

going to
This often shows an intention or what we expect to happen.

a)   It's **going to** rain any minute, so we must hurry.
b)   Mary is **going to** get some stamps for us when she goes out.
c)   The Government is **going to** build more low-cost homes next year.

Present Continuous tense
This shows what somebody intends to do or thinks somebody else will do.

a)   **I'm meeting** Mary at the Ocean Centre tomorrow afternoon.
b)   **Is** Uncle **coming** by train or bus tomorrow?
c)   We'd better get some petrol today. The price **is going up** on Monday.

Simple Present tense
This tense can refer to scheduled (habitual) future action. We also use it in some time and conditional expressions.

a)   His plane **leaves** next Thursday morning.
b)   The last train **goes** in an hour's time.
c)   Please give this key to Mary when you **see** her tomorrow.
d)   If anybody **phones** while I'm out, please take a message for me.

1   Make up five of your own sentences like the ones in section 3.
2   Make up five sentences similar to those in section 4.
3   Check and correct sentences made up by a student sitting near you in class.
    Give your sentences to somebody else to check.

5 'to be' + an infinitive

We can use a passive or an active infinitive after a suitable form of the verb 'to be'. Check that you understand this way of expressing a planned future event or an order about the future. In many cases the verb 'to be' + the following 'to' are similar in meaning to 'must'.

a)   This parcel **is to be delivered** by hand tomorrow morning.
     (= It must be delivered ...)
b)   If anybody comes while we're out, you **are** not **to open** the door.
     (an order)
c)   I'm not sure but I think these old shirts **are to be thrown away** soon.

6 The Future Perfect tense

active, non-continuous
He **will have finished** by tomorrow night.

active, continuous
By the end of this month, I **shall have been working** for this company for thirty years.

passive
The car **will have been repaired** by tomorrow so we can collect it in the morning.
The escaped prisoners **will have been caught** by the morning.

This tense expresses action that will be completed by some future time.

Exercise 3

Some of these sentences are correct. Others contain mistakes connected with future actions. Find the mistakes and correct them.

1   I hope our plane won't be delayed by the strike at London Airport.
2   This machine is not working properly. Tell the supervisor it is to be repaired immediately, and tell him I said so.
3   This factory is going to be close down at the end of next month. Eight hundred people will be unemployed then.
4   Hey, John! Will we go for a swim today? The beach won't be too crowded this evening. What do you say?
5   Mr Lee is on the phone now but he won't be long. I'll put you through to him in a minute. Do you mind hanging on a minute?
6   If you don't hurry, there'll be no food left. It shall all have been eaten.
7   Shall I pay that cheque in for you? I'll be going to the bank after lunch. It'll save you the journey.
8   Don't worry about Mary. Her work will improved when she will have more experience. After all, she's only been here a week.

9 The storm is approaching from the north and will probably arrived by about five p.m.
10 A property company is going to put up a block of flats over there. Then our view will block and we won't be able to see the sea any more.
11 The new wing of our school will be opened by the Minister of Education on Wednesday. About five hundred guests will be there.
12 What time does your plane leave tomorrow?

72 Gerunds

1 Forms

Gerunds are verbal nouns. This means that they are nouns formed from verbs. The most common type of gerund is the present active one, which ends in -ing.

	Active	Passive
Present Perfect	catching having caught	being caught having been caught

a) He is afraid of **catching** German measles.
b) Illegal immigrants are always worried about **being caught**.
c) The goalkeeper was blamed for not **having caught** the ball properly.
d) The men were angry at **having been caught** so easily.

In this chapter we will deal mainly with the present active form of the gerund, since this is the most common and useful one.

2 Spelling

In most cases, when you add -ing to a verb:

a) Omit a final 'e', for example, 'writing', 'making', 'arguing', 'blaming'.
b) Double a final consonant if a short vowel comes before it. (There are short vowels in these words: 'That pen is not much good'.) Examples include 'shopping', 'hitting', 'cutting', 'batting' and 'getting'.

3 Preposition + a gerund

This is probably the most common use of gerunds. Here are examples:

fond of eating	no intention of meeting	obtained by cheating
bad at drawing	stop him from going	tired of waiting
made by heating	look forward to seeing	used for making

When we refer to a past event, a perfect gerund is sometimes more logical but many people prefer to use a present gerund because it is easier and shorter. Compare these sentences:

a) He was angry at having lost all his money.
b) He was angry at losing all his money.

c) They complained about having been arrested by the police.
d) They complained about being arrested by the police.

Exercise 1

Look at the second example again ('He was angry at losing all his money'). Then say what gerunds we can put in the following blank spaces. Are there are sensible alternatives?

1　I look forward to _____ your friend tomorrow.
2　I look forward to _____ to your cousin on Monday.
3　Don't worry. We have no intention of _____ money.
4　He is a chef in a leading hotel, so he is capable of _____ a first class meal.
5　Mary is not happy in her present job, so she is thinking of _____ to another one.
6　Jack is thinking of _____ another job.
7　I heard some people arguing about _____ income tax.
8　Are you interested in _____ shells?
9　At airports, a special foam is used for _____ out aircraft fires.
10　If you are not used to _____ a car, let me do it.
11　Don't waste your money on _____.
12　Sometimes it is possible to listen to a speaker without _____ what he is talking about.

Exercise 2

What gerunds can we put in the following blank spaces? Are there any alternatives?

1　Peter is not accustomed to _____ in goal but I am sure he will do his best. If he succeeds in _____ the ball out, we are bound to win.
2　Thank you. We had no difficulty in _____ your house. We just followed the directions you had given us, without _____ any mistakes.
3　What's the use of _____ more money than you need?
4　Thank you for _____ my letters and for _____ the stamps.
5　Mrs Cresswell is a good dentist. She will deal with your teeth without _____ you and without _____ you an enormous bill.
6　Mary is thinking of _____ to Canada next year and of _____ a university there.
7　I am tired of _____ to people complaining about the weather. It's ideal for _____ crops.
8　When the suspect was charged with _____ goods from the shop, he insisted on _____ a lawyer.
9　It is better to refrain from _____ other people if you object to their _____ unpleasant comments about you.
10　On _____ at the hotel, the first thing we did was to check in at the reception desk.

---

4 Verb + gerund

We can use a gerund after the following verbs. An asterisk (*) shows that we can also use an infinitive after the verb but sometimes with a different meaning

admit	delay	give up	mind	regret*
advise	deny	be no good	need	remember*
attempt*	detest	hate*	omit*	resent
avoid	dislike	can't help	pardon	resist
bear*	enjoy	hinder	postpone	risk
begin*	escape	imagine	practise	not stand
burst out	be excused	intend*	prefer*	start*
confess	fancy	keep on	prevent	stop
consider	fear*	learn*	propose*	suggest
continue*	finish	like*	put off	try*
defer	forget*	love*	recommend	be worth

a) We burst out **laughing** when Peter came in, wearing fancy dress.
b) I can't help **admiring** the way Mary has dealt with the problem.
c) It's no good **worrying** about the money. You've spent it already.

Exercise 3

What gerunds or expressions introduced by a gerund can you put in each blank space? Discuss possible alternatives.

Example   Would you mind _____, Mrs Brown?

waiting hurrying
waiting a minute   moving a little
waiting in this room   sitting in the front
waiting until Mr Lee is free   passing me the sauce

1 When I get a chance, I like _____ with my friends.
2 Some people enjoy _____.
3 You ought to give up _____, John. Then your health will improve.
4 The man denied _____ but the policeofficer did not believe him.
5 Have you finished _____ yet?
6 Where are my glasses? I remember _____ them but I can't find them now.
7 My father always listens to the news and he cannot stand anybody _____ while the news is on.
8 The flood prevented us from _____.
9 Stop _____ and get on with your work.
10 These shoes are very old. They're not worth _____. You can throw them away.

---

73 Indirect (reported) speech

I Patterns using indirect speech

a) We often have to pass on a message, using such verbs as these:

She said (that)   She asked me to tell you (that)
He replied (that)   He claims (that)

b) There are many common sentence patterns in which we use indirect speech. Examples include:

I am quite sure that . . .	Some people believe that . . .
We cannot deny that . . .	It is not true that . . .
I am convinced that . . .	There is a rumour that . . .

2 Changing the punctuation

When reporting a statement, we omit the inverted commas in the original speech. We also omit the comma after the introductory speech verb.

Direct   She said, 'I'll bring my friend to your house tomorrow.'
Indirect   She said (that) she would bring her friend to my house the next day.

3 Making the place clear

In the above example, 'your house' has been changed to 'my house'. Similarly we sometimes make these changes:

Direct	**Indirect**
here	there
in my house	in his/her house
in this city	*in that city

*If both people are still in the same city, we would use 'in this city' in indirect speech. Use your common sense when you report a statement. Make the place clear.

4 Making identity and possession clear

Change words like 'I', 'he', 'she', 'my', 'your', etc. to make the situation clear. Look at the example in section 2 again. What happened to 'I', 'my' and 'your' when the statement was changed into indirect speech?

5 Making the time and date clear

Make any changes that are needed to make the time and date clear. Compare these examples:

At 10 a.m. on Monday, Mary said, 'It's Uncle's birthday today.' Mary was speaking to Anne. Later on, somebody asked Anne what Mary had said.

a) At 11 a.m. on Monday, Anne said, 'Mary said it is her uncle's birthday **today**.'
b) On Tuesday, Anne said, 'Mary said it **was** her uncle's birthday **yesterday**.
c) On Friday, Anne said, 'Mary said it was her uncle's birthday **last Monday** or 'four days ago').

Conclusion

Change references to time and date to make the meaning clear.

6 Changing the tense of verbs

If an action has not yet happened or is still happening, it may not be necessary to change the tense of a verb. This is true whether the tense of an introductory speech verb is in the present or past.

Direct	(10 p.m.) Mary said, 'I'm tired.'		
Indirect	(11 p.m.) Mary said that she is tired. (if she has not yet gone to bed)		
Indirect	(11 p.m.) Mary said that she was tired. (if she has gone to bed)		
Direct	(on Monday) 'I'll come tomorrow,' John said.		
Indirect	(on Monday) John says he will come tomorrow. John said he will come tomorrow.		
Indirect	(on Tuesday) John said that he will come today. (on Tuesday night) John said that he would come today. (on Wednesday night) John said that he would come yesterday.		

If an action has finished or has been changed, we often change tenses in this way:

	In direct speech	In indirect speech	
Simple Present	she wants	she wanted	Simple Past
Present Continuous	I am coming	he was coming	Past continuous
Simple Future	you will arrive	I/we would arrive	Present Conditional
Simple Future	it will rain	it would rain	Present Conditional
Present Perfect	she has finished	she had finished	Past Perfect
Simple Past	I lost it	he had lost it	Past Perfect
Past Continuous	I was walking	he had been walking	Past Perfect Continuous
Simple Past	I was caught	he had been caught	Past Perfect
	I can	he could	
	you may	I/we might	
	you must	I/we ought to	

Exercise 1

You work in an office and received the following messages for your employer, Mr Blank. You received the messages during the morning while Mr Blank was out. He returned after lunch. Use indirect speech to deliver each message.

Use a ruler. Cover up each possible answer. Make up your own message first. Then compare it with the answer.

1 'Please ask Mr Blank to phone me as soon as he gets in,' Mrs Blank said.
   Your wife wants you to phone her as soon as possible.
   or *Your wife phoned and wants you to phone her as soon as you return to the office.*
2 'The meeting with Export and Trading has been postponed from next Tuesday to the following day,' the Chief Accountant said.
   The Chief Accountant says/said that the meeting with Export and Trading has been postponed from next Tuesday to the following day. (... from Tuesday to Wednesday next week.)
3 'Ask Mr Blank if he can meet me for lunch at the City Club tomorrow at one,' Mr Wilson said.

Mr Wilson wants to know if you can meet him for lunch at the City Club tomorrow at one o'clock.

4 'I'm Frank Lee, Mr Blank's architect. Please tell him that the PWD has given the OK to my plans for his new house by the river. I'll phone him again this afternoon.'

Mr Frank Lee, the architect, says that the PWD has approved his plans for your new house by the river. He'll phone you again this afternoon.

5 'This is Mary Blank – you know, Mr Blank's daughter. Yes, that's right. please remind Daddy that I'm catching the 4.30 plane to San Francisco this afternoon. I hope he'll be at the airport to see me off.'

Your daughter, Mary, asked me to remind you that she's catching the 4.30 plane to San Francisco this afternoon. She hopes you'll be at the airport to see her off.

6 'This is David Evans, the auditors. Please tell Mr Blank that I'll come in to see him tomorrow at about ten. I've got some urgent queries to ask him.'

Mr David Evans – the auditor – will come to see you at about ten tomorrow morning. He's got some urgent queries he'd like to ask you about.

7 Commands, orders and requests

a) We can use an infinitive when we report a request or an order:

| **Direct** | Stop talking! |
| **Indirect** | She told us to stop talking. |

| **Direct** | Give me another chance! |
| **Indirect** | He begged us to give him another chance. |

| **Direct** | Give up smoking. |
| **Indirect** | She advised him to give up smoking. |

b) We can use 'not' + an infinitive in this way:

| **Direct** | Don't stop working. |
| **Indirect** | He told me not to stop working. |

| **Direct** | 'Don't touch the wire!' Mr Lee told John. |
| **Indirect** | Mr Lee told John not to touch the wire. |

| **Direct** | 'Don't be frightened,' Mrs Lee told Peter. |
| **Indirect** | Mrs Lee told Peter not to be frightened. |

Exercise 2

Change the following into indirect speech. Use any suitable introductory words, as in the examples above.

1 Shut the door quietly.
2 Get some rice and fish for me.
3 Keep away from the wet paint.
4 Put the keys in my bag.
5 Bring your money tomorrow.
6 Put your books away and turn the light off.
7 Don't leave your shoes by the door
8 Don't forget to bring your fees tomorrow.

9 Don't be angry with me.
10 Don't pay any attention to the rumours about me.

8 Verb + object + (not) + an infinitive

This is a common and useful pattern:

He (asked/told) told us (not) to wait for him.

We cannot use all speech verbs in this way. For example, we cannot put 'said' or 'demand' in place of 'told' in the above sentence. However, we can use these verbs in suitable situations:

asked	begged	told	advised
requested	ordered	urged	reminded

Exercise 3

Which of the verbs from section 8 can we put in the blank spaces below so that they make sensible sentences?

1 The accused man _____ the magistrate not to send him to prison. He promised to reform.
2 Sometimes I forget to take my PE clothes to school but my mother _____ me this morning, so I did not forget them.
3 The shop assistant _____ us not to buy the hi-fi set because it was an old model and spare parts were not available.
4 Mary is rather shy but her friends _____ her to enter the beauty competition. They felt sure that she would win.
5 The old watchman _____ the robbers not to hurt him.
6 The road was flooded, so a policeman _____ us not to try to drive through the water. He _____ us to turn round and take another route.
7 I _____ my brother not to touch the wet paint but he forgot and put his hand on the door.
8 A policeman _____ Mr Lee to move his car because it was blocking the entrance to somebody's house.
9 I _____ my brother not to turn the light out until I had finished my work.
10 The doctor _____ my grandfather not to worry about the operation. He said that it was only a minor one.

Exercise 4

Change the following into indirect speech. They are not commands or requests, so they do not follow the pattern in the previous two sections. Assume that you are reporting the speeches the day after somebody made them.

1 Mary said, 'I've left your camera in my house.'
2 My uncle told me, 'More than sixty huts were destroyed in the fire this morning.'
3 Mrs Lee said, 'I feel sorry for you.'
4 The policeman said, 'You must take your driving licence to the central police station tomorrow morning.'
5 The man said, 'I've come to check the telephone. Somebody has complained that it's out of order.'

6 My friend said, 'I'll come at about seven this evening and I'll bring Mary's photos with me.'
7 The fire officer told us, 'The fire started in the kitchen of the hotel.'
8 The girl said, 'I'm waiting for my friend. She's in the camera shop.'
9 Somebody told me, 'All the tickets for the concert have been sold already.'

74 Indirect (reported) questions

1 Patterns with indirect questions

Indirect questions are very common. We often use them in sentences like these:

a) She asked me **how old I am**.
b) I don't know **where Mary lives**.
c) I wonder **how much it will cost**.
d) I'm not sure **whether she will come or not**.

We often use indirect questions after these words:

She asked me …	when/what/why/how/where/whether/if/ …
I know …	I wonder …
I don't know …	We must find out …
Do you know …?	Does anybody know …?

2 Changing the tense, time, place, etc.

In Unit 73, we saw that it is often necessary to change the tense, time, place, etc. when we report a statement. We make similar changes when we report a question. In addition, there are two other problems:

a) Punctuation
b) Word order

We will consider these in the following sections.

3 Punctuation

We put a question mark after a direct question, i.e. a question which somebody can say. We do not put a question mark after an indirect question unless it occurs within a direct question. Study these examples:

Direct	Who lives next to Mary?
Indirect	He asked me who lives next to Mary.

But we can ask 'Do you know …?' and put an indirect question in the blank space. Then we use a question mark because of the words. 'Do you know'.

Direct and indirect together Do you know who lives next to Mary?

Here is another example:

Direct   What is happening?
Indirect   She wants to know what is/was happening.
Direct and indirect together   Do you know what is happening?

Exercise 1

Put a full stop or a question mark as required at the end of each of the following.

1 I wonder where Peter is
2 Mary knows where John is
3 When will lunch be ready
4 I am not sure how much a new tyre costs
5 Can you tell me the way to the railway station, please
6 I wonder when Uncle will arrive
7 Shall I close the windows
8 It must be possible to lock the door
9 Shall we go for a walk
10 It seems to me that the Government does not know how many people need a home of their own
11 He asked me if I had heard the news
12 We must try to find out why she has decided not to marry John
13 My friend asked me when the game started
14 Miss Smith asked me how old I am
15 How old are you, Mary
16 I'm not sure what this thing is
17 Do you happen to know what this thing is
18 What's this thing
19 I wondered what the strange thing was
20 Nobody knows how much oil there is in the ground

4 Word order

Normally the subject comes before the verb in a statement. In these statements and questions, the subject is in bold type:

Peter has a cold.
The postman usually comes at about eight o'clock.
Mary is happy.
Who is crying?
What is that strange thing?

In direct questions, the verb (or part of it) comes before the subject:

a) Has **Peter** got a cold?
b) Does **the postman** usually come at about eight o'clock?
c) Is **Mary** happy?
d) Is **that strange thing** a tool?

Indirect questions are statements, so we must put the subject **before** the verb. Compare the following. Notice the changes in the order of words.

Direct   He asked me, 'What is your name?'
Indirect   He asked me what my name is/was. (We can use either tense.)

Direct	She said, 'When are the rest of the girls coming?'
Indirect	She wanted to know when the rest of the girls were coming.

Exercise 2

Change these direct questions into indirect questions.
Start with 'She asked me' and make any necessary changes.

1 What's your name?
2 How much do oranges cost?
3 Where's your sister?
4 What time does the concert start?
5 How many eggs do you want?
6 When is Peter going to sell his motor-cycle?
7 How can I get to the market?
8 Why do you want to see the manager?
9 Where did your brother find the money?
10 How long will it take me to get to the railway station?
11 Why didn't you reply to David's letter?
12 When are you going to move to Canada?

5 Indirect questions using 'if' or 'whether'

We use 'if' or 'whether' (it does not matter which one) when we report a direct question that starts with a verb.

Direct	'Are you hungry?' she said.
Indirect	She asked me if/whether I was hungry.
Direct	'Have you lost your watch?' Peter asked m.
Indirect	Peter asked me whether/if I had lost my watch.
Direct	'Would you like a copy of the marriage certificate?' he said.
Indirect	He asked me whether I would like a copy of the marriage certificate.

Exercise 3

Make indirect questions. Start with 'He asked me' or any similar expression.

1 Are you thirty?
2 Are you over eighteen?
3 Is your brother still in England?
4 Am I in your way?
5 Is Mary at home now?
6 Is there much traffic at night?
7 Was anybody seriously injured in the accident?
8 Were you absent yesterday?
9 Am I the first to arrive?
10 Are you in charge of the maintenance department?

Exercise 4

Make indirect questions.

1 'Can Mary play the guitar?' Susan asked me.
2 John asked Anne, 'Does your brother like acting?'
3 'Have you finished all your work yet?' my mother asked me.
4 My uncle asked me, 'Has Susan got a job yet?'

5 David asked me, 'Would you like to join the Photography Club?'
6 My brother asked me, 'Will it rain on Sunday?'
7 'Do you know Peter's phone number?' Mary asked me.
8 I asked John, 'Have you found your keys yet?'
9 The manager asked me, 'Have you brought your testimonials with you.'
10 'Have you been to the cinema recently?' John asked me.

75 Infinitives

1 Forms

	stop	eat
Present		
active	(to) stop	(to) eat
passive	(to) be stopped	(to) be eaten
continuous	(to) be stopping	(to) be eating
Perfect		
active	(to) have stopped	(to) have eaten
passive	(to) have been stopped	(to) have been eaten
continuous	(to) have been stopping	(to) have been eating

Example 1

1 The policeman held up his hands **to stop** the traffic.
2 All this food must be eaten. Nothing must **be wasted**.
3 You ought **to be working** now – not watching television.
4 That driver was wrong. He ought **to have stopped** because the traffic lights were red.
5 Where's Uncle? He must **have been delayed** by the heavy traffic.
6 When I went into the classroom, the students ought **to have been working** but some of them were talking about a football match.

Native-speakers of English should be able to use all six forms of the infinitive. If English is not your mother-tongue, concentrate on using the forms of the infinitive shown in examples 1, 2, 4 and 5. The continuous forms are less important.

2 Using an infinitive without 'to'

Check that you are familiar with these uses of an infinitive without 'to'. (It is also known as a bare infinitive.)

1 After *can, could, do, did, may, might, must, shall, should, will* and *would*.
   a) When my father was younger, he could **play** football well.
   b) Anybody who breaks the law must **be punished**.

You can see from the first example that, even when we refer to the past, we do not add -ed to the infinitive. Past time is shown by 'could' and not by 'play'.

257

Put suitable active or passive infinitives in the blank spaces.

1 My friend can _____ chess better than I can.
2 I could not _____ to the radio because there was so much noise.
3 What do you usually _____ at breakfast?
4 Where did I _____ my key? I can't find it anywhere.
5 If you put several plugs in one electricity socket, you may _____ a fire.
6 If you ask Peter, he might _____ your watch. He repaired mine last month.
7 A referee must _____ neutral and not favour either side in a game.
8 Shall I _____ the light on? It's getting dark.

2 We can use a bare infinitive after such verbs as *see, watch, notice, observe, hear, listen to, feel* and *sense*.

Compare these two sentences:

completed action
I saw some men cut down a tree.
This means: 'I saw them finish the action.'

action not finished
I saw some men painting a building.
This means: 'I saw them working but I did not see the work completed.'

Sometimes an action happens very quickly, so we cannot easily tell the difference between a completed and an incomplete action. Then it does not matter whether we use a bare infinitive or an '-ing' word, for example:

a) I heard my mother *call* me.
b) I heard my mother *calling* me.

3 We can use a bare infinitive after *make* and *let*. Notice that we do not use 'to' after 'let'.

a) Sometimes Mrs Smith makes Mary stay at home to look after her baby sister.
b) The security guards would not let us enter the building.

It is a common error to use a 'to' infinitive after 'let'.

4 We can use a bare infinitive after the following expressions:

had better (I'd better)
We're late. We'd better **hurry**.
You had better **be** careful.

would rather/sooner
I would rather **go** by air than by sea.

need hardly
I need hardly **remind** you that he is rather deaf.

cannot but
I cannot but **admire** her determination.

What infinitives can we use in the blank spaces below?

1 In some countries, the Government will not let foreigners _____ in the country a long time.
2 There was a fire on the third floor of the building, so the police would not let people _____ the building.
3 In some toy shops, the shop assistants will not let small children _____ the toys.
4 I would rather _____ in a warm country than in a cold one.
5 Mary said, 'I'd rather _____ badminton than tennis.'
6 I watched a man _____ up a pole and sit on the top.
7 Last night, I listened to some people _____ education on the radio.
8 I saw the defendant _____ out of a car and _____ in the shop. Then I heard a shot and saw him _____ out again.
9 At the start of a race, the starter makes the competitors _____ until he fires his gun.
10 Please would you help us _____ this heavy cupboard?
11 When our car broke down, a stranger helped us _____ it. We were very grateful to him.
12 He was very rude. I dare not _____ you what he said.
13 You needn't _____ a key with you. I'll be here when you come home.
14 The first thing I'm going to do when I get home is _____ a drink.
15 Mary will probably let you _____ her typewriter if you ask her.

3 Expressing purpose

We can use an infinitive to show the purpose of an action.

a) I telephoned Mary **to ask** her about the meeting.
b) She bought some carbon tetrachloride **to remove** a stain from a blouse.

Complete these sentences in any sensible way. Add an expression which starts with an infinitive with 'to'.

1 I telephone my friend _____.
2 Mary went to the market _____.
3 Fishermen use bait _____.
4 The Government increased taxes _____.
5 John held up his hand _____.
6 Mary weighed the parcel _____.
7 Farmers use fertilisers _____.
8 They use insecticides _____.
9 I turned the radio on _____.
10 We stopped at a petrol station _____.

4 Adjective + an infinitive

a) This cupboard is too heavy for me **to lift.**
b) This cupboard is too heavy **to move.** (= for me to move)
c) He is too inexperienced **to be made** manager.
d) I am delighted **to meet** you. (at the first meeting)
e) I am delighted **to have met** you. (when leaving)

Exercise 4

Complete these sentences by putting in any sensible infinitives.

1   I'm sorry but you're too young _____ the competition.
2   We were not very pleased _____ that the price of electricity is going to be raised by 10 per cent.
3   I'll introduce you to David. He is very anxious _____ you.
4   The escaped prisoners are certain _____ soon. There is nowhere for them to hide.
5   It is dangerous _____ a match near a tin of petrol.
6   It is impossible for human beings _____ like a bird.
7   Arabic is not an easy language for a foreigner _____ quickly.
8   Her plane is due _____ at half past seven.
9   Are you old enough _____ a driving licence?
10 Patrick is a brilliant player. He is bound _____ for the national team.
11 I was lucky _____ a ticket for the concert. They were nearly all sold.
12 It was unwise of you _____ your money in such a risky scheme.

5 Able to, capable of

able to + an infinitive

She is able to use a computer.

capable of + a gerund

She is capable of using a computer.

6 How, when, where, what + an infinitive

How	I don't know how to do it.
When	They are not sure when to start.
Where	He wants to know where to put the machine.
What	I couldn't decide what to say.

7 Expressing obligation

Internal (moral) abligation

a)   We should be polite to other people.
b)   You ought to be kind to animals.

External obligation

a)   You must not enter another person's home without his permission. It is against the law.
b)   All vehicles have to stop when the traffic lights are red.

Exercise 5

Make up sentences showing what somebody should, ought to, must or has to do.
Use 'not' when necessary.

Example   That tap is leaking. You must repair it. You must not waste water.
         or   You should repair it.

1   Your driving licence has expired.
2   Uncle is coming to dinner this evening.
3   That tin contains petrol.
4   My brother is going to get married next Saturday.

5 You've left the door of the refrigerator open.
6 Tell Josh that smoking is bad for his health.
7 I've got to go now.
8 David has toothache.
9 Be careful! That water may not be fit to drink.
10 Your handwriting is horrible!

8 I am requested to inform you

These expressions are sometimes used in very formal letters. We can use an infinitive with 'to' after them.

I am requested	I am asked
I am instructed	I am obliged
I am directed	I am ordered

Example 1

a) I am directed to thank you for your letter and to inform you that it is receiving attention.
b) I am reluctantly obliged to warn you that any repetition of this conduct will lead to your dismissal.

9 About to

We can use an infinitive with 'to' after 'about' when we want to show that something will happen very soon.

Example 2

a) Peter was about to go to bed when somebody shouted 'Fire! Fire!'
b) Hurry up! The train is about to go. We don't want to miss it.

10 Intend to, no intention of

The above words are used in different ways:

a) I do not intend to visit London on my way to New York.
b) I have no intention of visiting London on my way to New York.

We can use 'intend' with or without 'not'. However, 'intention' is more common when used after 'no'.

11 I look forward to meeting him

Sometimes students think that we must use an infinitive form after 'to'. This is not always correct. Notice the following expressions:

a) I look forward to seeing/meeting/welcoming Mary next Monday.
b) I hope you don't object to waiting a few minutes.
c) They are opposed to moving to another district.
d) Her work is confined to giving advice – not money.

12 Except

These sentences show how we can use an infinitive after 'except'.

a) Mrs Lee has gone to Canada on business. There's not much we can do except wait for her to return.
b) According to the doctor, Susan is in a critical condition. He says there's nothing we can do now except pray that she recovers.

76 Participles

1 Forms

	Present	Past	Perfect
Active Passive Continuous	writing being written	written written	having written having been written having been writing

Examples

1 Sophie is in the other room, writing a letter to a friend.
2 Notes written in pencil are not always easy to read.
3 Having written to the company three times, and never having received a reply, I decided to go and see the manager myself.
4 There are some new shops being built not far from my home.
5 Never having been bitten by a dog, Mary is not at all afraid of dogs.
6 We stopped for a rest at eleven o'clock, having been walking for nearly five hours by then.

2 Common uses of participles

a) *As adjectives*, e.g. an insulting remark, an injured man.
b) *To form tenses*, e.g. she is writing, this was written.
c) *To introduce an expression which gives us information about a person or thing.* For example, in (1) above 'writing' starts an expression which tells us about Mary. In (2), 'written' starts a phrase which tells us about 'notes'.

Find the participle expressions in examples 3 and 6 above. Which words do they give us information about? Is each expression before or after the word it tells us about?

3 Noun + participle expression

We met these expressions in Unit 75:

a) I saw an old man cross the road. (completed action)
b) I saw an old man crossing the road. (not completed)

Exercise 1

Assume that the following actions were not finished. Put in any suitable present participle (ending in -ing).

1 On my home from work, I stopped to watch some men _____ a telephone cable.
2 I saw the men _____ in a shallow hole at the side of the road, so I guessed that they were from the telephone company.
3 Mary heard a noise, so she turned round. She saw a black cat _____ up a tall tree. She noticed a dog _____ at the bottom of the tree.
4 When I was travelling on a bus, I heard two ladies _____ about the high

prices at the market. (Remember that we do not use 'about' after 'discuss'.)

5 Peter heard a noise, so he looked out of the window. He saw a fire-engine _____ towards the industrial part of the town.

6 When you came in just now, did you notice anybody _____ outside?

7 Mary overheard two men _____ the people who live in this block of flats. She thinks the men may be burglars.

8 When Peter went round the corner, he was surprised to see a crowd of people _____ towards him. Then he noticed that they were chasing somebody.

9 Yesterday I heard two customers in a shop _____ French to the shop assistant. I stopped to listen to them _____ about a dress but I could not understand everything they said.

10 On television I saw a helicopter _____ two men who were trapped on the side of a mountain.

present participle
a) The boy **sitting** next to Peter is my cousin.
b) Vehicles **blocking** the traffic will be towed away.

past participle
c) The boy **injured** in the accident last week has fully recovered.
d) Vehicles **made** in Japan are usually very reliable.

Exercise 2

Put in expressions which start with a present or past participle, as in the examples above. Your expression can start with a participle made from the verb in brackets or you can choose your own words.

1 I'm sure the girl _____ is Mary's cousin. (sit)
2 The car _____ belongs to my father's friend. (park)
3 We have just bought a television set _____. (make)
4 People _____ sometimes find it difficult to get good medical attention. (live)
5 Who is that girl _____? (wave)
6 Listen to the birds _____. (sing)
7 The bridge _____ is going to be rebuilt. (destroy)
8 The notice in the store said: **People _____ will be prosecuted**. (catch)
9 The player _____ will probably be fined or suspended. (send)
10 The man _____ looks like Mary's brother. (stand)

4 Starting a sentence with a present participle

What does this sentence mean?
a) *Looking out of the window, I saw my friend.*
   Who was looking out of the window: the speaker or his friend?

What does this sentence mean?
b) *Climbing up a tree, I saw a grey monkey.*
   Who was climbing up the tree: the speaker or a monkey?

If you start a sentence with a present participle expression, make sure that it is not ambiguous. Usually the expression will refer to the noun or pronoun which starts the main clause, for example:

c) **Thinking** that he was the last to go to bed, John turned out the light.
d) **Not realising** that his sister was still writing a letter, John turned out the light as he left the room.

Express these sentences in a different way. Make one new sentence in each case, similar to the models above.

1 John did not realise that it was five o'clock. He got out of bed.
2 Mary felt rather tired. She decided to have a rest.
3 I hoped to catch the bus. I ran as fast as I could.
4 Mr Croal thought it was going to rain. He took an umbrella with him.
5 I did not realise that the telephone was out of order. I tried to telephone my brother.
6 Mary opened the door quietly. She tiptoed into the room.

5 Finishing a sentence with a participle expression

a) John rushed out of the room, **slamming** the door behind him.
b) Mary turned out the light, not **realising** that her brother was reading a book.
c) John rushed out of the room, **delighted** with the good news.
d) Mary turned out the light, **annoyed** by her brother's laziness.

As the examples show, we can put a participle expression at the end of a sentence. The expression does *not* refer to the noun immediately before it, so we use a comma to separate the expression from the preceding part of the sentence. Compare these two examples:

e) John rushed out of the room leading to the kitchen.
f) John rushed out of the room, nearly knocking his sister over as he did so.

Put in commas where necessary:

1 I picked up a wallet lying on the ground outside a shop.
2 I picked up a wallet wondering who had lost it.
3 We followed the path hoping that it would lead to the village.
4 We followed the path leading to the village.
5 Mr Lee looked at the water in the reservoir and frowned knowing that it would last only a few more days.
6 Mr Lee looked at the water in the well and frowned suspecting that it was heavily polluted.
7 The inspector went to take samples of water from the well supplying the whole village with drinking water.
8 This is the reservoir supplying the town with water.
9 When Mary got on the ferry, she spoke to a lady sitting next to her.
10 When Mary got on the ferry she spoke to a lady hoping to find out the best way to reach the Immigration Department.
11 The gangsters got out of their car and entered the shop not knowing that eight detectives were waiting for them inside.

12   The motor-cycle came round the corner on the wrong side of the road narrowly missing an oncoming taxi.

6   Using a perfect participle

These are the perfect participles mentioned at the beginning of this unit:

Verb	write	kick
Active Passive Continuous	having written having been written having been writing	having kicked having been kicked having been kicking

a)   Having written her essay as carefully as possible, Mary was disappointed when she did not get very good marks.
b)   Never having met Susan before, I was surprised to see how beautiful she was.
c)   Having been kicked deliberately, the goalkeeper was very angry.
d)   Never having been introduced to the girl, I did not like to say anything to her.
e)   Having been waiting half an hour, we finally decided to go home.
f)   Not having been working there very long, Mary did not know what to do when the manager was suddenly taken ill.

Exercise 5

This is a difficult exercise, so work slowly and carefully. Put in the correct perfect participle of the verb in brackets.

1   (lose) _____ all my money, I had to walk home.
2   (cheat) _____ before, Mrs Lee was very careful when she went to buy some jewellery.
3   Not (tell) _____ that there was no petrol in the car, Mr Smith was annoyed when he could not start the engine.
4   Not (live) _____ in the country many weeks, Mrs Brown found that many things were strange to her.
5   Never (fly) _____ in an aeroplane before, Mary was rather nervous when she got on and sat down.
6   (warn) _____ of the danger of snakes, we were careful when we went for a walk in the hills.
7   (finish) _____ his homework as quickly as possible, Peter rushed off to play football for his club.
8   Zoë was delighted when she first visited Malta, never (be) _____ there before.
9   We had to walk home, (miss) _____ the last bus through our own carelessness.
10   (wait) _____ more than a fortnight, Mary was relieved when she finally received a letter from her brother in Canada.

77 Prepositions

In this unit, we will consider prepositions, adverbial particles, some phrasal verbs and some short adverbs.

1 Time and date

in	on	no preposition
in the morning in the evening in July in 2004	on Monday on Monday morning on Sunday on Sunday evening on 4th July on Christmas Day on my birthday	last Monday last Monday morning next Sunday next Sunday evening last/next July yesterday tomorrow

Exercise 1

Correct any errors in these sentences:

1 My friend arrived at Christmas Day.
2 There was a severe storm on last Monday evening.
3 Our holiday begins from next Monday.
4 My mother's birthday is at 31st October.
5 I saw her on last Sunday.
6 We moved to a new flat at 2001.
7 It is very humid at the summer.
8 On next Sunday we are going to visit my uncle.
9 What are you going to do in Saturday morning?
10 We are going to have a party in Tuesday evening.

Check that you can use these expressions correctly:

Note: *Some Americans omit 'on' before a day of the week. For example, in American English one would say 'Sunday we went to San Francisco'. In British English one would say 'On Sunday we went to San Francisco'.*

early in the morning
early one morning/day
in the early afternoon/evening
in the day-time
at the same time
at half past seven
at night (during the night)

during the day
for four days
for a few minutes
since (last) Monday
since five o'clock
during the week
during August

2 No preposition is needed

'To lower' means 'to put down'. Therefore we do not need 'down' after 'lower'. 'Retreat' means 'go back'. Therefore we do not need 'back' after 'retreat'.

Exercise 2

Take out any words which are unnecessary.

1 We visited to the museum last Thursday.
2 The increase in the number of people can match with the increase in the number of homes.
3 We all stopped talking when Mary entered into the room.
4 I heard some men discussing about a fire at a factory.
5 My friend returned back to his own country last Friday.
6 All that rubbish must be removed away as soon as possible.
7 Mrs Brown wants to speak to you concerning about your career.
8 Susan asked me to accompany with her to the party.
9 The doctor advised me to take in the medicine twice a day.
10 The policeman looked up and saw that a car was approaching to him.
11 They have a holiday for every seven days.
12 Ships leave here and sail to everywhere in the world.
13 Yes, I know Cyprus quite well. I went to there last year.
14 Our company made a loss last year but this year we recovered back the sales we had lost previously.
15 Most tourists travel by air in nowadays because it is cheaper and quicker.

3 Some problem words

Sometimes students confuse two words or two different uses of the same word. Check that you know how to use the following words:

Problem word	Example
sympathy for	We felt a lot of sympathy for her.
sympathise with	We all sympathise with her.
sympathetic towards	They were sympathetic towards her.
lack (noun)	He shows a lack of enthusiasm for his work.
lack (verb)	He lacks enthusiasm for his work.
is lacking in	He is lacking in enthusiasm for his work.
regret (noun)	Now he is full of regret for his decision.
regret (verb)	Now he regrets his decision.
contact (noun)	We must get in contact with Mary.
contact (verb)	We must contact Mary.
demand (noun)	There is not much demand for asbestos now.
demand (verb)	They demand an explanation.
request (noun)	He submitted a request for an increase in salary.
request (verb)	He requested an increase in salary.
discussion	They are having a discussions about the plan.
discuss	They are discussing the plan.
stress (noun)	We must put more stress on marketing.
stress (verb)	We must stress marketing much more.
emphasis (noun)	Put more emphasis on hygiene.
emphasise (verb)	Emphasise hygiene much more.
claim (noun)	He submitted a claim for $2,000.
claim (verb)	He claimed $2,000 as compensation.

suspicions (noun)	The police have their suspicions about him.
suspect (noun)	He is a suspect in the crime.
suspect (verb)	They suspect him of having robbed a bank.
enter a room	My grandfather entered the room slowly.
enter into an agreement	We have entered into an agreement with an overseas company to assemble cars here.
investigation	There was an investigation into the fire.
investigate	They investigated the cause of the fire.

Exercise 3

Put in any missing words. In some cases, no word may be needed.

1 What you must do is emphasise _____ the importance of agriculture.
2 The Immigration Officer demanded _____ my passport.
3 Miss Lee is very hard-working and intelligent but perhaps she is lacking _____ experience.
4 I sympathise _____ you. Is there anything I can do to help?
5 If you have any queries, please contact _____ the Service Manager.
6 Mary probably regrets _____ her hasty decision to resign.
7 Most people are sympathetic _____ animals and try to prevent anybody from being cruel to them.
8 Do you think we have put enough emphasis _____ the advantages of the scheme?
9 The police suspect _____ that his injury was caused by another employee, so they are going to investigate _____ the matter.
10 Sometimes a pilot is used when a ship enters _____ a harbour, especially if the captain is not familiar with it.
11 The customer claimed _____ $500 as compensation for the damage caused by faulty spare parts.
12 What were you and Susan discussing _____?
13 Living in a large block of flats puts a certain degree of stress _____ the people there.
14 The police suspect the men _____ having set fire to the factory deliberately.
15 Please get in contact _____ me if I can help in any way.
16 Don't emphasise _____ their mistakes so much.
17 The prisoner demanded _____ a re-trial on the grounds that the judge had been prejudiced.
18 Now my brother regrets _____ his rudeness to you.
19 This stamp is different _____ the rest.
20 What is the difference _____ 'reticent' and 'reluctant'?

4 Two prepositions

Interested in	He is very **interested in** cycling.
Good at	He is very **good at** cycling.

When you use two words together, two different prepositions may be necessary, for example:

a) He is very **interested in**, and **good at**, cycling.
b) He is very **good at**, and **interested in**, cycling.

This sentence is wrong:

c)   He is very interested and good at cycling.

5 Preposition + pronoun

Remember that we use the object case of a personal pronoun if it follows a preposition. These examples are correct:

a)   Between you and **me**, I think he has made a mistake.
b)   It was kind of **her** to help us.
c)   I hope you're not angry with **him**.
d)   She complained about you and **me**.

6 Some common uses of prepositions, etc.

Check that you are familiar with these expressions. If necessary, make up sentences containing some of them.

about

9.58 is about ten o'clock
worry about something
be curious about it
write about education
he is about eighteen

to wander about the town
to quarrel/argue about something
They are about to leave.
to complain about it
I'm sorry about the accident.

above

in the examples above
in the sky above him
Above all, be honest.

He lives above us.
We could hear him above the noise.
See section 6 above.

across

Go across a road/harbour.
He lives just across the road.
I came across this old letter yesterday when I was clearing out a file.

after

Don't hit the dog. After all, it was only trying to protect us.
Look after yourself in Canada.
look after a baby
He came after lunch.
After that, there were no more wars.

against

a law against stealing
to vote against it
It's against my conscience.

to lean against a wall
He is against gambling.
to warn somebody against something

along

to run along a road
Hurry along now!
She knew the truth all along.

I'll go along with them.
(support them or join in a plan)

among(st)

We live among(st) friends.
to argue amongst yourselves
Amongst other reasons, I support the plan because it is efficient.

Divide it among(st) you.
to quarrel amongst yourselves

around
to walk around a tree   to travel around the world
He wrapped a blanket around the sick man.

at
good/bad/weak at English   delighted at passing
clever at mathematics   driving at high speed
at noon/midnight/night   buy shoes at $100 a pair
at once   at home/work
useless at most subjects   to be at war with a country
stare/point/look at   at first sight
at first/last   do two things at the same time
at least sixty   at the beginning/end of the month
to arrive at a place   at six o'clock
I met her at Christmas.   at my friend's house
She came at Easter.   at the moment
He is at a loss to know what to do.   work hard at it
disappointed at failing   at dawn

before
He came before Christmas.   We must finish before 5 p.m.
She will arrive before long.   Look before you leap.
I had never been to Mauritius before,   Wash before you go to bed.
so I was very surprised.   He was born before 1960.

behind
behind the door   behind with the rent (in arrears)
in the car behind us   say things behind a person's back
behind the times (old-fashioned)

below
see below   below the belt (unfair)
in the example below   below the surface
below the knee   below him (in position)
He lives below us.   His mark is below average.

between
between him and me   a quarrel between two people
between $50 and $60   Share it between you.
Don't let anything come between us.   a choice between two alternatives
We can do the work between us.   Leave a space between the desks.

beyond
beyond (any) doubt   Don't live beyond your means.
beyond my power   beyond your expectations

by
made by hand   It works by electricity.
signed by Peter   Divide/multiply it by two.
learn by heart   live by painting pictures
travel by sea/bus/train   We mush finish by Wednesday night.
little by little   two metres by four by three

By the way, what is his name?
She did it by herself.

paid by the hour/day/week/month
I cut my hand by accident.

Exercise 4

Put in any missing words. Some of these sentences are based on the above words but many are not.

1 If 50 per cent is the pass mark in a test, 48 is _____ the pass mark and 52 is _____ it.
2 If a share is issued at a price of $10, when its price is $9.50, we can say that the price is _____ par.
3 Don't quarrel _____ the money. Share it _____ the five of you.
4 My father is going to get rid _____ his old car. It has never been the same since it was damaged _____ an accident.
5 I saw Mary just _____ lunch but I haven't seen her since noon.
6 My cousin used to be a waiter _____ a restaurant. Now he is the owner _____ several restaurants spread _____ the country.
7 _____ accordance _____ the rules, there will be a meeting next Friday evening _____ the company's offices _____ the tenth floor _____ City Building. You are invited to be present _____ the meeting.
8 _____ all the actors I know, Peter is _____ far the best.
9 I can't do two things _____ the same time _____ making a mistake.
10 This type of spanner is superior _____ that one and is much more useful _____ mechanics.

down

run down a hill
fall down the stairs
climb down a tree
lie down and have a rest
Please sit down.

Put your pens down.
He is down with the flu.
Calm down! It's not serious.
The fire will soon die down.
He won't let us down.

except

a) Except for Mary, everybody was present. (We must use 'for' here.)

b) Everybody was present except for Mary. (Here 'for' is optional.)

for

It is good/bad/suitable/fit/ready/ impossible for you.
pay for something
ask for the bill
look for a friend
wait for a bus
He's gone out for a walk/ride/drive.
Is there enough food for us?
He left for Rome yesterday.
It is rather the worse for wear.
He was punished for lying,
exchange A for B
He is the agent for a toy company.
That flat is for sale/rent.
It is used for making shoes.

I booked a table for six people.
Don't take his help for granted.
This letter is for Mary.
She works for her uncle.
He is the worse for drink.
They searched for treasure.
Who is responsible for this mess?
What plans have you made for the future?
Will they compensate him for his loss?
Mary applied for a job.
I have lived here for twenty years.
to prepare for something
This medicine is good for you.

He comes from Australia.
He is descended from …
from my point of view
retire/resign from work
different from
He received $50 from an uncle.
free from disease

to escape from
to be absent from work
say it from memory
It prevented him from leaving.
He stopped us from entering.
From my room, we can see the hills.
to suffer from a disease

in

in a box/pocket/bag/bottle
in London/New York
in my opinion
blind in one eye
deaf in one ear
in other words
in English
written in ink

in trouble/danger/distress
in the army/navy/air force
in a muddle/mess
in love/pain/tears
in a hurry
I'll be back in a fortnight.
in poor/excellent health
get in a taxi/car

We do not use 'in' in these expressions.

concentrate on reading
live on the tenth floor
according to custom
at the corner of the road
live on an island
He is not at home now.

The house was broken into.
We looked everywhere.
popular throughout the world
at the bottom of the hill
adapt yourself to changed conditions

into

get into trouble
get into difficulty
rush into a room

look into a problem
let somebody into a secret
put your back into your work

near

Our house is near the sea.
The tiger came nearer and nearer to us.

He is near the limit of his endurance.
I live near my school.

of

a new kind/sort/type of car
the Minister of/for Education
think of, be sure of, be certain of
How kind/cruel/wise/silly of you!
the top of the hill
the back of the bus
the best of the songs
in case of need/fire
to get rid of something
to dream of a person
to hear of a job
in spite of the storm
inform him of a change

a knowledge of Chinese
a little/great help to us
How careless/generous of him!
made of, full of, short of
a shortage/surplus of food
children of the same race/age
jealous/envious of somebody
to be aware of something
to be accused of a crime
She approves of you.
It consists of three parts.
It is composed of two parts.
without the help of your brother

off

fall off the table/ladder
Take your shoes off.

Turn/switch off the light.
put a meeting off until later

put off making a decision
Finish your work off.
to get off for a place
get off a bus
Keep off the grass.

They are well off (rich).
Break a piece off.
Don't leave the cover off.
The effects will wear off.
Let off a firework.

Exercise 5

Correct any mistakes in these sentences. You may have to change words, take some out or add some.

1 Claire sat down at a quiet corner of the room and read a book.
2 My friend did not want to go to the concert but I succeeded to persuade her and she finally agreed to go.
3 It is not easy to give a definition for many words used in political discussions.
4 Take a deep breath and try to blow all the candles off at one time.
5 Languages are more difficult to boys than to girls.
6 In the last fifty years, there has been a growing interest of trade in my country.
7 We thought we would miss the train but we managed to catch it in the last minute.
8 Early in one morning, my dog started to bark furiously, so I guessed that somebody was in the corridor outside.
9 Mary is very sincere on her belief that women are more suitable for some types of work than men are.
10 In a debate, it is sometimes necessary to remind speakers the main points which are being considered.
11 We ought to use more locally-made products instead foreign ones.
12 My grandmother is very old-fashioned and she objects the use of some modern inventions at home.
13 My father was walking so quickly that it was difficult for us to keep up him for most of the way.
14 When a child is very young, he starts to experiment his language and find out what he can use it for.
15 There is a limit to the amount of food a human being needs every day. If he exceeds beyond this level, he will get fat.
16 I enjoyed the film at the Ocean Cinema last night but it did not end up until nearly half past eleven, which was rather late.
17 The workers at that factory have gone on strike and they are demanding for a 15 per cent increase in their basic rate of pay.
18 This house is leasehold, so when the lease expires it will revert back to the owner.
19 Some of the players in our team lack of skill, so we need an experienced coach to help them.
20 Would you mind recording down the score for us?

on

on Monday evening
on purpose
on fire
on the table
put it on the notice-board
to concentrate on

on the contrary
on the other hand
spend money on it
keen on swimming
put your socks on
turn the light on

to put emphasis/stress on
get on a bus/train/plane
He is on holiday/leave.
on my way to
on sale
on good grounds
keep on talking
go on working

live on rice and fish
congratulate her on
there is a tax on
on time
on guard
on the whole
on my right

opposite

He lives opposite us.

His house is opposite ours.

out

out of stock
out of practice
out of reach
get out of bed
out of your mind
out of town
to set out for Rome
to be out (not at home)
to sort out a problem

to put a fire out
to find out the reason
to take your books out
to hold/hang out
to call/shout out
to go out of a room
out of a job
to burst out laughing
a bone out of joint

over

look over a wall
jump over a fence
think it over
to fall over
to turn a page over

to hand it over
overweight
over the limit
over sixty
over age

past

at half past seven
I walked past a hotel.

He ran past me.

per

per annum
$20 per kilogram
per month

$10 per litre
per capita (per head/person)
per cent

round

go round the shops
go round a bend
round the corner

round the clock
somewhere round here
round and round

through

get through a test
fly through a window
work through lunch
get it through a friend

go through (on the phone)
We went through a tunnel.
a deal fell through
go through a city

to

go to school
go the west of
give it to him
kind/cruel to

ready to start
sorry to
the first to come
curious to know

274

fix it to

made to order

have to stop

glad to

the last to go

anxious to help

get used to it

easy/difficult to

ten to four

reply to a letter

known to us

inferior to

made to measure

be alert to it

walk to and fro

sentenced to death

to his surprise

valuable to them

equal to

too hot to drink

want/like to go

delighted to

object to it

pay attention to

agree to help

towards

sympathetic towards him

towards the end of June

walk towards the sea

a contribution towards a new building

under

under the influence of

under the age of 18

under the carpet

under the bridge

under the control of

under these conditions

under the impression that

See under 'Prepositions'.

up

put up the price

put up your hands

get up in the morning

stand up

climb up a tree

bring up a child

keep up with a person

draw up a plan

It's up to you.

stay up late

grow up

Hurry up!

up to now

clean up

make up your mind

look a word up

Cheer up!

Shut up!

What's up?

catch him up

tie a parcel up

with

go with him

walk with her

play with a ball

mix A with B

agree with him

disagree with

quarrel/argue with

provide him with

be careful with it

keep up with him

deal with him

compared with it

experiment with

find fault with

have difficulty with

be familiar with

supply them with

with any luck

without

travel without a ticket

go without food

go without saying goodbye

Without doubt, he is right.

do it without help

Do it without fail!

I can't live without you.

without taking advice

Exercise 6

Put in suitable words.

1 This application falls _____ the third category and will be dealt _____ later on.
2 The explanation you want is _____ the top of page 47.
3 The plan had many advantages. _____ brief, it looks good _____ me.
4 Nicola says she has no intention _____ being present _____ the meeting _____ Monday evening since she is not _____ favour _____ the proposal.
5 I have promised to support Mary by voting _____ the proposal, and I agree _____ her that it has many defects. Indeed, it may be harmful _____ the club as a whole.
6 It is not polite to leave a party _____ thanking your host or hostess.
7 He doesn't have much knowledge _____ the facts of the case, so we can't rely too much _____ his opinion.
8 Nevertheless, _____ my opinion he is a trustworthy witness and you can have confidence _____ what he says.
9 Can you translate _____ French _____ English fluently? There is a vacancy _____ a simultaneous interpreter _____ the legal department _____ our company.
10 Peter usually writes _____ us _____ least once a fortnight and tells us how he is getting _____ _____ his new job _____ California.
11 _____ any doubt, this is the finest example _____ Shang pottery _____ exhibition today.
12 The train left _____ six o'clock, exactly _____ time. Jake was held _____ in a traffic jam but he just managed to jump _____ the train before it left.

---

78 Pronouns

I PERSONAL PRONOUNS

a) Use the object form of a personal pronoun after a preposition.
b) Make sure that your pronoun agrees with its antecedent (the word that comes before it and to which it refers).

Exercise 1

Correct any mistakes (in the use of pronouns) in these sentences.

1 Mary likes classical music and often listens to them at home.
2 One evening, my friend and me were going to a concert when it suddenly started to rain.
3 When we make friends with other people, you must keep them and treat them fairly.
4 Somebody fell in the water, so a man jumped in to save he or she and he succeeded after a struggle.

5　Although the food did not taste very nice, we ate them all because we did not want to offend Uncle.

6.　Most people will agree that traffic problems are very difficult for the Government to solve them.

7　We saw two beautiful boats with red sails on it.

8　Mary stood between he and I, wondering what had happened and determined to prevent us from arguing any more.

9　It was me who was to blame for the mistake – not you.

10　I and my friend decided to go shopping last Saturday.

11　The manager wrote Mrs Smith a letter, informing that the machine would be delivered in a week's time. He hoped she would be patient.

12　New York is a large city and she is still developing.

13　Some parents rely on their children to look after themselves when they are too old to work and have very little money left. Then the children can repay their parents for the love and care shown when they were young.

14　It is not easy to translate ideas into English and then write it down correctly.

15　Students spend a long time studying mathematics at school but when he leaves school, he gradually forgets most of what he has learnt.

2 REFLEXIVE PRONOUNS

The reflexive pronouns are **myself, yourself, himself, herself, itself, ourselves, yourselves, themselves** and **oneself**.

a)　We call these pronouns 'reflexive pronouns' when they are the object of a verb or come after a preposition:
   (i)　Mary accidentally cut **herself** when she was opening a tin.
   (ii)　Look after **yourselves** on the journey, boys!

b)　We do not use the ending -selfs for any of these pronouns.

c)　Some verbs are often followed by a reflexive pronoun, for example:
   (i)　We all enjoyed **ourselves** at the picnic.
   (ii)　Mary blamed **herself** for the mistake.

d)　These pronouns are called 'emphasising pronouns' when they emphasise a word.
   (i)　The President **herself** opened our new school building.
   (ii)　The fire damaged a lot of equipment in the store but the building **itself** was not very badly affected.

Exercise 2

Put in suitable reflexive or emphasising pronouns:

1　Control _____, Anne! Don't get hysterical!

2　My brothers agreed to go swimming but I _____ decided not to go.

3　At first, I thought the dogs were going to jump into the flooded river but they just managed to stop _____ at the edge of the river.

4　Don't prick _____ with that needle, Mary.

5　The girls really enjoyed _____ when they went on a tour of Europe.

6　Now my brother is earning enough money to be able to support _____ without having to borrow money.

7 Don't try to lift that log by _____, boys. You'll only strain _____ if you do.
8 There is nothing wrong with the country _____ but the climate is unpleasant at some times in the year.
9 Mary: What did you say?
John: Nothing. I was just talking to _____.
10 One must learn to look after _____ in a strange city.
11 *John:* What's the matter?
Mary: Oh! I'm so mad I could kick _____. I've left my key on the table in the lounge. Now we can't get in!
12 You're looking very pleased with _____, girls. What have you done?
13 Sometimes Paul cannot express _____ clearly because he insists on using long or rare words.
14 Cats are clean animals. They spend a lot of time washing _____.
15 We don't need any help. We can move the cupboard by _____.

3 POSSESSIVE PRONOUNS

The possessive pronouns are **mine, yours, his, hers, ours** and **theirs**. We never add an apostrophe to these pronouns. They are used in place of a possessive adjective and a noun.

a) You've got my book. This is **yours**. (= your book)
b) That's not your bicycle. It's **mine**. (= my bicycle)

4 RELATIVE PRONOUNS

You already know that we can use a pronoun in place of a noun. If the pronoun relates two statements about the same person or thing, we call it a 'relative pronoun'.

As the subject of a clause

Use 'who' or 'that' + a verb when you refer to people.

a) I know the girl. That girl found the money.,
b) I know the girl **who/that** found the money.

Use 'which' or 'that' + a verb to refer to animals and things.

c) This is the bus. This bus goes to the station.
This is the bus **which/that** goes to the station.

Exercise 3

Join each pair of sentences to make one sentence, as in the examples above. You can use ' that' in all sentences or choose between 'who', 'which' and 'that'.

1 Where is the key? The key opens this cupboard.
2 That is the man. That man sold me the watch.
3 I'll speak to the lady. She owns the shop.
4 Do you know the girl? She is standing next to Mary.
5 Some men have built a car. The car runs on solar energy.
6 I think this is the path. This path leads to the river.
7 Rabies is a disease. It can be fatal to human beings.

8 Is this the train? This train goes to London.
9 What happened to the cow? It escaped from some men and ran through the streets.
10 Soldiers will soon recapture the prisoners. They escaped from prison during the night.
11 That is the tree. That tree is dangerous and should be cut down.
12 I don't know the name of the lady. She gave away the prices.

Look at this sentence:

I know the girl **who found your watch**.

We call 'who found your watch' a relative clause (or an adjectival clause). We can put this type of clause early in a sentence.

The girl **who found your watch** is Peter's cousin.
The bus **which goes to the station** has not come yet.

Exercise 4

Make these sentences longer by putting in relative clauses in the blank spaces. Start with 'that', 'who', or 'which' + a verb. Use 'who' (or 'that') for people. Use 'which' (or 'that') for animals and things.

1 The boy _____ is my best friend.
2 The train _____ is half an hour late.
3 Anybody _____ may be arrested by the police.
4 The police believe that the fire _____ was started deliberately.
5 Do you know the man _____?
6 I can't find the key _____.
7 People _____ should not throw stones.
8 Make up your mind. He _____ is lost.
9 The man _____ is the father of an old friend.
10 Vehicles _____ have to pass a fitness test every year.
11 People _____ may die of lung cancer or another disease.
12 During the night, the road _____ was blocked by a landslide.

As the object of a clause

Use 'whom' or 'that' when you refer to people.

a) I know the girl. The Inspector congratulated that girl.
    I know the girl **whom/that** the Inspector congratulated.

Use 'which' or 'that' when you refer to animals and things.

b) This is the bus. A lorry hit this bus.
    This is the bus **which/that** a lorry hit.

Important notes

Especially in speech, we often omit the relative pronoun in sentences like those above. Thus we can say and write:

a) I know the girl the Inspector congratulated.
b) This is the bus a lorry hit.

Do not repeat the object in the relative clause:

Wrong	This is the camera which I bought it yesterday.
Right	This is the camera (which) I bought yesterday.
Wrong	Those are the men I saw them near your car.
Right	Those are the men I saw near your car.

Exercise 5

Experiment with these sentences. In each place put a subject + a verb (+ more words if you like) and try to make sensible sentences.

Example   The man ... lives in the same building as I do.

he is speaking to	the referee warned
Mary saw	my friend told us about
the police arrested	Mrs Lee mentioned
the dog bit	the lorry hit
the tree fell on	you met yesterday.

1 The boy _____ is my friend's brother.
2 Do you know the name of the man _____?
3 The wallet _____ belongs to an American tourist.
4 What did he do with the wallet _____?
5 The law _____ will not be very popular.
6 That strange light _____ might have come from a UFO.
7 Where is the book _____?
8 What are you going to do with the money _____?
9 The policeman _____ was very helpful.
10 My mother likes the picture _____.

After a preposition

This is a difficult pattern. It is given here for recognition purposes only. You can make up similar sentences if your English is extremely good.

Use 'whom' to refer to people.
Use 'which' to refer to animals and things.

1 I must thank the man **through whom** I got the job.
2 That is the boy **with whom** Peter once had a fight.
3 There is the man **to whom** you must apply if you want a job.
4 The lady **from whom** I heard the news is a friend of the judge.
5 The house **in which** Mary used to live has been pulled down.
6 Tell us about the game **in which** you scored two goals.
7 The hotel **at which** we stayed was an excellent one.
8 Do you happen to know the time **at which** the film ends?

Using 'whose'

We can use 'whose' to refer to a person or an animal. It is followed by a noun and verb. This is another difficult pattern. it is given here for recognition purposes but you can make up similar sentences if your English is good.

a)   The player **whose arm** was broken is Paul's cousin.

b) What happened to the man **whose name and address** were taken by the police?

c) The cat **whose paw** was injured has recovered completely.

Defining and non-defining clauses

Check that you know the difference between a defining and a non-defining relative clause. The punctuation and way we say these clauses are different.

defining clauses

Consider this sentence: 'The man is very rich.'

We do not know which man this sentence refers to. We can add a clause which defines 'the man': 'The man who owns this hotel is very rich.'

Here are further examples of sentences containing defining clauses:

1 The dog **which Mary is playing with** belongs to a neighbour.
2 You ought to speak to the man **who is in charge of the Accounts Department.**
3 Anybody **who steals goods from this shop** will be prosecuted.
4 I'll introduce you to the lady **who will produce the play.**

non-defining clauses

Consider this sentence: 'My uncle is very rich.'

We know which man the sentence refers to. He is the speaker's uncle. If we add some more words, they will not define the man because the word 'My' has already defined him:

'My uncle, **who owns this hotel**, is very rich.'

In written work, we put a comma before and after a non-defining clause. In speech, we lower the voice when saying the words in the non-defining clause:

'My uncle,   is very rich.'
              who owns this hotel,

Sometimes writers put a non-defining clause in brackets to show that it is not essential to the meaning of the sentence:

'My uncle (who owns this hotel) is very rich.'

Then the brackets take the place of commas.

Here are further examples of sentences with non-defining clauses:

1 That dog belongs to my neighbour, **who has several pets.**
2 You ought to speak to Mr Lee, **who is in charge of the Accounts Department.**
3 I'll introduce you to Mrs Lee, **who will produce the play.**
4 My younger sister, **who is very good at mathematics,** wants to be an accountant.

In this unit, we will consider common problems with the use of punctuation marks (including the hyphen).

Using a full stop

With abbreviations

The use of a full stop after many abbreviations is now optional. Some years ago, people put a full stop after these abbreviations and ones like them:

Mr.	Capt.	Ltd.	Dr.	A.D.	U.N.O.
Mrs.	Sgt.	Co.	Col.	B.C.	B.A.

Not long ago, some people omitted the full stop if the first and last letters of an abbreviation were the same as those in the full word. Then we had:

Mr (Mister) but Capt. (Captain)
Sgt (Sergeant) but Co. (Company)

In modern times, some people omit full stops after all abbreviations. In an examination, it is perhaps safer to use a full stop after an abbreviation.

In sentences

Put a full stop at the end of a sentence:

   a)   He turned off the light. Then he went to sleep.

If you join two sentences together, use a conjunction:

   b)   He turned off the light and then he went to bed.

If you join more than two sentences together, put a conjunction before the last one:

   c)   He locked the door, turned off the light and then went to bed.

Do not punctuate a subordinate clause or phrase as if it is a separate sentence.

Wrong	We could not go to work yesterday. Because the road was flooded.
Right	We could not go to work yesterday because the road was flooded.
Wrong	I have several hobbies. For example, stamp-collecting, playing the guitar, and cooking.
Right	I have several hobbies as, for example, stamp-collecting playing the guitar, and cooking.
	(The comma after 'guitar' can be omitted.)
Wrong	I phoned my friend. Hoping to find out if he was free to play badminton.
Right	I phoned my friend, hoping to find out if he was free to play badminton.

There is often a difference between the punctuation of formal prose and that used in dialogue. Sometimes we do not speak in complete sentences, for example:

Mary: What did you think of the play?
Mary: Not bad at all. The acting was excellent and so was the scenery. Not much of a plot. Very ordinary and obvious. Never mind. I quite enjoyed it.

A few authors use this type of writing even in continuous prose. It is not a suitable method for formal and examination work.

Using a comma

These sentences show some of the more important uses of the comma:

- My best friend, Mary Smith, has a very cheerful and friendly nature.
- Are you ready, Peter?
- 'I don't like geometry', Mary said. 'It's very difficult.'
- 'I don't like trigonometry,' Anne said, 'because it's very difficult.'
- As we all know, agriculture is very important.
- To his great disappointment, the shop did not sell spare parts.
- I usually watch the news on television. However, I could not watch last night because I had to go out.
- To obtain the best possible result, wash this garment in warm water.
- You are too young for this job. Besides, you do not have any experience.
- The price of fuel has affected the economy, and the result has been disastrous for many people.

We do not use a comma in these sentences:

- The building in which I live has twenty floors.
- The problem is that they have no gas supply.
- Much of the work is done by machinery so that not many men are needed.
- That is why the traffic problem is such a difficult one to solve.
- We Catholics do not believe in divorce.
- Everyone in the country has a responsibility for its safety.
- Dogs do not often attack people although they often bark at them.

Exercise 1

Punctuate these sentences correctly, and put in capital letters when necessary.

1 I saw Mary Anne Susan and Margaret at the wedding last Saturday.
2 Money is all they are concerned with, it is very important to them.
3 Mr Brown is an engineer, he works in a factory, however he is also a very good painter.
4 John is a very pleasant and helpful boy not a bit like his father I quite like him.
5 My grandmother likes to read quietly, that is why she prefers to live by herself.
6 I started to get out of bed, then I remembered that it was a holiday.
7 The sky grew darker and darker, the wind increased in strength blowing all the papers off the table.
8 The need for coats is limited in this area. For the winter is not very cold as it is elsewhere.

9 My sister hopes to be a social worker when she is older, she wants to go to a university.

10 After the operation Peter could not eat or sleep very well a short walk made him feel faint. So he often had to rest.

Using a colon

Two common uses of the colon (:) are:

a) To introduce a list of numbered items, as shown in the line above.

b) To define, explain or give examples of a preceding word. However, compare the following examples. They are both correct.

   (i) He has many hobbies which include photography, cycling and underwater swimming.

   (ii) He has many hobbies: photography, cycling and underwater swimming.

In (i) we do not use a colon because the list is an integral part of the sentence. Here are two more correct examples:

   (iii) Examples of important currencies include the US dollar, the yen, the German mark and the Swiss franc.

   (iv) I can think of at least four important currencies: the US dollar, the yen, the German mark and the Swiss franc.

Using a semicolon

Not all writers use the semicolon (;) in the same way. It marks almost as long a break as a full stop. It separates grammatical sentences which are closely related in their ideas. In a passage of prose, we should be able to replace all the semicolons with full stops without changing the meaning of the passage. However, a few writers seem to use a semicolon frequently, while other writers hardly ever use it.

We can also use a semicolon to separate items in a list when we wish to use a comma within separate items, for example:

I can think of at least four important currencies: the US dollar, which has risen sharply in recent months; the Japanese yen, which relies on the strength of the Japanese export market; the German mark, supported by a strong economy and tight control of expenditure; and the Swiss franc, traditionally a very stable and reliable currency.

Using a question mark

Put a question mark after a direct question. Do not put one after an indirect question unless it forms part of a question. Please see Unit 74 (under the heading '3 Punctuation') for full details of this point.

Using an apostrophe

a) We use an apostrophe to show that a letter has been left out or that more than one letter has been omitted. Check that you know the full form of these common speech forms:

1	can't	4	I'd finished	7	shan't
2	o'clock	5	I'd like one	8	they've
3	didn't	6	won't	9	they're

| 10 he's here | 12 it's hot today | 14 he'll help you |
| 11 he's gone home | 13 it's run away | 15 we've finished |

b) The word *it's* has two possible meanings, as in 12 and 13 above.
    12 it's – it is
    13 it's – it has

The possessive adjective **its** never has an apostrophe, for example: **its tail**.

c) When an apostrophe is used to show possession, we follow these guidelines:

(i) Don't use an apostrophe at all unless you mean 'of'. Thus there is no apostrophe in such sentences as these:
- Small boys sometimes sail boats across this pool.
- Mary likes oranges and pears very much.

(ii) Put an apostrophe before the 's' if a noun is singular or forms its plural without adding an 's', for example:
- Where is Uncle's car? It's next to Mrs Lee's.
- There is a children's park not far from where the fishermen's nets are drying.

(iii) Put an apostrophe after the 's' if the noun is plural and forms its plural by adding 's', 'ies' or 'eys'.
- I can hear the ladies' voices. They must be talking about the tournament.
- Mary goes to a girls' school.

(iv) In most cases, use 'of' and not an apostrophe for lifeless things.
- The end of the pier was damaged by a ship. (not 'the pier's end')
- The roof of that house is made of tiles. (not 'the house's roof')
- She says the rear of the bus was damaged in the collision.

However, an apostrophe is used in these common expressions:

in a month's time	the sun's rays	a nation's glory
in two months' time	a month's pay	a ship's doctor
at arm's length	at one's finger tips	out of harm's way
at death's door	to one's heart's content	for goodness' sake
New Year's day	a stone's throw away	at one's wits' end
yesterday's news	the earth's surface	the cat's tail

(v) No apostrophe is needed in these sentences:
- Music was more progressive in the 1960s than in the 1990s.
- The Chans and the Browns are coming to dinner this evening.
- There were several JPs at the meeting.

But it is useful to put an apostrophe in this type of sentence:
- Mind your p's and q's. Dot your i's and cross your t's.

Exercise 2

Correct these mistakes

1 the building's walls
2 the sentence's meaning

3 the class's attention
4 drama's influence

5 the car's wheels	8 the hut's roof
6 the licence's number	9 a town's life
7 the saying's truth	10 the fire's cause

Exercise 3

Punctuate correctly:

1. Draw a circle with a diameter of 12 cm and calculate it's area.
2. You can use somebody elses book Mark if yours is at home.
3. I can hear the birds singing can't you.
4. Next week well get two days holiday.
5. One should always try to keep ones word dont you agree Mary.
6. The discovery of oil off the coast of our country will certainly increase its prosperity there is no doubt of this.
7. One should be ready to defend ones country when it is attacked by its enemies.
8. There will be a children's concert at the community centre on Saturday.
9. In science fiction the writers creative ability can make a book very successful.
10. Did you go to Peter and Marys wedding David.

Using a hyphen

If you look up 'dressing gown' in different dictionaries, you will see 'dressing gown', 'dressing-gown' and 'dressinggown'. Dictionaries do not always agree about the use of hyphens.

Use your common sense. Put a hyphen in when this helps to make your meaning clear. Compare these expressions.

He is an ill mannered boy.
He is an ill-mannered boy.

In the first, a reader might think that the boy is ill. The hyphen in the second makes the meaning clear.

Compare these two correct sentences:

She is a well-known singer.
She is well known in America.

The following words are correct:

sitting room	man eater	email	a nearby school
sitting-room	man-eater	e-mail	midnight
cooperate	passer-by	human beings	a caretaker
co-operate	hard-working	newspaper	a native-speaker

Using inverted commas (quotation marks or speech marks)

In printed material, we use single inverted commas for direct speech. Then we use double inverted commas for a quotation within direct speech, for example:

■   'The name of the book,' she said, 'is "Airport".'
     In writing, we can use the above method or this one:

■   "The name of the book," she said, "is 'Airport'."

Normally the words of a new speaker start a new paragraph:

At first, I could not see anybody in the shop. Mary and I waited patiently for somebody to appear. Then an old lady hobbled from a room at the rear of the shop.

'Yes?' she said. She spoke as if we had woken her up and she resented having to deal with a customer.

'Can we use the phone, please? It's an emergency.'

The old lady seemed to think for a moment, as if wondering whether to refuse or not.

'It's over there,' she said at last, pointing to the end of the counter.

Exercise 4

Punctuate these sentences correctly. Be careful because some of them contain indirect speech while others contain direct speech.

1 Mary said if it rains the sports meeting will be cancelled then it may be held next week
2 if there is a storm mary said the concert will be postponed until next saturday
3 there was a severe storm peter told us the final match was abandoned it will be played next monday
4 my friend told me that the game had been cancelled because of the rain he said that the game might be played later
5 excuse me the stranger said could you tell me where the nearest police station is mary gave the man directions and then said youd better go by taxi theres a taxi rank just over there many thanks the man said he turned and walked across the road to get a taxi
6 I wonder if youd do me a favour Peter asked his sister certainly she replied what is it ive got to go out Peter said but im expecting a phone call from David if he phones would you mind taking a message for me no problem Ann said
7 the sales assistant told me that he did not know when the manager would be back he did not know where he had gone
8 I dont know where the manager has gone the salesman said and I dont know when hell be back sorry I can't help you
9 we must find out which plane uncle is arriving on my mother said then we can phone the airport and find out if its on time
10 does your brother still work in a bank Mary asked me yes I said hes an assistant manager now he was promoted after he passed the final exam of the institute of bankers oh thats good news Mary said do congratulate him for me when you see him

1 Write ei after c. Write ie after other letters.

Notice that this rule applies only when *ei* and *ie* are spoken with an /ee/ sound. Thus words such as 'weight' and 'height' are outside the rule. An exception to the rule is 'seize'.

Check that you can spell these words:

ei	ie
deceive	believe
receive	achieve
conceive	thief
receipt	niece
deceit	piece
conceited	reprieve
ceiling	shriek
perceive	view
foreign	ancient
leisure	deficient
their	friend
freight	science
weight	society
neighbour	field

2 Adjectives can end in -ful. Adverbs can end in -fully.

Adjective   He is a careful driver and very helpful to us.
Adverb   He drives carefully. She smiled at us cheerfully.

Note the spelling of these words:

- skill, skilful, skilfully
- fulfil, fulfilled, fulfilling

3 Omit a final silent 'e' when you add a suffix starting with a vowel.

But retain the silent 'e' if the suffix starts with a consonant. Don't worry about words like 'judgement' and 'acknowledgement' because you can retain the 'e' or omit it, as you wish. Both 'judgement' and 'judgment' are used.

make – making   hope – hoping   shine – shining
write – writing   dine – dining   phone – phoning

4 Short vowel + single consonant – double consonant + -ing/ -ed.

After a short vowel + a consonant, double the consonant when you want to add -ing or -ed.

Short vowel	hop – hopping
	stop – stopped
Long vowel	hope – hoping
	hope – hoped

Exercise 1

Put in ei or ie.

1 Did you rec__ve my letter?
2 What a dec__tful person!
3 She has lost w__ght.
4 What's his h__ght?
5 Do you bel__ve him?
6 He is very conc__ted.

7 That's a big f__ld.
8 Mary is my best fr__nd.
9 I rec__ved your card last week.
10 They have lost th__r cat.
11 The c__ling is cracked.
12 What's the charge for fr__ght?

Exercise 2

Put in a suitable form of the verb in brackets.

1 Tell us what (occur) after the game.
2 You have (omit) a vital point.
3 (a notice) NO (SMOKE)
4 We stopped to watch some men (dig) a trench at the side of the road.
5 The man (admit) his offence when he was arrested.
6 We spent a long time (plan) the exhibition.
7 Mrs Collymore has (refer) your complaint to me.
8 More crimes were (commit) last month than in any previous month.
9 We'd better hurry up. It's (begin) to rain.
10 Mary and Anne have gone (shop). They'll be back for lunch.

5 American English

These examples show you some of the differences between American and British ways of spelling some words.

British	American
metre	meter
centre	center
theatre	theater
colour	color
honour	honor
behaviour	behavior
cannot	can not
programme	program
favourite	favorite
travelled	traveled
quarrelled	quarreled
skilful	skilful
aluminium	aluminum
cheque	check

6 Don't omit a silent letter

Check that you can spell these words correctly:

Wednesday	unconscious	soften
February	exhibition	answer
moisten	sarcastic	vehicles
discipline	doubtful	separate

7 Common errors

Check that you can spell the words in these lists. They contain words that are often spelt wrongly.

List 1

cinema	opinion	definitely	conscience
business	magnificent	beneficial	conscious
mathematics	familiar	reputation	robbery
instruments	similar	explosion	wealthy
argument	famous	explanation	valuable

List 2

invitation	recognise (or	restaurant	absurd
language	recognize)	competition	assembly
rhythm	excitement	messenger	library
rhyme	whether	modern	continuously
until	noisily	extend	reputation

List 3

destruction	mysterious	pronunciation	guidance
bargain	magnificent	immediately	sandwich
despised	privileges	temporary	collision
existence	pedestrians	temporarily	television
intelligent	exclamation	surprised	thorough

List 4

occasionally	forty	disappointed	collapse
accommodation	ninth	disagreeable	solemnly
approach	twelfth	committee	punctually
eliminated	organise (or organize)	definition	distributed
exaggeration	measured	grammar	appropriate

List 5

envelope	glimpse	incidentally	relatives
develop	clarify	superstitious	humorous
embarrassed	audience	interested	honourable
successful	lightning	necessary	appearance
headquarters	available	necessarily	encouraged

THE SIMPLE PRESENT TENSE

1 Active forms

The Simple Present tense (active) has two forms:

for normal statements: for emphasis: in questions: in negatives:	He grows rice. He does grow rice Does he grow rice? He does not like it.	You grow flowers. You do grow flowers. Do you grow flowers? You do not like it.

Notice that when we use 'does', we do not add an 's' to the second part of the verb.

A statement form can be used to ask a question. This is common when a speaker seeks confirmation, for example 'You *do* know him?'

2 Responses and incomplete verbs

We use 'does' or 'do' in these sentences:

a) Mary likes apples and so **does** her sister.
b) Mary likes apples and so **do** I.
c) *Peter*: **Do** you know the way to the river?
     John: Yes, I **do**.
d) David works much harder and gets better results than I **do**.

3 Uses

The main use of this tense is to express habitual actions. Thus we often use such words as *every day*, *often*, *never*, *rarely*, *seldom* and *frequently* with this tense.

a) My father usually gets up at six o'clock.

If we refer to past time, we do not normally use this tense. We use the Simple Past instead.

b) When he was young, my father always got up very early.

We can use this tense to express scheduled future action. This is common in referring to travel plans because the movements of buses, trains or aeroplanes are regarded as habitual.

c) Your plane leaves here tomorrow and reaches London on Monday.
d) What time does the plane for New York leave on Monday?

The Simple Present tense is also used in these types of conditional expressions;

e) If he has too much to drink, he behaves badly. (habit)
f) If anybody phones while you're out, I'll take a message.

This tense is used with *after*, *before*, *when* and *until* when we refer to future action in sentences like these:

g) We can play badminton after he **comes**. (= will have come)
h) You can't go out before Uncle **leaves**. (= will have left)
i) You must be polite when Mr Lee **comes**.
j) Wait until Mary **comes**. Then she'll help us.

We use this tense if a verb has no continuous form.

k) Who **has** the key now?
l) Mary **seems** very happy.

Some writers use the Simple Present tense when giving a list of dates and events in this way:

m) 1939: Hitler **attacks** Poland.
   Britain and France **declare** war on Germany.

n) 1941: Germany **attacks** Russia.
   Japan **attacks** the USA.

This is common usage in history charts but we do not normally use the Simple Present tense when writing about past events. Some writers occasionally change into a present tense to try to make their work more dramatic but this is not an easy technique. Only skilled writers can use it correctly.

Commentators sometimes use the Simple Present tense on the radio or on television.

o) Happy Horse **goes** to the front, followed by Lightning Prince. Sure Win **moves** up from fourth to third position.
p) Jones **runs** up and **bowls**. Smith **hooks** it to leg. Brown **dives** but **fails** to catch the ball.

This tense can be used to express eternal truths.

q) The earth **goes** round the sun.
r) Moisture **causes** iron to rust.

These are both habitual actions.

The Simple Present tense is also used:

When reporting a statement: Mary says she is very busy now.

When making a suggestion: Why don't you get a new watch?

In exclamations of this type: Here comes Uncle! There they go!

4 Problems in using the Simple Present tense

a) Check that the subject and verb agree, particularly when the subject is separated from the verb.
   ▪ The main reasons for this unsatisfactory state of affairs **seem** to be a lack of money and poor planning.
   ▪ After this, the water which is stored in the reservoirs and later **passes** through a treatment plant **comes** to us through metal or plastic pipes.
b) Use a singular verb with 'every' and its compounds.
   ▪ Every person **needs** air, food and water.
c) Use a singular verb with 'more than one'.
   ▪ There **is** more than one reason for this delay.

292

d) When 'not' follows 'need' or 'dare', do not add an 's' to the verb.
    ▪ He **dare** not tell anybody about it.
    ▪ Tell Mary she **need** not wait for us.
e) Use this tense with 'already' and the verb 'know'.
    ▪ Peter already **knows** what to do.
    ▪ This is something which most people **know** already.

Exercise 1

Put in the Simple Present tense of the verb in brackets.

1   The amount of rain (not vary) very much from year to year.
2   Everybody (have) to learn at least one language.
3   If he (not come), we shall have to play without him.
4   My father usually (read) a newspaper.or (watch) television after dinner.
5   Such careless acts as David's sometimes (cause) accidents which, in turn, (cost) lives.
6   As everybody (know) quite well, more than one planet (move) around the sun.
7   ... (live) your friend ... near you?
8   ... (belong) the rest of these books ... to your friend?
9   Where ... (stay) most tourists from Europe ... when they come here?
10 Such phrases as 'with a long beard' and 'in the back of the car' often (follow) the noun.
11 We can't start the meeting until the chairman or vice-chairman (come).
12 Waiting for buses (waste) a lot of time and (make) people impatient.
13 Peter or one of his friends (know) the answer to that question.
14 Neither the boys nor the girl (live) in this building.
15 Wait until the bus (stop) before you (get) off it.

5 The passive form of the Simple Present tense

The passive is used when the action is done to the subject. We can use 'by' to show the agent, but in many cases we do not mention the agent.

a) Many babies **are born** each year. They **are** usually **inoculated** against such diseases as poliomyelitis and measles.
b) A lot of rice **is grown** in Thailand and **exported** to neighbouring countries. (exported = is exported)

The passive form is made with 'is' or 'are' + a past participle. You can see from the second example above that when two verbs are used with the same subject, we can omit 'is' or 'are' before the second verb. Here is another example:

c) In all countries, robbers **are arrested** and eventually **taken** to a court. They **are given** a fair trial and **sent** to prison if they **are found** guilty.

Exercise 2

Put in the passive Simple Present form of the verbs in brackets.

1   In most large cities, many cars (steal) each year and not all of them (recover) by the police. Apparently, some (export) to neighbouring countries and quickly (sell).
2   When a ship reaches a sport, it (search) if the Customs officers think

there may be drugs on it. If drugs (found) on the ship, somebody may be arrested.

3 If safety precautions (not take) on building sites, a company may be prosecuted by the Government.

4 In the morning, vegetables (take) to the market and (buy) by housewives. Usually, these vegetables (wash) before they (sell). Poor quality or bad vegetables (throw) away.

5 Rain (collect) in reservoirs and (store) until it (need). The water (take) from the reservoirs and (treat) to ensure that it is pure. Chemicals (add) and dirt (remove). Then the water (pump) to service reservoirs near centres of population.

Exercise 3

This time you must decide whether the active or passive form of the verb is required. Put in a suitable form of the Simple Present tense of the verbs in brackets.

1 This report (consist) of three parts. It (believe) to have been written by an expert in horticulture.

2 That car (belong) to my father. It (clean) every day, so it always (look) in excellent condition.

3 It is unfortunately true that crime (exist) almost everywhere. In some cases, crimes (cause) by poverty or unemployment.

4 Before these radios (leave) the factory, they (inspect) to see that they (not contain) any flaws. Unsatisfactory products (reject) by the quality controllers, who then (enquire) into the causes of the defects. When necessary, improvements (made) in the production process.

5 These are very reliable machines but they (inspect) every week and (repair) or (overhaul) if they (have) defects. Our engineer (think) very highly of the machines and (recommend) that we buy additional ones from the same manufacturer.

6 *Mary:* When (arrive) Uncle, Anne?
Anne: His plane (expect) to land at six o'clock if it (not delay) by the storm.

7 Many traffic accidents (happen) every day. Some (cause) by carelessness or impatience. Strangely enough, a large number of accidents (occur) on straight roads and in fine weather. It thus (seem) that we must blame drivers in many cases.

8 The large hotels are full, so tourists (advise) to try small hotels and boarding-houses, but they (warn) that they may have to sleep at the airport if they (have) no reservations.

9 Each year a tree (shed) most of its leaves. These (fall) to the ground and (break) up by bacteria in the soil. The leaves (turn) into food for the tree. The roots of a tree (reach) out as far as its branches and (rely) on decayed leaves for food.

10 My sister (work) in a large bank. Each year some members of staff (promote) to more senior positions, so Mary (hope) that one day she will obtain a more responsible post.

THE PRESENT CONTINUOUS TENSE

Forms

Active Passive	
I am following She is following They are criticising	I am being followed She is being followed They are being criticised

In the active form, the subject is doing the action. In the passive form, somebody is doing the action to the subject.

Uses

The main use of this tense is to express temporary action, i.e. something which is happening at the moment of speaking but which will stop later on. We can compare the two tenses in this way:

Present Continuous It is raining now. (It will stop soon.)
Simple Present It always rains in May. (This is a habit.)

With a word such as 'always' or 'continually', we can express a repeated action in this way:

She is always reading a book when we arrive home.
People are always complaining about the cost of living.

This tense is used to express planned future action, especially when it concerns movement.

Uncle is leaving for London tomorrow evening.
We are meeting Mary at the City Hall next Friday morning.
Those goods are being flown to California tomorrow morning.

Notes

1   Do not use a continuous form of 'to have' if the verb refers to illness or possession. Use a non-continuous form.
    a)   Peter is absent today because he has a cold.
    b)   *Mary*: What's the matter?
         John: I've got toothache.
    c)   *Peter*: Who has the key to the cupboard?
         David: Miss Lee has.

2   Some verbs are not normally used in a continuous tense (unless they have a special meaning). These verbs include the following and we use non-continuous forms of them.

thinking

believe	remember	know	think
mean	understand	forget	

senses

hear	recognise	see
notice	smell	

desire	hate	love
wish	forgive	dislike
like	want	refuse

others

concern	consist of	own
belong	possess	seem
keep	contain	appear

■ This stew consists of meat and vegetables.

■ She seems to be very happy about something.

3 When replying to a spoken question, we often omit the verb 'to be' in this way:

Peter: What are you doing?
Mary: Looking for my keys.

or

Anne: What are you doing here?
Susan: Waiting for my mother. She's in the shop.

The answers shown above are normal ones. Only a foreigner would reply 'I'm looking...' or 'I'm waiting...'

Exercise 4

Put in a suitable present form of the verb in brackets. You may have to use the Simple Present tense or the Present Continuous tense.

1 *Mary*: What does the lady want?
  Anne: She (want) to speak to Mrs Wong. I (not know) why she (want) to speak to her.

2 *Peter*: Where's the television set?
  Anne: There's something wrong with it. Two men took it away. It (repair) now but it'll be back tomorrow.

3 (On the telephone)
  David: Can I speak to Anne, please?
  Mary: I'm sorry. She (wash) her hair now. Shall I ask her to phone you later?
  David: No, thanks. I'll try again later.

4 Peter is not at school today. He (have) a high temperature. His mother (think) he may have influenza.

5 Most of our goods (export) by air because they (need) urgently. A new warehouse (build) at the side of the factory. It should be ready by the end of March.

6 (In a science laboratory)
  David: What (keep) in that cupboard?
  Peter: Dangerous acids and poisonous substances. They (store) there so that the students cannot hurt themselves.
  David: Who (have) the key?
  Peter: I don't know. I (expect) the science teacher (have) it.

7 One result of the higher prices of fuel oil is that many countries (search) for oil and gas beneath the sea. Wells (drill) in numerous coastal areas and geologists (investigate) vast areas off Africa, Europe and Asia.

8 In a recent letter to a newspaper, a reader complained that not enough (do) to help disabled people. They still (face) difficulties on public transport. Getting into public buildings sometimes (present) problems. However, a Government spokesman said that this problem (consider) by various Government departments and improvements (made).

82 Verbs – past tenses

In this unit, we will revise three tenses which express past actions. It will be helpful to start with a simple explanation of the basic differences between these tenses.

BASIC DIFFERENCES BETWEEN TENSES

Present Perfect tense

(he has kicked; he has been kicked; he has been kicking)

The most common use of this tense is to express past action when the point of time at which the action happened is not mentioned.

a) I have been to London twice. (The writer does not mention the date or time.)
b) She has finished her work.
c) Somebody has been injured.
d) We have been waiting a long time.

Simple Past tense

(he kicked; he was kicked)

This tense is used to express past action when the point of time is mentioned or is known.

a) I went to London in 1999 and in 2001.
b) He finished his work ten minutes ago.
c) Somebody was injured in the accident last night.

Past Perfect tense

(he had kicked; he had been kicked)

This tense is used to show which of two past actions happened first. In most cases, it is used with a verb in the Simple Past tense and helps a reader to understand the sequence of past events.

a) He told us (on Monday) that he had just been to London (the week before).
b) I watched television after I had finished my homework.

c) The man said (at 6 p.m.) that somebody had been injured in an accident (at 5.50 p.m.).

Now we will consider these tenses in greater detail.

THE PRESENT PERFECT TENSE

Forms

Active	he has kicked; they have stopped
Passive	he has been kicked; they have been stopped
Continuous	he has been waiting; we have been working

In all cases, we can insert 'not' after 'has' or 'have'.

Uses

a) Do not state the exact date or time of a past action if you use this tense. The following sentences show very common errors:

Wrong	I have seen him last year.
Right	I saw him last year.

Wrong	He has hurt his leg when he was playing football.
Right	He hurt his leg when he was playing football.

b) Do not omit the final -ed if one is necessary.

Wrong	My brother has been offer a good job in Canada.
Right	My brother has been offered a good job in Canada.

c) Check that you choose 'has' or 'have' to agree with your subject.

Wrong	Everybody have gone home.
Right	Everybody has gone home.

d) We can use this tense with *already, just, now* and *recently.*

I have already finished. The film has just started.
Now you've made another mistake.
This road has been repaired recently.

e) We use this tense after *This is the first/second time* ... even if the action has not yet happened. This sounds illogical but it is idiomatic English.

Peter sat down to play chess with David. He stared at the board for a moment and then said, 'I'm sure I'll make a lot of mistakes. This is the first time I've played chess.'
Later on, Peter told his sister about playing chess with David. He said, 'I was lucky. I won two games although that was the first time I had played chess.' (Notice the use of the Past Perfect tense instead of the Simple Past tense.)
Half way through a game of badminton with her friend, Mary said, 'This is fun. Do you know this is the first time I've ever played badminton?' (Notice that Mary did not say 'I'm playing' although she was playing when she spoke.)

f) We can use the Present Perfect tense to refer to completed future action. We do this in some adverbial clauses of condition or time.

I'll take you for a drive when I've passed my driving test.
Put all your books away after you have finished your work.

g) We often use this tense with 'for' and 'since' in sentences like these:

I haven't seen Anne since she was fourteen.
We've been waiting (for) more than an hour.

h) We also use this tense with 'ever' (in questions) and 'never' (in statements).

Have you ever tried to swim across the harbour?
I've never been to Brazil. What's the climate like there?

Exercise 1

Put in the Present Perfect form of the verbs in brackets. You may need to use the active, passive or continuous form.

Examples:
Active   he has finished, we have gone
Passive   he has been caught; they have been arrested
Continuous   we have been waiting; she has been working

1 Somebody (take) my bike! I think it (steal)!
2 In recent years, greater efforts (make) to protect wild animals. As a result, some quite rare species (manage) to increase in numbers. This (achieve) despite the growth of towns.
3 *Mary*: What (do) you with my radio?
  John: Nothing. I (not see) it and I certainly (not touch) it.
4 According to the radio, a ship (sink) near the Paracel Islands. Two lifeboats (see) in the area but nobody (rescue) yet. A helicopter (go) to help in the rescue work.
5 In some countries, people (try) to emigrate for several years but (not succeed) yet. Sometimes they (refuse) permission by their own governments. In other cases, they (fail) to satisfy the immigration standards of overseas countries.
6 How long (work) you for your company? (promote) you yet?
7 Somebody (borrow) my dictionary. (get) you it, Mary?
8 Something (happen) to Uncle's car. There's a large dent in the driver's side. It looks as if he (have) an accident.
9 You can pay this invoice. It (check) twice and I (confirm) that we (receive) the goods.
10 Ah, there you are, Peter. I (look) for you for the past twenty minutes. If you (finish) your work, we can go out for lunch.

Exercise 2

Give possible responses to the questions below. Use the Present Perfect tense or the Simple Past tense, depending on the situation.

1 *Mary*: Have you ever been to America?
  a) *Anne*: Yes, and I (be) to Canada, too.
  b) *Joan*: Yes, I (go) there a couple of years ago.

2 *Mary*: Have you read this book?
  a) *Anne*: Let me see. No I don't think I (read) it before.
  b) *Joan*: Yes, I (read) it when I was in hospital last month.

3 *Mary:* Where's my badminton racket?
  a) *Anne:* I think Sue (borrow) it but I'm not sure.
  b) *Joan:* Sue (borrow) it this afternoon to play in a tournament.

4 *John:* What's happened? Why are all those people crowding round that car?
  a) *Tom:* The driver (knock) an old woman down a few minutes ago.
  b) *Bill:* I'm not sure. I think there (be) an accident.

5 *John:* Have you had dinner yet?
  a) *Tom:* Yes, we (have) it half an hour ago.
  b) *Bill:* No, we (not have) anything to eat for some hours.

THE SIMPLE PAST TENSE

Forms

Active   He stopped; he did stop.
Passive   He was stopped; they were stopped

The active form with 'did' is used a) for emphasis and b) to make negative statements and questions. Remember that we do not add -ed to a verb if we use 'did' before it.

Uses

a) The most common use of this tense is to express a completed (past) action when the time of the action is known or stated.

   ▪ He arrived last night. We met him at the station.
   ▪ Our house was built twenty years ago.

b) We use the Simple Past tense in generalised (less likely) conditional statements.

   ▪ If motorists drove more carefully, they would have fewer accidents.
   ▪ If the Government increased income tax, production might fall.

c) The Simple Past tense is also used in these patterns.

I would rather I wish If only It is time It's high time	I would rather you did not sell the car. I wish I lived in Australia. I wish Mary had a sister. If only we knew where he lives! If only we had more time! It is time we found the answer to this problem. It's high time you learnt to type.

d) We can also use this tense for habitual actions in the past.

▪ When my mother was young, she often sang at concerts.
▪ Men hunted animals to obtain their food centuries ago.

300

Irregular and difficult verbs

Check that you know the principal parts of these verbs:

Verbs which have the same form in the present and past

bet	put	cost	hit	thrust	split
let	cut	hurt	burst	forecast	upset
set	shut	shed	spread	broadcast	cast

Verbs which have the same form for the Simple Past tense and the past participle

bend	bent	feel	felt	lend	lent	sit	sat
bind	bound	fight	fought	light	lit,	sleep	slept
bleed	bled	find	found		lighted	slide	slid
bring	brought	get	got	lose	lost	spend	spent
burn	burnt	have	had	make	made	spill	spilt
buy	bought	hear	heard	mean	meant	stand	stood
catch	caught	hold	held	meet	met	stick	stuck
creep	crept	keep	kept	pay	paid	strike	struck
deal	dealt	kneel	knelt	say	said	sweep	swept
dig	dug	lead	led	sell	sold	tell	told
dwell	dwelt	learn	learnt	send	sent	think	thought
feed	fed	leave	left	shine	shone	win	won
				shoot	shot	wind	wound

Check that you know these verbs:

Infinitive	Simple Past tense	Past Participle
arise	arose	arisen
be	was	been
bear	bore	born(e)
beat	beat	beaten
become	became	become
begin	began	begun
bite	bit	bitten
blow	blew	blown
break	broke	broken
choose	chose	chosen
come	came	come
do	did	done
draw	drew	drawn
drink	drank	drunk
drive	drove	driven
eat	ate	eaten
fall	fell	fallen
fly	flew	flown
give	gave	given
go	went	gone
grow	grew	grown
hide	hid	hidden
know	knew	known

301

ring	rang	rung
rise	rose	risen
run	ran	run
see	saw	seen
show	showed	shown
sing	sang	sung
sink	sank	sunk
speak	spoke	spoken
steal	stole	stolen
swim	swam	swum
take	took	taken
tear	tore	torn
throw	threw	thrown
wake	woke	woken
write	wrote	written

These verbs form their Past tense by adding -ed but students often make mistakes with them:

complain	complained
destroy	destroyed
explode	exploded
flow	flowed
raise	raised
weigh	weighed

Exercise 3

Assume that we are making sentences about things which happened a week ago. Make short sentences with the Simple Past tense of the verbs below. Add any suitable words. Do not use 'not'.

Examples: forget: I forgot my books (last Saturday).
flow: The water flowed down the side of the hill.

1	blow	6	feel	11	mean	16	understand
2	meet	7	lend	12	slide	17	drive
3	teach	8	flow	13	spend	18	fell
4	strike	9	complain	14	spill	19	steal
5	dig	10	destroy	15	arise	20	wake

Exercise 4

Put in the Simple Past tense (active or passive) of the verbs in brackets.

1 During the fire last night, some gas containers (explode) from time to time and (be) a hazard for firemen. Clouds of black smoke (rise) from the scene and (blow) across the valley. The fire (bring) under control by 9 p.m. and the last flames (extinguish) by 9.30 p.m. Streams of water (flow) between the huts and (find) their way to the nearest drains.

2 Inflation (rise) steadily during the year but (fall) slightly in the last two months. Utility charges (reach) new peaks and (create) problems for housewives and manufacturers. Imported food (cost) more and even the price of water (increase). Meanwhile, overseas countries (raise) tariff

barriers against imports. These (make) it more difficult for exporters to find markets.

3 Last year I (spend) three months in London during the winter. It (be) very cold. There (be) ice on many roads, and the children (slip) and (slid) about on the ice happily. They (throw) snowballs at one another and (build) a snowman. I (not like) the weather at all. I (shiver) with cold sometimes and (wear) warm clothing.

4 Last week a distant relative (come) to stay with us. He is a rather mean man and always pays as little as possible for things. He (go) shopping and (want) to buy a watch. When he (find) a suitable one, he (bargain) with the sales assistant and (drive) the price down as low as possible. He (take) the watch home with him when he (leave) us. Two months later, he (write) an angry letter.

'The watch (stop),' he wrote, 'so I (take) it to a watch repairer. He (say) the watch wasn't Swiss at all. The case was Swiss but the cheap movement inside it (make) in another country.'

When I read his letter, I (think) to myself, 'Sometimes it's not wise to bargain too much.'

5 Yesterday the young daughter of a neighbour (take) to hospital in an ambulance. A week earlier, her father (put) some kerosene in a bottle. He (not stick) a label on the bottle. The little girl was thirsty, so she (drink) some of the kerosene by mistake. She (feel) ill almost immediately, so her mother (get) an ambulance.

THE PAST PERFECT TENSE

Forms

Active	he had finished; they had stopped
Passive	it had been finished; they had been stopped
Continuous	we had been waiting; he had been working

Uses

a) This tense is used to show which of two past actions happened first.

When I **had finished** my work, I went to bed.
The prisoner confessed two days after he **had been arrested**.
A bus arrived after we **had been waiting** about ten minutes.

Warning: *If there is only one verb in a sentence, you will probably be wrong to use the Past Perfect tense. Use it only when you want to tell your reader which action happened first.*

Sometimes we can tell which action happened first because there is a word such as 'after', 'when' or 'before' in a sentence. Then some native-speakers use the Simple Past tense, especially in speech. In written work, it is better to follow the pattern shown above. However, we do not need the Past Perfect tense if we use 'and then'.

We waited ten minutes and then a bus arrived.
I finished my work and then I went to bed.

b) We can also use the Past Perfect tense in indirect speech. Then it replaces a verb which was in the Present Perfect or Simple Past tense in the original speech.

My brother said that birds had pecked the tops off the tomato plants.
I asked her where she had been.

c)   We use this tense in conditional sentences which refer to the past:

If you had put a label on the bottle, Mary would not have drunk from it.
If we hadn't taken her to hospital immediately, she might have died.

d)   This tense is also used when we speak about a past event and use *I wish, I would rather, I would sooner*, or *if only*.

I wish I had not written that letter.
I'd rather you had not sold your bicycle.
If only we had bought a house when prices were low!

Note: This pattern is common when we want to show which of two past actions happened first:

when/after + Past Perfect, + Simple Past

After we **had walked/had been walking** for an hour, we stopped for a rest.

We can change the order of the clauses and write:

'We stopped for a rest after we had been walking for an hour.'
If the verb in the main clause is not in the Simple Past tense, we do not use the Past Perfect tense in the subordinate clause.

We usually stop for a rest after we have been walking for an hour.
We will stop for a rest after we have been walking an hour.
I go to bed when I have finished my work.

Exercise 5

Change into indirect speech:

1   He said, 'I've finished cleaning the car.'
2   She told us, 'I lost my bracelet last Saturday.'
3   I thought, 'I've lost all my money.'
4   'Have you seen Peter?' Mary asked me.
5   'Did your father sell his car?' Anne asked me.
6   I told her, 'No, he hasn't sold it yet.' (Ignore 'No'.)
7   My friend asked me, 'How long have you been waiting?'
8   I told him, 'I've been here half an hour at least.'
9   John said, 'My bicycle has been stolen.'
10 We told him, 'The thief was caught ten minutes ago.'

Exercise 6

In each of these sentences there are two verbs in brackets. Put one verb into the Simple Past tense. Put the other verb (showing which action happened first) into the Past Perfect tense.

1   I (realise) that I (leave) my keys at home.
2   Mary (not know) that her friend (go) out.
3   The policeman (warn) us that the bridge (knock) down by the flood.
4   About half an hour after we (go) to bed, the telephone (start) to ring.

5 My uncle (decide) to buy the car after he (be) for a trial drive in it.
6 After she (plant) the seeds, Mary (water) them carefully.
7 The accused man (deny) that he (drive) carelessly.
8 When I saw the results of the test, I (wish) that I (work) harder in the previous weeks.
9 Mary (admit) that she (make) the dress herself.
10 An old prospector (find) gold after he (look) for it for nearly twenty years.

PART 6

Oral English

A PRONUNCIATION

1 Check that you can pronounce the letters 'qu' correctly in these words:

/kw/   queen   quiet   aquarium   squatter   question
       quaint   quite   banquet   squashed   equality

/k/   queue   mosque   unique   bouquet   grotesque
       quay   mosquito antique   conquer   picturesque

2 Check that you can pronounce the letters 'et' in these words:

/it/   pocket   packet   market   banquet   bracelet
       rocket   racket   assets   locket   triplet

/ay/   buffet   chalet   parquet   bouquet   tourniquet
       ballet   duvet   gourmet•   valet   crochet

Americans pronounce the last syllable of 'fillet' to rhyme with 'they' and 'day'.
British people pronounce 'fillet' in the same way as 'fill it'.

Answer these questions about the words above.

1 Which word means 'food put on table so that each person can help himself/herself to it'?
2 In which activity does a woman need a special hook or needle?
3 He looks after his employer's clothes. What do we call him?
4 If you are cold at night, you can put this on your bed. What is it?
5 This is used to stop blood from coming out of a cut or wound. What is it?
6 Which word is the name of a type of wooden floor?
7 A ship can load or unload goods at this place. What is it?
8 Which word can refer to a small bungalow at a holiday camp or a large home in Switzerland?
9 _____ goods are often valuable because they are old. What is the missing word?
10 What do we do at a banquet?

B READING ALOUD

When you have to read a dialogue or a passage of prose aloud in a test, these guidelines will help you.

1 If possible, read the passage silently first. Read it through to find out what it is about.
2 Be prepared to read in groups of words like this:

Yesterday evening, / Mary had dinner with her family / at a new restaurant / not far from her home. // Mary was wearing / one of her best dresses / and she looked very pretty. // During the meal, / a friend passed Mary / some sauce. // Unfortunately, / he knocked over a glass of tea. //

3 When you are reading dialogue, notice whether you should sound angry,

sad, happy, annoyed, irritated, surprised or frightened. Try to show the right emotion when you speak.

4   Don't speak too quickly. If you are nervous, force yourself to slow down a little.

5   If the passage contains short forms (I'll, don't, it's), don't say the long form.

   Some students will see *I'll* in a passage but say 'I shall' or 'I will'. That is wrong. Say the short form.

6   Make sure that you know how to pronounce final -ed and -s clearly. Don't leave them off when you are reading aloud.

Read this passage silently. Then read it aloud. *It is taken from a recent GCE O-level examination.*

When I was a young and inexperienced teacher, I often got landed with the job of taking a party of small children on trips to places of interest. These, of course, were places that children were expected to be interested in. Sometimes, I confess, I wondered why they had been chosen.

Problems would begin before the expedition had even started. Someone – or two or three – would always be missing when it was time to board the bus, involving last-minute searches and cross words when the culprits were found.

When we finally got started, the children would always discover that something vital had been left behind. Then there was the seating problem. The popular children would have a great queue of 'friends' hoping to sit next to them. At the other end of the bus, another child would be weeping because no one wanted to share his or her seat.

The visits to museums were the worst. Despite the warning notices 'DO NOT TOUCH', little fingers would be all over the place, moving closer and closer to some priceless object, much to my anxiety and the anger of the museum staff.

The journey and the arrival back at school would be a time of great relief for me. 'Never again!' I would say to myself.

But when the children – some of them at least – said 'thank you' as they left the bus, I would relent and be prepared to consider the possibility that I might be fool enough to do it once more – perhaps!

From UCLES, GCE O-level English Language, Oral Test, Day 9, Test 1, November 1998.

Listen when somebody else is reading the passage aloud. Underline any words that he or she pronounces wrongly. Then help the person to say the words correctly.

C PICTURE DISCUSSION

Imagine that you are looking at a picture of a scene during a women's football match. You can see one player being taken off on a stretcher. A first aid person is holding what looks like a metal bottle of oxygen. A lead from it goes to a mask over the player's mouth. One of the other players is waving an angry fist at an opposing player. We can see some spectators looking at the injured person on the stretcher. Their faces show shock, surprise, curiosity or anger.

In an examination, an examiner might give you this picture and say:

Describe what you can see in this picture.

Then you could:

a) Give a general impression of the scene, e.g. 'A player at a football match has been injured. Some first aid people are taking her off the field.'
   Then you could describe some of the people and make a guess about how the injury happened.

or

b) You could start with the focal or most important part of the picture, i.e. an injured person on a stretcher. Then you could describe people farther and farther away from the focal point.

or

c) You could describe the picture, starting with the foreground and moving to the background.

or

d) You could start with one side of the picture and work across to the other side.

Other possible questions include these:

- ■ Choose one of the people in the picture and describe the person in detail.
- ■ At what time of the day did this event take place? How do you know?
- ■ Where did this happen? How can you tell?
- ■ What is this man/woman doing/thinking/trying to say?

Then the examiner could start a discussion by asking about any of these things:

- ■ Do you ever play football?
- ■ Is it a good or a bad thing for girls to play football?
- ■ Do you think soccer is a dangerous game?
- ■ What game/sport are you interested in?
- ■ Do you watch any sport on television?

Practice

Discuss the picture on the next page with a classmate. You can take turns to be an examiner and a candidate taking the GCE examination.

D CONVERSATION

Look again at the description of a scene at a football match at the start of section C. Read this conversation between an examiner (E) and a candidate (C) who does not know how to hold a conversation with an examiner. This is an example of what not to do in an examination.

E: Do you ever play football?
C: No.
E: What is your favourite sport?
C: Er . . .
E: What game do you like to play? (continued on page 312)

C: Cards.

(The examiner has to change the topic.)

E: Do you ever watch sport on television?
C: No.
E: Do any members of your family watch sport on television?
C: Yes.
E: Who watches sport?
C: Brother.
E: What does he watch?
C: Don't know.

(The examiner is working hard but the candidate is not cooperating.)

E: What do you watch on television?
C: I like to watch detective and mystery films. I like science fiction films also.

(The candidate had memorised those two sentences. The examiner is not impressed.)

E: When do you watch television?
C: At home.

(The candidate thought the examiner said, 'Where do you watch...?' The examiner has already decided to give the candidate a very low mark.)

What mistakes did the candidate make?
1 His answers were too short. If you answer 'Yes' or 'No' to a question, give your reasons for your answer.
2 He has not given the examiner any evidence to justify even a pass mark. He is not cooperating with the examiner. If you have to take a conversation test, say two or three sentences each time. Then wait for the examiner to continue the conversation.

Read this conversation between an examiner and a different candidate. Then act it with a classmate. Act it two more times. Take turns to be the examiner and the candidate.

E: Do you ever play football?
C: No, not now. I used to play two or three years ago but now I play badminton with my friends. We can play in a park or at school.
E: Do you play singles or doubles?
C: Doubles usually. Then more players can play at the same time. Sometimes I play mixed doubles at school. Now I'm learning to play tennis as well but I'm not very good.
E: Do you ever watch games on television?
C: Yes, when I get a chance. I like to watch football, cricket and athletics but this year I haven't had much chance because I've been preparing for this exam.
E: Do you take part in athletics yourself?
C: Yes. I like to do the 100 metres and the 400 metres. I like to do the long jump as well.
E: How far can you jump?

Now work with a classmate. Continue the conversation.

84 Practice 2

A PRONUNCIATION

1   Check that you can pronounce the short /i/ sound or the long /iː/ sound: *ship* and *sheep*.

Say these words clearly:

/i/ as in 'sit'

1	fit	6	living
2	rich	7	pill
3	this	8	will
4	it	9	sit
5	sick	10	dip

/iː/ as in 'seat'

11	feet	16	leaving
12	reach	17	peel
13	these	18	wheel
14	eat	19	seat
15	seek	20	deep

Say these sentences:

21   Don't eat this peel. It will make you feel sick.
22   These shoes will fit you if your feet are not too big.
23   If you take this pill with your food, it will keep you fit.

Listen when somebody says some of the words 1–20. Write down the numbers of the words you hear. Then check with the person who said the words. See if you wrote down the correct numbers.

2   Check that you can say words containing the sound /v/. Don't confuse the /v/ and /w/ sounds.

/w/   When you pronounce the /w/ sound, push both lips forward slightly.
/v/   When you say the /v/ sound, touch your bottom lip with your top teeth. Do NOT push your lips forward at all.

Say these words:

1	verb	4	vehicle	7	valuable	10	province	13	revolver
2	vote	5	reverse	8	vividly	11	thieves	14	nervous
3	valley	6	preserve	9	valve	12	shelves	15	driver

B READING ALOUD

Read this passage silently. Then read it aloud. It is taken from a recent GCE O-level examination. In this passage, two children have a frightening experience as they fish for tadpoles.

The two children crept through the long grass. In their hands they held sticks with fishing nets attached and some plastic containers. It was late afternoon and the sky was just beginning to turn dark. Apart from the rustling of the bushes and the cracking of twigs under their feet, there was no sound to be heard.

They had walked for about four hundred metres when the bushes began to get thinner. Very soon they found themselves in an open space beside a small lake. The water was still; there was no breeze and no sound of birds singing. It was growing darker. In front of them was a notice which read,

'No Fishing Without Permit'. They were not fishing; they had come there to search for tadpoles and frogspawn for their school's Nature Corner.

They walked around the edge of the lake until they found a suitable spot. Beneath the water's surface they could just make out small, black creatures wriggling around. The older child gave one more look behind but there was no sign of human life anywhere. They gripped the handles of their nets and plunged them into the lake. Suddenly, from across the lake, something shot towards them at an incredible speed. They did not stop to see if it was a creature or a boat, but ran, scared, through the bushes to the safety of the main road.

From UCLES, GCE O-level English Language, Oral Test, Day 10, Test 2, November 1998.

C PICTURE DISCUSSION

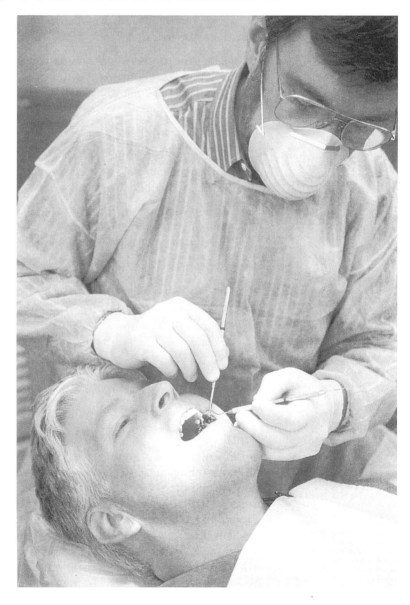

D ROLE PLAY – GREETING PEOPLE

There are many ways of greeting people. Use a method that is suitable for the situation.

You are going to interview somebody of your own age or younger than you are.

a) You have met the person before, so you know him/her.
   You can say:
   Hallo, John.
   Hallo, Mary.
   Hi, Anne.   (No surname is used.)

b) You have not met the person before but he/she is about your age.
   Hallo, I'm Peter King. What's your name?

c) You have stopped a stranger in a street or store when you are making a survey.
   Excuse me. Can I ask you a few questions?
   Excuse me. I'm doing a survey. Can you spare a minute to answer some questions?

d) You are going to interview somebody who is older and/or senior to you.
   Good morning.   (You can add 'Sir', 'Madam' or 'Miss' if you do not
   Good afternoon.   know a person's name but this is not necessary. If
   Good evening.   you know the person's name, use the method below.)

or

   Good morning,   Miss Wilson.   (No given name is used.)
   Good afternoon, Mrs Lee.
   Good evening,   Ms* Smith.   (*'Ms' is pronounced /miz/.)
                   Mr Rahman.

Practice

How can you greet each of these people?

1 You are a reporter. You are going to interview somebody who witnessed a serious traffic accident.
2 You are an Immigration Officer and you are interviewing a tourist who has just arrived from a foreign city which is believed to be a drug-smuggling centre.
3 You are a committee member of the English Language Club at your school. You are going to interview a member to get suggestions for improvements.
4 You are a Form 5 student and you are going to interview a foreign teacher who has just come to teach at your school.
5 You are on a visit to the UK. You are going to speak to a travel agent to get information about flights to Paris and Rome.
6 You work in the Customer Services Department of a large store. A foreigner has come to you with a complaint. You need to get information from her.
7 At a community centre, you have to interview teenagers who are 2–3 years younger than you are. You need to get information from the teenagers and have not met them before.

8 You want to get some information from an English-speaking neighbour. You have seen the neighbour before but have never spoken to her.

9 You telephone a large store one afternoon because you want to get some information about a special offer of software for a computer. You hear a woman's voice at the other end of the phone.

10 You are working during the school holidays. You are helping to carry out a survey of bus passengers to find out when and where they use a bus.

85 Practice 3

A PRONUNCIATION: SILENT LETTERS (1)

Check that you know that the following letters are silent in some words.

b   debt, doubtful, subtle, climb, limb, bomb, comb, tomb
dumb, numb, thumb, crumbs, plumber

The letter 'b' is pronounced in these words: cucumber, number, jumble, member.

Match these explanations with the words above.

1 very small pieces (usually) of bread or cake
2 with no feeling in part of your body
3 somebody who can repair a leak in a pipe
4 often dropped from an aeroplane, it can destroy buildings and people
5 unable to speak
6 an arm or a leg
7 used to make your hair tidy
8 some people call it your first finger

c   muscle, Gloucester, Leicester, Worcester, indictment
ch yacht
d   grandfather, grandmother, grandson, handsome, Wednesday, handkerchief
g   gnome, gnat, gnash, gnu, sign, resign, foreign, campaign, champagne
gh although, bought, daughter, slaughter, naughty, sigh, delighted, straight, weigh
h   vehicle*, exhausted, heir, hour, honest, honour, honorary, exhibit, rhyme, rhythm, rhinoceros, silhouette, rheumatism, oh, verandah
k   know, knew, knowledge, knife, knee, kneel, knit, knock, knuckle, knot

*The 'h' is pronounced in 'vehicular' but not in 'vehicle'.

In the sentence, 'You have left out an "h", we **say** *an* /aych/. We do **not** say /h/ before /aych/.

Match these explanations with the words above.

9   the shape of somebody or something seen through a sheet, curtain, etc, so that only the outline is visible.
10 showing that a ferry carries cars and trucks
11 a special type of wine originally made in one part of France
12 a heavy, armoured animal with a horn on its head, now almost extinct
13 on your hands, the place where two bones are joined in a flexible way
14 use needles to make a garment with wool
15 the mother of your sister's mother
16 decide to leave employment (or be forced to leave)
17 a painful disease with inflamed joints
18 a mythical small goblin which lives under the ground

B READING ALOUD

Read the following passage silently. Then read it aloud. Two boys are discussing the problems of homework.

Rene and Jean were on their way home from school. During the journey they started to talk about homework.

'The work we are given by teachers to do at home,' said Rene, 'can be enjoyable, but I often find it's a bit of a burden. Some hardworking students enjoy it because they know it improves their knowledge and increases their chances of doing well in examinations. On the other hand, a lazy student may find it boring, irritating – even pointless.'

'I enjoy homework,' replied Jean. 'It gives me the opportunity to think about the work we have done at school, and to make sure that I have understood it. It also helps to pass the time. After all, I can't spend all my leisure time with my friends or slumped in front of the television, eating snacks and getting fat.'

'That's all very well,' persisted Rene, 'but too much homework may do more harm than good. If I had to spend all my spare time studying, I would not be able to meet my friends and to keep up with the various pastimes and hobbies I enjoy. Having fun is important too so that one's mind is fresh, and exercise keeps the body fit and active.'

Jean thought for a while; then he said, 'In the end, I suppose, it's all a matter of balancing one's life so that there is enough homework to keep right on top of the school work, enough fun to keep the mind fresh, and enough exercise to keep fit. I wonder if I have got the balance right.'

'I'm sure I don't know,' said Rene, 'but if we don't get off the bus now we'll miss our stop.'

From UCLES, GCE O-level English Language, Oral Test, Day 3, Test 1, November 1998.

C DISCUSSION

1 Do you think the discussion in Section B above is genuine? Did this conversation ever take place between two boys or has it been invented by somebody? What are your reasons for your answer?

2 With which of the boys do you most agree: with Rene or with Jean?

3 If you were on the bus with the two boys, what would you say to **one** of them in reply to something he has just said?

4 What do **you** think about 'the problems of homework'?

5 Do you think it is possible to abolish homework by (a) slightly lengthening the school day, (b) slightly shortening the annual holidays, or by (c) combining (a) and (b)?
Would this change have any effect on the standard of achievement of students?

6 Make up a timetable schedule, showing how long students in each secondary year should spend on the whole of their homework each day. There is no need to mention separate subjects. What we need here is a figure for the **total** amount of homework per day.

Does your school have guidelines for the amount of homework each day? If so, are the guidelines followed by teachers and students?

D WHAT'S THE DIFFERENCE?

Study the two pictures below. Make a list of any differences between the two pictures. Then, when everybody is ready, tell the class about the differences you have found.

Practice 4

A PRONUNCIATION: SILENT LETTERS (2)

Check that you know that the following letters are silent in some words:

l half, calf, chalk, folk, palm, salmon, colonel, almond, psalm, talking, walking

n column, solemn, autumn, condemn, government, hymn

p cupboard, raspberry, receipt, corps, psalm, pneumatic, pneumonia, psychology

r tired, careful, iron, heart, sailor, inspector, bored, arm

Match these explanations with the words above.

1 a type of soft red or pink fruit which grows on canes and may contain pips
2 a fish which can live in the sea or in a river and tastes very nice
3 an army rank below a brigadier
4 a member of the crew of a ship
5 If a police sergeant is promoted he may become an ...
6 a sacred poem or song (often in praise of God)
7 a heavy metal which can rust
8 proof that you have paid for something
9 the scientific study of the mind, emotions and behaviour
10 a serious disease of the lungs (which can be fatal)

s debris, précis, island, aisle, corps, bourgeois, isle, rendezvous

t castle, whistle, thistle, bristle, gristle, rustle, wrestle, Christmas, often, mortgage, moisten, hasten, soften, fasten, listen, bustle

w write, wreck(age), wrong(ly), wrist, wrap, wretched, wriggle, wring, wrinkle, answer, sword, two, Greenwich, playwright, twopence, wretched, shipwreck

Match these explanations with the words above.

11 what the hair on a dog does when it is angry
12 a very large defended building where nobles used to live
13 a person who writes plays
14 a crease on your face
15 a district in the south-east of London
16 rubbish left behind after a storm (or a fire)
17 a metal weapon for fighting
18 what somebody wants when he asked you a question
19 a space between rows of seats in a church or on a plane
20 a meeting-place

B READING ALOUD

Read the following passage silently. Then read it aloud. In the passage, a teacher remembers taking part in a play at the school where he worked.

I have always admired people who perform in public. To stand up on stage, as an actor, and pretend to be someone else for two or three hours, is something I can never imagine myself doing.

However, I did once appear on stage. The school at which I teach put on a production of Shakespeare's *Hamlet*. I was the director. We thought it would be a nice touch for members of the teaching staff to play some of the minor parts. The Head Teacher volunteered to play the First Gravedigger and everybody thought it would be a good idea if I played his assistant.

The Head Teacher took his responsibility very seriously; by the first night he was word-perfect. He was an academic, dignified man but, for the performance, he had made himself look suitably comic by wearing a ridiculous orange wig and a shapeless hat. I was dressed in an old string vest and dirty, baggy trousers. We thought it would not be in keeping with the character he was playing for the Head to wear his glasses. This meant that I had to lead him into the orchestra pit (which was our 'grave') in pitch darkness while another scene was taking place. We crashed into scenery and other objects and by the time we were in position my nerves were frayed.

When the lights went up, the Head gave an impressive speech and the audience rocked with laughter; he turned to me, gave me my cue ... and I stared in silence. My words had gone completely out of my head.

C SPEAKING AND LISTENING

Choose somebody in your class. Say the number of one of the sentences below. Then everybody else in the class can listen and make a note of any words pronounced wrongly when your classmate reads the sentence aloud.

1   A vehicular ferry collided with a pier because of the negligence of two labourers on the quay.
2   The bad man grabbed the bracelet and ran away but an off-duty detective witnessed the incident and promptly arrested the robber.
3   This film is based on a novel by Daphne Browning. It is quite impressive and was described in glowing terms in a local newspaper. The heroine received considerable praise for her performance.
4   All the produce from these farms will be loaded on that vessel and exported to Europe next week.
5   Officers from the Preventative Service discovered drugs on the ship, and several members of the crew are believed to be involved in a smuggling ring. Two of them are known to be addicted to heroin.
6   In all probability, advertisements for cigarettes will be banned eventually, as has already happened in Singapore.
7   In modern warfare, helicopters are often used for reconnaissance in rural areas, and they sometimes obtain information of strategical value.
8   The squatters and hawkers evacuated the site in an orderly way after they had been offered temporary accommodation at a transit camp.
9   There used to be a freshwater pool full of frogs here, but the ducks have eaten the frogs and made the pool filthy.
10   The beggar was very cunning and pretended to be lame. Each day he collected several dollars from gullible tourists and mocked them behind their backs.

D PICTURE DISCUSSION

Discuss this picture (a) as a class or (b) in small groups or (c) with a classmate.

87 Practice 5

A PRONUNCIATION

1   Check that you can say the /sh/ sound correctly in these words:

sh	fishing, pushed (*pusht*), finished (*finisht*), shared, ashore, shelves
ss	Russia, permission, admission, confession, discussion, transmission
ch	parachute, chauffeur, machine, moustache, champagne, chaperon, chef, cache
s	sure, sugar, comprehension, insurance, tension, extension, diversion
c	ocean, vicious, electrician, efficient, special, socialist, sufficient
sc/sch	conscious, conscience, schedule (Amer: *skedyool*), Schubert

t   ratio, patience, auction, information, initial, nation, cautious, partial

2   Check that you can say the /ch/ sound in the words below:

(t)ch   chapter, achieve, beach, fetch, watch, ditch, franchise, stretch

t   question, suggestion, nature, adventure, capture, signature, creature

Notice that the letters 'ch' are spoken with a /k/ sound in many word, e.g. character, chemistry, choir, chorus, stomach, ache, anchor, archaeology, architect, bronchitis, echo, mechanic, orchestra, orchid, technique

B LISTENING PRACTICE

Write down the numbers of the sentences you can hear when somebody reads them aloud.

1   Please wash the baby while I'm out.
2   Please watch the baby while I'm out.
3   Get some French bread when you go out.
4   Get some fresh bread when you go out.
5   The doctors managed to save him.
6   The doctors managed to shave him.
7   Peter is a sure loser.
8   Peter is a sore loser.
9   One of the players had a deep cut on his shin.
10 One of the players had a deep cut on his chin.
11 The story was all about three witches in ancient China.
12 The story was all about three wishes in ancient China.
13 Which of these is Kelly's share?
14 Which of these is Carrie's chair?

C ROLE PLAY

Read these dialogues silently. Then act one or both of the dialogues with a classmate. A, B, C and D are four different people. It does not matter whether they are males or females. If there is time, take turns to be different people.

A   Somebody (A) is talking to a friend (B) about something funny that happened.

A: I must tell you what we saw on the beach yesterday. It was so funny! In fact, it really gave me a pain in the tummy just laughing...

B: Well, come on. Don't keep it a secret! What was it?

A: You know that boy, David King, in 5B?

B: The one who is always playing football and practising kung fu on everybody?

A: That's the one. Well, he left his clothes on the beach while he went for a swim. He was just getting out when a stray dog came along...

B: Oh dear! What happened? Some of those strays are really vicious.

A: It's not as bad as you think. The dog didn't attack him. It just picked up

David's shorts and strolled off with them.

B: Ha! Ha! I wish I'd seen that. What did David do?

A: He called the dog but it just ignored him and trotted away. Then David started to chase it. That made the dog frightened, so it started to run.

B: Did he catch it? He'd look funny going home in his swimming trunks.

A: I don't know what happened. I was with some friends. We had to go and catch a bus. When I looked back, the dog was leading by about forty metres.

B: I bet David will be more careful with his clothes next time. We'd better not say anything about it when we see him.

B David is talking to a friend about the same incident.

C: Hey, Dave. Is that true that you've been out catching dogs? What are you going to do with them: eat them or sell them? Is it a very profitable business?

D: Very funny! Who told you that story?

C: Peter. He said he saw you chasing a dog along Silver Beach on Saturday. He heard you shouting. He was sure you weren't playing.

D: I wasn't! A silly dog stole my shorts while I was in the sea. I asked it very politely to bring them back but it took off like a rocket.

C: I wish I'd seen that. Perhaps he was hungry or taking them back to his master to sell. Maybe he's been specially trained to steal people's clothes. What did you do?

D: What could I do? I ran after the dog. The faster I ran, the faster it ran. A lot of people thought it was very funny but I didn't. Running on sand is not easy.

C: What happened in the end? Did you catch the dog?

D: Not a hope! It was too fast for me. Somebody tried to stop the dog for me, so the dog dropped the shorts and ran away. That's the last time I go swimming by myself!

D PICTURE DISCUSSION

Look at this picture. Then answer the questions below.

What are the people doing? Is anything going wrong? Are the people enjoying themselves? Who is *not* happy? Have you ever been to a school fun fair? Can you tell us about it?

88 Practice 6

A PRONUNCIATION

1 Stress in exclamations

In the following exclamations, the word in colour is often stressed.

    1 What a *silly* thing to do!   *or*   *What* a silly thing to do!
        What a *nice* dress!   *or*   *What* a nice dress!

2	What a *shame* !	*or*	*What* a shame!
	What a *pity* !	*or*	*What* a pity!
	What a *nuisance* !	*or*	*What* a nuisance!

3*	How *stupid* of him!	*or*	How stupid of *him* !
	How *kind* of Mary!	*or*	How kind of *Mary* !

*The first type is more common. The second type has a different meaning.

Exclamations such as 'Oh!' and 'Ah!' can be spoken in different ways, depending on whether they express surprise, anger, disappointment or another emotion.

2 The letters 'th' in 'thirty' and 'path'

When you pronounce the /th/ sound in 'thirty' and 'path' put the tip (end) of your tongue slightly between your teeth. If you find that the sound is difficult to make, poke your tongue out a little way between your teeth. Then you will not make an /f/ or an /s/ sound by mistake.

Say these words and sentences clearly:

1	think	4	thing	7	path	10	bath
2	thirst	5	thin	8	mouth	11	both
3	three	6	thank	9	fourth	12	thunder

13 Shall I get thick or thin bread at the store?
14 You should follow this path through the village for thirty or forty metres.
15 On Thursday night we had a lot of thunder and lightning.
16 Ruth's birthday is on the third or fourth of next month.

3 Listening practice

Listen to somebody saying these sentences. Underline any words that are not pronounced correctly.

1 Those verbs end with an 'e' and there is no literal translation of them.
2 In preparation for the annual sale, the price of most garments was marked down a great deal.
3 The gale brought an unbelievable amount of rain and prevented bathing for some time.
4 We were impressed by his scheme and attracted by his offer but he failed to convince Ms Green.
5 The engineers are concerned about the pressure on the wall and are considering making changes.
6 Uncle smiled and looked very pleased when he told us how much money he had managed to save during the past few months.

B READING ALOUD

Read the following passage silently. Then read it aloud. Listen when other students read it aloud. Underline any words which they pronounce wrongly. (This passage is taken from a past examination paper. The writer is discussing how our attitudes towards birthdays change as we grow older.)

When we are very young, we don't really understand birthdays. We hear our parents using the word and then, one day, all our friends come to our house.

They are dressed in clothes we have not seen them wearing before. They are carrying brightly-wrapped parcels called presents which they give to us. For the next two hours or so, we play games organised by the adults. If we are lucky, we may have a visit from a professional children's entertainer. We spend quite a lot of time eating sandwiches, jelly and cake and drinking fizzy lemonade. When the fun is over, all our friends go home with little bags stuffed full of cakes and sweets. We have all learned the word 'party'.

As we grow older, our birthday celebrations become larger and more expensive. Our parties are held at more exciting venues than our homes, such as fast-food restaurants. Sometimes we have swimming or bowling parties and when we become teenagers our parties take place in discotheques or similar places and cost our parents even more money. However, we can invite more friends and receive even more presents.

When we are older still, we reach the stage where we want to forget birthdays. They remind us of the years that are passing. We cannot escape the fact that we are growing older. We no longer have parties although we might buy cakes for our workmates. Sadly, birthdays are no different from any other days – but it is still fun to receive presents.

From UCLES, GCE O-level English Language, Oral Test, Day 9, Test 2, November 1998.

C PLAYING 'BINGO' (LISTENING CAREFULLY)

Play the game **Bingo**. This is how you can play.

a) First you must draw a large square or box with 9–16 smaller boxes in it, as in the diagram opposite.

b) Then choose a topic such as any of the following:
   - numbers 1–20 or 1–30 or more
   - the names of vegetables
   - the names of fruit
   - the names of countries or cities
   - the names of rivers
   - the names of tools
   - the names of things in the sea
   - flowers or plants
   - boys' or girls' names
   - words containing the /sh/ or /ch/ sound
   - words containing 'pl', 'pr', 'bl', or 'br'
   or anything else that is suitable

c) On the blackboard, make a list containing more words than the number of boxes drawn.

d) Each student must write one of the words in each small box until all the boxes contain a word.

e) Then somebody (your teacher or a student) will say some of the words – slowly and clearly. If you hear a word that is in one of your boxes, put a cross through it.

Malta	Singapore	China	Jordan X
Brazil X	Mauritius	Egypt	India
Jamaica	USA	Australia X	Kenya
Zimbabwe	Nigeria	Pakistan	UK

f) The winner of the game is the first person who can cross out all his or her boxes. He (or she) can shout out 'Bingo!'

g) The teacher or caller will check the winner's box. Then you can start again, using different words.

D ARE YOU DESCRIBING A PICTURE OR DISCUSSING IT?

In an examination, you may have to **describe** a picture or – more likely – **discuss** one. We considered techniques for describing a picture in Practice 1. Different techniques may be necessary when a picture is used to start a discussion.

1 An examiner may ask you to give your own opinion of something.
2 He (or she) may ask you whether you think something is wise or not, safe or dangerous, good or bad.
3 You may be asked about your own experience and interests – or about what your friends do.
4 You may be asked about things you like or dislike.
5 Don't try to push a prepared speech into a discussion. It may annoy an examiner and cause you to lose marks. Speak naturally – almost as if you were speaking to a friend.
6 Don't just say 'Yes' or 'No' as your answer. Give a reason, an example, an opinion or details of some kind.

Practice

All the answers to the following questions are too short. Try to make each answer longer by adding one or two sentences.

1 Q : Do you ever watch television or listen to the radio?
  A : Yes, sometimes.

2 Q : Which channels or stations do you watch?
  A : The one with the news on it.

3 Q : The news? Why do you like that?
  A : It's interesting.

4 Q : What was on the news yesterday?
  A : A fire.

5 Q : Do you listen to the radio at all?
  A : Yes, sometimes.

6 Q : What kind of music do you like?
  A : Country and western.

7 Q : Can you play any instrument yourself?
  A : I beg your pardon?

8 Q : Can you play the piano, the guitar or any other musical instrument?
  A : No.

9 Q : What do you do during the school holidays?
  A : Help my parents.

10 Q : How do you help them?
   A : I work in the shop.

11 Q : What sort of work do you do?
   A : Serve the customers.

12 Q : How do you serve them?
   A : I sell them goods.

Remember: *The answers given above are bad ones because they are too short. Try to give more information in your answers during an examination.*

89 Practice 7

A PRONUNCIATION

I Saying the letter 'x'

The letter 'x' is pronounced in these ways. Say the words.

/eks/   X-ray
/ks/   six, exercise, box, galaxy, oxygen, taxi, exit, maximum
/gz/   examine, exhaust, exaggeration, anxiety, example, exact, exist

328

| /ksh/ | luxury, anxious, complexion, connexion, crucifixion, obnoxious |
| /z/ | xylophone, Xerox, Xerxes |

2 Syllable stress

In the following pairs of words, we stress the **first** syllable if the word is used as a **noun**. We stress the **second** syllable if the word is used as a **verb**:

| noun : | an 'object | a 'rebel | a 'permit | a 'protest | a 'record |
| verb : | to ob'ject | to re'bel | to per'mit | to pro'test | to re'cord |

Say these sentences. Be careful how you pronounce the words in bold type.

1 We are going to a studio to **record** a new song.
2 A disc jockey is a person who plays **records** most of the time.

3 We **import** many goods from China and other countries.
4 There is no duty on most **imports**.

5 Nobody is allowed in this part of the building without a **permit**.
6 I doubt whether the security guard will **permit** us to enter the building.

7 In some countries **rebels** are quickly executed.
8 If a player **rebels** against the team manager, he may lose his place in the team.
9 The tenants **protested** when the landlord **increased** their rent by 50%.
10 The landlord did not take much notice of their **protest** because he thought that the **increase** was justified by the cost of repairing the building.

3 Short speech forms

When some students have to read out a short speech form, they wrongly say the full form of the words. For example when they have to read out 'He's' they say 'He is' or 'He has' instead of the correct pronunciation /hi:z/. Say these sentences correctly.

1	Don't touch it.	7	Mary hasn't finished yet.
2	I'm ready to go.	8	It's time to go home.
3	He isn't here.	9	She's Tom's sister.
4	She'll help us.	10	I'll go with you.
5	We've finished.	11	John didn't break it.
6	We'd better wait.	12	I'd rather stay here if you don't mind.

B READING ALOUD

Read each dialogue silently. Then work in pairs and read the dialogue aloud. Take turns to read each part.

1 A woman (W) is telling her husband (H) what happened when she went shopping.

W: It was all very exciting and happened so quickly...
H: Well, you'd better start at the beginning and tell me what happened.
W: I was walking along Market Street towards the bus depot. Then suddenly I heard a bang, like somebody firing a gun...
H: Did you see anybody fire a gun? Where was the man?

W: Wait a minute! Don't be so impatient! Suddenly some men rushed out of a goldsmith's shop.

H: Oh! A robbery! You were lucky you weren't hurt. What happened?

W: Apparently it was an ambush. The police were waiting inside the shop, disguised as shop assistants and customers. Other policemen – in uniform – were hiding in nearby shops. They rushed out, too.

H: I hope they caught the robbers!

W: Yes, they did. I saw three men taken away in a van. They had paper bags over their heads. They were all handcuffed.

H: We must watch the news on TV this evening. Perhaps they'll show us something about the robbery. Anyway, I'm glad they caught the men. Somebody must have tipped them off.

W: There's too much crime these days. I blame the TV for it. There's too much violence on it.

H: Yes, maybe you're right. It's bound to have a bad influence on young men.

2 A tourist (T) is telling a friend (F) what happened when he was buying a gold bracelet.

T: As a matter of fact, I thought there was something strange when I went in the shop.

F: Why? Was there anything wrong?

T: Well, yes and no. There was nothing definite but the sales assistants all looked very strong and healthy. They didn't speak exactly like shop assistants. One of them didn't know what a hallmark is.

F: That doesn't surprise me. I'm not 100% sure what a hallmark is. Anyway, what happened then?

T: I'm not sure because it all happened so quickly, and I wasn't really expecting any trouble. Suddenly I heard somebody shout in a language which I couldn't understand. I saw a man holding a gun and another one with a long knife.

F: What did you do? I bet you were scared! I would have been.

T: I was too astonished to be really frightened. Anyway, there was nothing I could do because the 'sales assistants' turned out to be detectives. Somebody fired a shot. There was a quick struggle and it was all over.

F: Was anybody hurt? What did the police do with the robbers? Where were the real sales assistants?

T: Oh, they were in a back room, out of the way. No, nobody was hurt, as far as I could see. The police took the robbers away in a van. It was all over in a few minutes.

F: Well, I still think you were lucky to be at the scene and yet not get hurt. Will you have to give evidence?

T: I don't know. I have to go to the police station tomorrow morning to make a statement and maybe to identify two of the robbers. I didn't see the face of the third man. But I don't see how I can appear in court...

F: Why not?

T: Well, we're leaving in three days' time, so I won't be here when the case comes to court.

C PICTURE DISCUSSION

Use this picture as the start of a discussion. You can talk about the people in the picture and then about anything related to it, e.g.

crime and punishment the causes of crime dangerous jobs
the work of the police gold and jewellery anything else relevant

90 Practice 8

A PRONUNCIATION

1 Saying the letters 'th' in 'that' and 'brother'

If you put the end of your tongue between your teeth when you say /th/, you will not say /d/ by mistake.

Say these words clearly. Then listen when somebody else says some of them. Write down the numbers of the words you hear.

1 they	4 dare	7 breathe	10 fed her
2 day	5 southern	8 breed	11 loathes
3 there	6 sudden	9 feather	12 loads

2 Saying the sounds /l/, /n/ and /r/

Say these words. Then say the number of a word when somebody says it.

1	file	6	right	11	a gain	16	labour
2	fine	7	line	12	a game	17	neighbour
3	fire	8	nine	13	sale		
4	light	9	Rhine	14	sane		
5	night	10	a gale	15	same		

3 American English

Some words are pronounced in different ways in American and British English, e.g.

word	American English	British English
pass	/pæs/ (short 'a')	/pa:s/ (long 'a')
route	/rowt/	/root/
leisure	/li:dʒə/	/ledʒə/
tomato	/təmaytou/	təma:tou/

But notice that there are several different dialects within the USA and UK. In the USA, people in San Francisco, New York and Houston do not all speak in the same way. Similarly, in the UK, people in London, Liverpool and Newcastle often speak in different ways.

B VOCABULARY

Check that you know these differences between American and British English.

British	American	British	America
petrol	gas(oline)	frying-pan	skillet
boot (of a car)	trunk	torch	flashlight
bonnet (car)	hood	wedding ring	wedding band
bumper	fender	catapult	slingshot
gear level	shift	fire station	fire house
a nappy	a diaper	a $5 note	a $5 bill
to post	to mail	postman	mailman
a shop	a store	a flat	an apartment
a biscuit	a cracker	paraffin	kerosene
sweets	candy	a tin	a can
a lorry	a truck	curtains	drapes
a holiday	a vacation	a lift	an elevator
a vest	an undershirt	a chemist	a druggist
a cupboard	a closet	a pram	a baby carriage
a caretaker	a janitor	rubbish	garbage, trash

C READING ALOUD

Read this passage silently. Then read it aloud. The passage comes from a past examination paper.

Tara was an outstanding athlete when she was at school. At the annual sports day she would always win her races easily and lead her relay teams to victory.

When she reached the age of sixteen, her sports teacher suggested that she ought to take her running talent seriously. 'You could just be good enough to race in international competitions,' he said.

Tara discussed her teacher's ideas with her parents. They knew how much hard work could be involved. Her father had been an athlete in his youth, but had retired from the sport early when he suffered a leg injury that couldn't be permanently cured.

'I wouldn't dream of discouraging you, Tara,' said her father, 'but you have to remember two important things. The first is that your school work mustn't suffer while you are training. Whatever happens to your athletics you will have to earn your living later on, and for that your exam qualifications are vital.

'Secondly, all the hard work may be for nothing. Hundreds of young athletes try, and try hard, to get to the top, but only a few make it. I suppose that your chances of running for your country are really quite small.

'But,' he added, 'if you don't try you will never know what you might have achieved. So there it is, the choice is yours.'

Tara went away to think carefully and to make her decision.

From UCLES, GCE O-level English Language, Oral Test, Day 2, Test 1.

D THINKING ABOUT IT

Think about the following.

1 Imagine that you are one of Tara's best friends. She came to you and told you what her sports teacher had said. Then she said, 'Do you think I should take up serious athletics as my career? A successful athlete can become very wealthy.'
   a) What information do you need before you can give Tara the best possible answer?
   b) Where will you get this information?
   c) How will the information help you to decide on your answer?

2 If Tara becomes a successful international athlete:
   a) What benefits will her career bring her?
   b) What dangers will she have to deal with in her career?

3 All you know about Tara is what is in the passage. If she asks you for advice about taking up athletics as a career, what will you say to her? Why?

E PICTURE DISCUSSION

Work in pairs. One student can pretend to be an examiner and lead the other student in a discussion which starts by looking at the picture on page 335. It is not necessary to confine the discussion to the scene shown in the picture.
Then change roles and discuss the second picture on page 336.

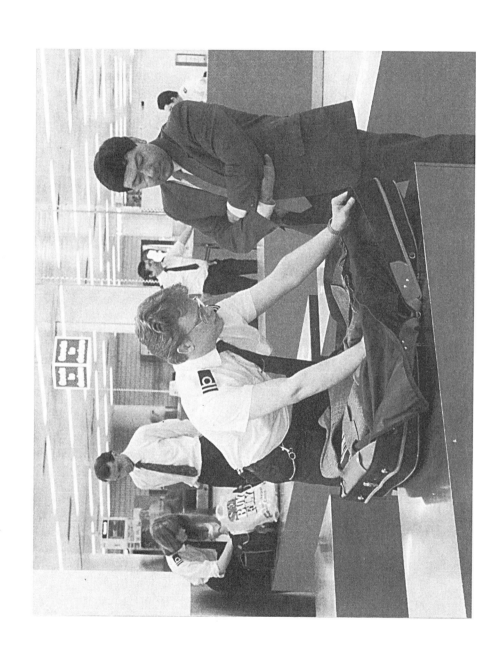

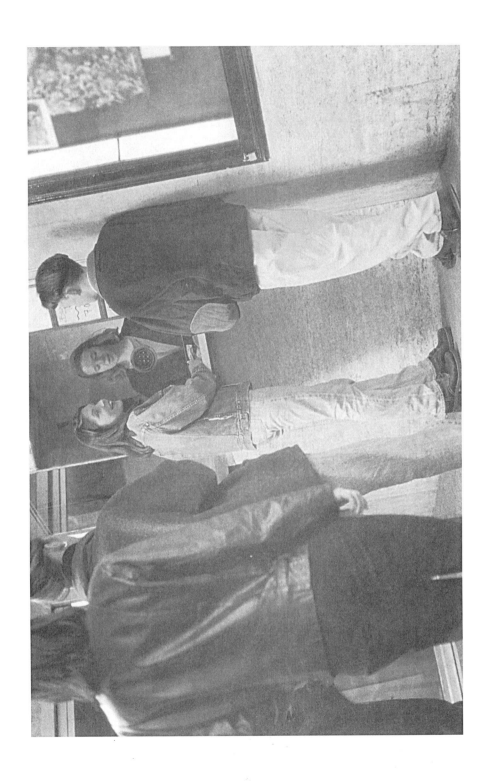

Composition Topics

The following composition topics are mentioned in this book. Some of them are considered in detail.

Index